MW01040738

Systems-Centered Therapy for Groups

SYSTEMS-CENTERED THERAPY FOR GROUPS

Yvonne M. Agazarian

THE GUILFORD PRESS
New York   London

This book is dedicated to my brother,
Jack (1915-1945), who died for
his values, and whose stubborn
courage I remember when
I am running short of my own.

© 1997 The Guilford Press
A Division of Guilford Publications
72 Spring Street, New York, NY 10012

All rights reserved

No part of this book may be reproduced, stored in a retrieval system, or transmitted, in any form or by any means, electronic, mechanical, photocopying, microfilming, recording, or otherwise, without written permission from the Publisher.

Printed in the United States of America

This book is printed on acid-free paper.

Last digit is print number : 9 8 7 6 5 4 3 2 1

Library of Congress Cataloging-in-Publication Data

Agazarian, Yvonne.
    Systems-centered therapy for groups / Yvonne M. Agazarian.
      p. cm.
    Includes bibliographical references and index.
    ISBN 1-57230-195-3
    1. Group psychotherapy.   2. Social systems.   I. Title.
RC488.A6227   1997
616.89′ 152—dc21   97-3418
                                                    CIP

Acknowledgments

*M*any thanks to Anne Alonso, Jay Fidler, Don Brown, Helen Durkin, Len Horwitz, Dave Jenkins, Malcolm Pines, George and Vasso Vassiliou, and Dorothy Whitaker for their confidence in my ability to develop a coherent group systems theory, particularly through the times when I was losing confidence in myself.

An individual thank you to each and every one of the members of the therapy groups, training groups, work groups, and seminars, whose work in making the transition from group-as-a-whole to systems-centered groups has contributed to the development of systems-centered practice as it is today—with particular gratitude to the generosity of the members of the "Friday" Training Group, who contributed to my own leadership training; and the perseverance of the "New York" Training Group, which contained chaos long enough to make sense out of it.

Special thanks to the members of my primary subgroup, Claudia Byram, Fran Carter, and Anita Simon, who have helped to shape every chapter in this book. To my friend, colleague, and cotherapist, Dick Peters, who copioneered the changes in our therapy group throughout the nearly 30 years we have worked together; and to Berj Philibossian, my constant companion, who asks all the hard questions that must be answered.

Gratitude to all my friends over the past three years for their understanding when I related to this book instead of them, and especially to Ken and Barbara Eisold for making room for me in their family and the joys of their garden, and to Zebbie Schactel for her forbearance and the peace of her salt marsh.

Thanks to Peggy Greenlee for catching all the bits and pieces that fell through the cracks, for her loyalty, and for her extraordinary talent in proofreading.

Particular thanks to Seymour Weingarten of The Guilford Press for his confidence that a 1,100 page manuscript could be transformed into a book. Thanks to Rochelle Serwator, who had to understand what I was trying to say before she could help me to say it. It is a particular pleasure to join the ranks of the authors who are indebted to their editor.

Contents

Introduction:
Autobiography
of a Theory

F was the homicidal and suicidal ward of the "Female Chronic" building at Essondale, the large mental hospital outside Vancouver. I was a 19-year-old student working a summer job with no experience and no training. I arrived at the hospital on my first day of work, changed into a nurse's uniform, and instantly became a nurse! (In 1947 there were no candy stripers.) I then went to work on the ward to which I had been assigned.

There were 150 patients in two huge day rooms joined in the shape of an L. At each end of the L was a large porch. At the center was the nurses' station, from which the first of the two wards could be viewed. Opposite the nurses' station in the other direction were the dormitories, bathrooms, and the long corridor out of the ward to the elevators, side rooms, and the "disturbed wards." The noise was indescribable! In 1947 the only treatments available were electroconvulsive and insulin shock, paraldehyde, restraints, and side rooms.

The matron introduced me to my charge nurse (she had a black eye!), who sent me immediately onto the ward telling me that it was the "ladies'" cigarette time and my job would be to light their cigarettes. I walked through the door onto the ward. I joined the nurse handing out the cigarettes and lit a match, trying to hold my trembling hand still enough so that the patients could light their cigarettes. One of them put her arm around my shoulder. "Don't be frightened, nurse," she said. "We won't hurt you." That was how it began.

I was, in fact, superbly trained for the job. At my convent the nuns managed difficult students by giving them responsibility, and I had been "in charge" of the junior school dormitories and study halls (and manners in the refectory) since I was 10. I was good at managing the younger ones and at keeping the most difficult ones out of trouble. I also had a clear idea of chain of command: I did what I was told by authorities (ours is not to reason why!). I had the manners taught to British children: "Always be polite to people less fortunate than yourself." I had no preconceived ideas about mental patients. Moreover, I liked the people I met on the ward very much indeed. At the end of my first 12-hour day, I went to bed in the nurse's residence feeling that for the first time in my life I had been involved in something that I could do, that I liked, and that mattered both to me and to others. As the junior nurse I had no privileges. I did not take the women walking, dancing, to church, or to the cinema. I was the "day-room nurse" from 7:30 in the morning until 7:30 every evening for a 4-day shift with one day off in between.

By the end of my first 2 months at Essondale, I had organized the ward. First I tidied it up: I cut toenails that had grown down and painfully under, French-braided hair, found lost clothes, and did a lot of "tucking in." I set out to clean the lavatories—"You do not ask others to do what you will not do yourself"—and was joined by patients. I organized groups for bridge, for sewing and knitting, and for solving jigsaw puzzles. I learned how to hold the women's bodies so that they did not get hurt during shock treatment. I joined the "emergency squads" when they grappled violent patients into a side room—and then went back and visited those patients during my breaks.

I also set my mind to organizing the work that I could not do by myself. There were many patients in the ward who could do little but manage themselves; others were so agitated that they roamed the day room in a stream of noise and activity. But there were also many patients who could manage themselves quite well. It was they who joined me to organize "our" ward. When patients had seizures, they often came out of them displaying combative behavior and thus risking confinement in a side room. The higher-functioning patients and I experimented with ways of holding patients as they came out of a seizure so that they were contained. Sometimes there were patients trying to cut or hang themselves on both porches at the same time. We set up a suicide detail that could spring into action and reach both porches simultaneously. In the bathrooms at night, often the place of most chaos, I stood a trustworthy patient by each plug, ready to pull it out if the bather tried to drown herself by putting her head under the water. And every night I pushed three or four of the catatonics into the bathroom, raised their arms so that they formed towel racks, and turned their palms up so that they could hold the soap.

Then one day a new resident came into the bathroom, took one look, turned a withering blast of disapproval and disgust toward me, and said, "Nurse, how can you use human beings this way?" My world, seen through his eyes, changed. My stomach filled with iced water and horror.

For a long, disoriented moment I thought I was going to faint. Then, a metallic, machine-like voice, rusty from long disuse, came from one of the "towel racks." It said: "On Nurse Agazarian's ward, everyone works."

During my 4 months at Essondale as an untrained but commonsensical and practical 19-year-old who knew no better than to take responsibility for 150 unmedicated psychotic patients, side room admissions dropped, fewer fights occurred, and there was less violence. One patient was even discharged—at that time an unusual event. What were the key variables behind this improvement? I had no training. I certainly could not interpret a person's psychodynamics: I did not know any! So what did I have? I had good English manners, and I had a genuine feeling for my fellow human beings. I also had a clear understanding of role in relationship to authority (and I left knowing, in a way I would always remember, how important it is to have the role, the title, the uniform—*and the key to the doors*). I had a basic belief that one is responsible to and for one's environment. I knew how to provide structure and how to delegate responsibility for its maintenance. I was clear about goals and could give clear guidelines for work. Essondale was the beginning of a lifelong journey for me in the field of mental health. What follows is the journey itself.

I came to America from England in 1960 to educate my 7-year-old son, who was not likely to pass the "11 plus" in England; born blind, bright, and rebellious, he was refusing to learn braille and was heading for trade school. For myself, I came to America to change careers and to finish the psychoanalytic training I had begun in London. I was accepted as a second-year student in the Psychoanalytic Studies Institute in Philadelphia, which was affiliated with the Philadelphia Mental Health Clinic.

I also decided to register for courses in the psychology department at Temple University. Luckily, I went to the wrong building and discovered Temple's Group Dynamics Center instead. By the following summer I was teaching in it. Dave Jenkins, the chairman of the department, had studied with Kurt Lewin and introduced me to Lewin's field theory (1951). He also taught the first research course I had ever taken, a course in which I was required to define constructs and make operational definitions for everything, including my poetry. I became intensely interested in the fact that there was no common set of definitions for group and individual dynamics, which made it almost impossible to research the dynamics of groups as separate and discrete from the dynamics of individuals or to address the important question of interdependence between the two. I was determined to remedy this. (Fools rush in where angels fear to tread!) There was, however, some firm ground upon which to stand.

THEORETICAL FOUNDATIONS

The Force Field

Lewin's (1951) field theory defines *life space* as a person's perception of his or her environment. Lewin postulated that all behavior is a function of the life space. Thus, perception *now* is behavior *next*. It struck me that Lewin's concept of life space could serve as a map for both individual and group therapy. Korzybski (1948) portrayed man as a map maker who is often so reluctant to revise the map to fit the territory that he is apt to revise the territory to fit the map instead. Festinger's research on his theory of cognitive dissonance (1957) demonstrated that people often deny, change, or lie about their perceptions of reality to ward off the anxiety that is generated when their cognitive maps are invalidated by reality (Festinger & Aronson, 1960). I thought all of these observations applied well to the human tendency to resist change.

Howard and Scott's (1965) theory of stress proposes that all human behavior is goal oriented and can be explained as either approaching or avoiding the problems that lie along the path to the goal. Putting all these concepts together, I adapted Lewin's formulation (behavior is a function of perception of the environment) to read "behavior is a function of perception of the problems that lie along the path to the goal." By redefining problems in terms of the permeability of the boundaries in the life space and by translating approach-and-avoidance behavior into the driving and restraining forces of Lewin's force field, I could see the potential for generating life space maps of group or individual resistance to change. When the restraining forces are the greater, the boundary becomes a barrier. By reducing the restraining forces, permeability to the forces that drive toward the goals of change is regained (Agazarian, 1986). It is a short conceptual step (but a long journey in real time to develop the concept) to define (1) defenses common to both group and individual behavior, (2) which defenses are generic to which phase and subphase of group development, and (3) the methods and techniques for systematically weakening the specific phase-appropriate restraining forces at each boundary between regions at all levels of the life space (see Table 4.3). These concepts are the foundation for both a theory of living human systems and the practice of SCT.

SAVI: An Empirical Approach to Group Communication

All the time that I was immersed in developing theory, I continued my interest in research. In 1963, Anita Simon and I began to develop a system for observing group and individual dynamics by classifying verbal behavior neutrally. Unlike most observation systems in the field, our coding system is based purely on theoretical constructs, not on human judgment. We based our "system for analyzing verbal interaction" (SAVI; Simon & Agazarian, 1967) on constructs from Shannon and Weaver's (1964) information theory and from Howard and Scott's (1965) theory of stress.

According to Shannon and Weaver, noise in the communication channel is entropic to the information it contains. They discovered that their formula for measuring the amount of information in the channel was the negative reciprocal of the entropy formula. Noise (entropy) in the communication channel (defined in terms of ambiguities, contradictions, and redundancies) reduces the probability that information will get from the sender to the receiver. Since this formulation translates easily into a Lewinian force field, I used these ideas to define restraining forces in terms of noise in the communication (Agazarian, 1989d, 1992a).

The concept of noise has several important implications for communication. It goes without saying that information must be goal oriented if it is to be useful. However, if the problem of noise is not addressed, it reduces the potential for the transfer of information. Worse still, the noise itself introduces dissonance, which will then reduce the person's ability to process information even if it does get through (Agazarian, 1969a).

In constructing the theory for SAVI, I assumed that verbal behavioral acts can be coded in terms of ambiguity, contradiction, and redundancy. Each act is also classified in terms of the two kinds of information that exist in every message: *what* the person is communicating and *how* the person is communicating. The relationship between the person and topic information in the message can be coded as either "clear" or "noisy." Noisy communications gave us the criteria for our "avoidance" (entropic) verbal behavior, and clarity in a message constitutes "approach" (negentropic) behavior. Thus, there are two dimensions for the SAVI coding system: approach–avoidance and topic–person. Using these criteria, we generated discrete classes of verbal behavior that could be classified in a matrix called the SAVI grid (Agazarian & Simon, 1967).[1] When the SAVI matrix was used to record a frequency count of our classes of verbal behavior, we were pleased to find that it gave us a snapshot of the approach-and-avoidance character of a person's communication.

Our first informal research using SAVI involved role behaviors as the bridge construct between group and individual dynamics

---

[1]By adding two more variables in the classification of verbal behavior, namely, contingent on the flow (called *contingent*) and orienting the direction of communication (called *orienting*), we arrived at the 3 × 3 matrix that we use today.

(Agazarian, 1982). The first role behaviors we analyzed were the communication patterns that characterized the autocratic, democratic, and laissez-faire leadership behaviors described in the leadership styles researched by Lewin, Lippit, and White (1939). We found that different SAVI patterns characterized the different leadership styles. These patterns stayed the same even when different people demonstrated the styles. We also found that the communication patterns of the groups changed as the leaders changed—whether or not the population of the groups stayed the same. It was an easy conversion to translate those SAVI patterns into force fields analysis. Next we used SAVI to see if the different phases of group development had different communication patterns. (Anita and I were graduate students then, and we submitted all this work as term papers. We had no idea that it might be important or that it was worth preserving.)

SAVI and the Phases of Group Development

In his experiences in groups, Bion (1959) recognized that group behavior is influenced more by the underlying flight, fight, and pairing dynamics of groups than by the psychodynamics of its individual members. Building on this concept, Bennis and Shephard (1956) developed a theory that group development is driven by these underlying forces, which manifest themselves in a predictable sequence. They observed that an early phase of flight is followed by fight and that fight culminates in a scapegoating of the leader and is in turn succeeded by a phase of pairing in intimacy. We used SAVI to code these phases. We once again found that we obtained consistent patterns that characterized each phase. We also coded the communication patterns of the characteristic roles (e.g., "overdependent" and "counterdependent") that group members play within the phases. I later generalized Bennis and Shepard's phases of development to the predictable events in group psychotherapy, and still later I used the SAVI instrument to illustrate empirically the relationship between the phases of group development and the characteristic defenses of each phase.

Anita and I then performed a SAVI microanalysis of the shifting patterns that characterize the life of each phase of group development. We marked the transitions from one phase to another as well as the transitions through the regions of each phase. We called our method "taking a talk for a walk," as it enabled us to follow the flow (as one follows a musical composition by reading the score) between approach and avoidance communications. We used this method when we joined Andy Beck and her research team, applying SAVI, as one of several measures, in a joint analysis of a tape of a psychotherapy session that was presented to the General Systems Theory Panel at the 1985 American Group Psychotherapy Association Conference (Agazarian & Simon, 1989).

From the SAVI data, as well as the literally thousands of hours of working with therapy groups, it became abundantly clear to me not only that there is a predictable rhythm and sequence to the underlying developmental events of a group's life but that how these events are manifested has more to do with the way the group is led than with its composition. In other words, I found that as I, in my role as group leader, varied the group structure, the behavioral norms that developed in the group varied. Thus, in Bennis and Shepard "Training Groups" where my leadership style created a power vacuum by leaving it to the members to solve their own group problems, preoccupation with the power of the leader and competition between members outweighed almost all other considerations (Agazarian & Peters, 1981). When in later Tavistock groups I, as leader, addressed only the group-as-a-whole and ignored members' questions, the ambiguity and deprivation manifestly set off both yearnings to be dependent and reaction formations to rebellion (Agazarian, 1993a). At this stage of my experience as a group leader, I was taking group scapegoating for granted as an inevitable part of group life. I was to discover later that under a systems-centered leadership style the group rarely actively scapegoats.

In spite of the fact that both my research orientation to group dynamics and my practice of group psychotherapy was predominantly Lewinian, I continued to practice as a Freudian psychoanalyst.[2] Therefore, I used psychoanalytical thinking when I sat behind the couch and group dynamic thinking when I worked with a group. As a Freudian, I interpreted all behavior as a function of unconscious repetitions of the past. As a Lewinian, I interpreted all behavior as a function of perception of the present. As a Freudian, my own unconscious was my guide. As a Lewinian, I was guided by the research methods of reality testing and empirical observation. As a group therapist, I observed the group from the group-as-a-whole perspective in the context of phases of group development; as an analyst, I observed individual members in the group psychodynamically. As a Freudian, I listened with a third ear to the individual voices. As a Lewinian, I listened to the voice of the group-as-a-whole. I was, in effect, now between two disciplines, and I often felt split. I did not know then what good training I was get-

[2]As a psychoanalyst, I could rely on a significant and growing body of literature on theory and practice. In group psychotherapy work, on the other hand, the promise of the group theory and research that had enriched the 1950s (Cartwright & Zander, 1960) was not fulfilled in the '60s and '70s.

ting in being able to contain significant differences while looking for bridges into similarity.[3]

SYSTEMS THINKING: FROM THEORY TO PRACTICE

The next important influence in my life was systems thinking. I spent some weeks in 1979 with George and Vasso Vassilliou in their Athenian Institute of Anthropos. On one occasion, when I was talking about bridging between group and individual dynamics, George threw a bit of hamburger into his pond. One goldfish, faster than the others, reached it first and swam off with it. As it was too large for him to swallow, the other goldfish darted after him and nibbled away at his prize. Pointing to the goldfish, George said "from the perspective of the fish in general, we see an efficient distribution and feeding system; one fish is playing a role for the whole shoal of fish by catching the hamburger and holding it in his mouth while the whole group of fish feed." "However," George continued, "we see something different when we take the perspective of the individual fish, who is having his dinner stolen from him before he can eat it" (Agazarian, 1987b).

In 1980 I joined Helen Durkin's American Group Psychotherapy Association General Systems Committee just after the committee finished writing its book (Durkin, 1981). We met twice a year, and for the first time since working with Dave Jenkins, I had colleagues with whom I could regularly discuss both the systems concepts and how to put them into practice. When we met for the last time, in 1984, Jay Fiedler urged us to make systems theory operational in practice. It seemed impossible, but I was determined to try.

My first step toward implementing systems theory resulted from a change in my perception of myself and my own work. People had always claimed that I was an exceptional group and individual therapist. I was not equally impressed with myself. It seemed to me that, however well the individual and group sessions seemed to go, my results were not significantly different, in terms of treatment outcomes, from those of colleagues whose work I respected—whatever their discipline! I accepted that I had charisma, that I had learned well how to manage the dynamics of large and small groups, and that I was completely involved and dedicated to the individuals with whom I worked. At the same time, I was disappointed not only in myself but also in the inability of therapy to make predictable or systematic change in the patients.

---

[3]One of my first psychoanalytic papers (1963) reinterpreted Seche Heyes's "Renee Case" (1951) in terms of "transformation through the discrimination and integration of differences."

There was always a part of me that continued to try to build a theory. In my heart I rejected much of what was traditional and accepted theory in the field, but I continued to use it because I knew nothing better. Tolerating and containing the chaos of persistent internal skepticism about one's life's work is not easy; I had many points of departure from traditional beliefs and was often terrified of the direction my ideas were taking me. I wanted to settle for the known, to turn back to the security of a shared discipline, yet I found myself continually turning away from the known toward the unknown.

A turning point in this process came when I was preparing to be the discussant for Sampsom and Weiss's presentation of their work to the 1989 American Group Psychotherapy Association. The Sampson and Weiss hypothesis was that pathogenic beliefs are the source of inhibitions, symptoms, and anxiety. As I prepared my paper, the idea came to me that there is an unconscious cultural pathogenic belief that man is the center of the world. I then hypothesized that this unconscious pathogenic belief is acted out, in both individual and group therapy, by treating the patient as if he or she is the center of the world and that the patient is thus unconsciously encouraged to take things personally. Then I realized that there is an even more fundamental unconscious pathogenic belief, common to both the therapist and the patient, namely, that it is the therapist who is really the center of the world. The acting out of these contradictory unconscious pathogenic beliefs in therapy would explain why so many therapies founder on unresolved transferences (see Pennov's [1978] book on love addiction). Worse still, the egocentricity of this focus would generate the very narcissistic pain, shame, and survivor guilt (in both the patient and the therapist) that was identified in Sampsom and Weiss's research. The idea that much of the suffering in therapy (my own as well as my patients') could be iatrogenic held such cognitive dissonance for me that I dreaded to present it publicly. (Revolutionary though it was to me, it was hardly noticed in my presentation!)

In the short run, this reasoning process made me look closely to see which dynamics in therapy groups were generic to group development and which could be iatrogenically induced by leader behavior. In the long run, it contributed to formulating the goals for SCT as transformation from self-centered to systems-centered.

Then came a demonstration I did for the Eastern Group Psychotherapy Society (EGPS) meeting in New York in 1985. The meeting consisted of demonstrations by volunteers of four different leadership styles. My demonstration, of the Tavistock method, was last. I worked with the group as a whole, without individual interpretation; helped the group to hear its own voice; contained the scapegoating; and helped the group take back its projections and come to closure. The response from the audience was enthusiastic and complimentary. I was elated, but still unable to understand their enthusiasm (Agazarian, 1987a).

That same evening I was told that before their session with me the demonstration group had felt themselves to be in sufficient trouble to ask the conference coordinators to help them integrate the rather overwhelming experience of four different leaders in 2 days. After my session, however, the group cancelled their request saying they felt they had integrated the experience in their session with me! This was outcome feedback of sufficient objectivity for me to take in. Clearly, I had done something that many other group therapists were not doing. But what?

In 1980 I had started a group-as-a-whole training group in Philadelphia, and in 1985 I formed a similar training group in New York. After the aforementioned EGPS meeting, the members of these training groups went through great turbulence while I tried to identify the variables that I had been using that were working so well. By then I was taking for granted that the same principles of group dynamics operated in all groups, whether large or small, and that there was an underlying coherence to human dynamics that applied just as well to groups as to individuals. By 1990, members from my training groups and I were exploring together the theory we were developing. All the members, from all my training groups, began to meet formally twice a year, and I had the opportunity to experiment with groups as large as 40 and 50.

For large group work I have a great debt of gratitude to Lionel Kruger (1975) and to Pat de Mare for their years spent differentiating the dynamics of the large group from the small. One important difference Pat formulated is that large group dynamics are relatively free of the family transferences that are so easily stimulated in the small group. In his work on the function of hatred in large groups, Pat reconceptualized hatred from superego pathology to a natural response to the frustration endemic to large group processes (de Mare, Piper, & Thompson, 1991). His recognition that hatred contained is transformed into creativity has now become one of the foundations of my systems-centered therapy, or SCT. His work altered my understanding of the hatred that erupts in the fight phase of groups in the form of scapegoating, first of each other and then of the leader. I began to deliberately encourage the group's exploration of the impulse to act out the hatred, as well as of the underlying conflicts that generate it.

When, in 1990, I did my first "how to do it" videotape (generously role played by the Philadelphia training group), what I demonstrated was a group-as-a-whole leader approach, which, like *The Visible and Invisible Group* (my first book; Agazarian & Peters, 1981), is half oriented psychodynamically and half oriented to systems. I had not then developed the method of "functional subgrouping," one of the unique features of SCT (see Chapter 2 for more detail).

It would require a major change in orientation on my part to depart from my lifelong style of following a group and interpreting its dynamics as they emerged to actively and even intrusively intervening to structure the group process. This transition was begun when I attended a conference on short-term dynamic psychotherapy (STDP) led by its developer, Habib Davanloo. Davanloo teaches STDP by presenting videotapes of clinical interviews (the very idea of videotaping patients was shocking to me). If I had not seen with my own eyes the results that Davanloo achieved in his "breakthrough interview," I doubt that I would have had the courage to explore, discover, and develop the methods that now characterize SCT.[4] The virtue of STDP's insistence that all sessions be videotaped is that a comparison can be made between what the therapist thought was going on dynamically in a session and what actually did go on (the two are often shockingly disparate!). Furthermore, videotape makes it possible to observe the patients' "intention movements," or signals of their intention to act (Tinbergen, 1951). I had been working with Dick Peters in cotherapy since 1968, and had been informally joined in private practice by Anita Simon and Claudia Byram in the 1970s. In 1990 we were still working together when the four of us started supervision in the STDP method with Mike Alpert and watched videotapes of our own patients. Making the transition from a therapeutic approach that respected defenses to one that confronted them elicited great resistance in all of us. However, the acuity of our perceptions increased to the point that we came to rely on the empirical data to make our clinical judgments about how much pressure to put on patients' defenses without risking decompensation,[5] regression, or stubborn resistance.

---

[4]Dr. Davanloo's work served, for me, as an umbrella for many other influences that I had not been able to incorporate in therapy: The layman's suggestion that when in doubt one should ask the patient (a revolutionary idea to a young trainee analyst!); Wolpe's (1958) pioneering work on deconditioning anxiety; Tinbergen's (1951) contributions to the science of ethology and the function of animal intention movements; Berne's (1964) simplification of psychodynamic concept; the work of the committees that translated psychodynamic diagnoses into behavioral descriptors for the American Psychiatric Association's *Diagnostic and Statistical Manual of Mental Disorders* (DSM); neurolinguistic programming (Bandler & Grindler, 1979) and the interpretation of the signals of facial movements and color; and Ekman's (1992) research about the interdependence of facial expression, body posture, and emotional experience.

[5]For example, motoric movement with anxiety signals a patient's central nervous system involvement, which is a signal to proceed in the direction currently evolving in the therapy. This is in contrast to a patient's verbal confusion, which signals a cognitive disruption and is a signal to stop until the anxiety reaction is deconditioned.

In 1992 the four of us were invited to join a research project for the University of Pennsylvania that involved treating individual patients with generalized anxiety disorders with 16 sessions of STDP. We were required to review the videotapes of our clients weekly to maintain reliability with each other and to reinforce the consistency of the techniques of the research approach. Since the case manager and supervisor for our section, Leigh McCullough, was writing the guidelines for adapting STDP to a 16-session framework (1995), we had the opportunity to develop not only our clinical techniques but also the theory. I am grateful for these sessions, for much of the groundwork in refining my own theory was done as we six (Fran Carter joined us in private practice at about this time) thrashed out the differences and similarities between STDP and SCT. This research work on STDP marked the final transition for me into doing what I had not dared to do before, namely, develop and formalize an approach to therapy based on the theory of living human systems.

Key Concepts of Systems-Centered Therapy

Like STDP, SCT is modeled around a formal and systematic treatment plan that progresses, step by step, toward undoing defenses in a systematic hierarchy. In SCT, the first module in the hierarchy of defense modification is similar to STDP's foundation work toward the "breakthrough" (Davanloo's term for the point in the initial interview when the patient's authentic murderous rage *breaks through* his defenses against it). The major difference is that defense modification in STDP is essentially carried out in a traditional physician–patient relationship (in which the therapist knows what is best for the patient). SCT, on the other hand, is a partnership in which the therapist governs the structure of the therapy so that the patient is confronted with a series of forced choices (the "fork-in-the-road" technique) between exploring the defense itself or what is being defended against. The patient governs the choice as to which "fork-in-the-road" they will explore first. The patient does not have a choice about whether to explore or not. The SCT therapist does not choose which fork the patient should explore first.

By rigorously keeping the therapeutic work appropriate to the context of system development, we discovered the importance of sequence and timing and began to understand that certain work can only be done when it is in context. Mastering the techniques for undoing the defenses in the flight subphase lays the groundwork for the more complex work of the fight subphase. It became obvious that each developmental phase provides the most relevant context for modifying the defenses specific to it. It also became clear to us that as long as simple conflicts are addressed before more complex ones are, and as long as affect is contained within here-and-now reality, the more serious flooding of underlying dedifferentiated regressive experience, which so often threatens groups, can be contained, explored, and integrated. Thus, working in the appropriate context enables regression in the service of integration and avoids dedifferentiation.

A major impetus to my increasing pressure on myself to formalize SCT was the growing influence of managed care in the mid-1990s. I wanted to see whether I could develop an SCT treatment plan in which each therapeutic session would serve as a self-contained therapy that could stand alone or take its place in one of a series of sessions, each of which built upon the work in the session before it and prepared the ground for the one that came next. If this turned out to be possible, then SCT might well serve as a short-term therapy which could survive the the interruptions and resumptions that so often accompany the requirements of managed care.

What became formalized from this ambition is the hierarchy of defense modification which serves to reduce the restraining forces to system development at all system levels of the therapeutic hierarchy. Because SCT is a therapy based on an ongoing series of choices the patient is *able* to make, resistance is largely bypassed. Each session is a minitherapy in and of itself. Stalemated sessions are rare. If the patient has to stop therapy because insurance coverage stops, therapeutic gains have still been made and are maintained. When the patient returns to SCT, the next experience of therapy can begin where the last one left off. What is more, because SCT is technique based rather than person based, it can be continued at another time with a different SCT therapist, trained to make the same kind of authentic relationship as the therapist of the patients' previous treatment.

SCT therapists are currently testing out systems-centered groups to learn how best to help people make the transition from being self-centered to systems-centered. It is an SCT belief that relief from the suffering of self-centeredness comes when members can experience their roles in the subgroup and the group-as-a-whole and observe their individual selves mirrored in the structure and function of the hierarchy of living systems.

A THEORY OF LIVING HUMAN SYSTEMS

An Overview of the Theory and Its Practice

R uth Benedict (1934) in her *Patterns of Culture* pointed out that *who* anyone is has as much or more to do with one's environment than it has to do with one's nature. The "good" person of one culture is the "bad" of another. Thomas Szasz (1970) noted that the person who is "made mad" in one culture is "made wise" in another. The Milgram (1974) experiments demonstrated that marked shifts from "good" to "bad" can be elicited in a matter of hours or days in any culture.

The nature of the culture and the behavior and life experience of the people within it are all determined by the norms that govern what people do and what they do not do. This is true for the entire hierarchy of living human systems, whether the system is an individual; a collection of individuals that form a group; or a collection of groups that make up an organization, a country, or the world.

The major issue for systems-centered practitioners is not whether the conditions we design for our patients in therapy elicit the patient behavior that we treat (it is our opinion that they do) but, rather, that we take explicit responsibility for the conditions we design and that we design them with explicit goals in mind. The norms of a systems-centered group are directly and deliberately induced rather than indirectly influenced or simply allowed to emerge.

The people who enter a systems-centered group learn specific techniques in order to become systems-centered members. However, membership alone does not make a systems-centered group. A systems-centered group is formed through developing subgroups. Subgrouping (which is defined and described in detail in Chapter 2) is the intervening variable that brings into being the systems-centered group. Members develop the subgroups, and the subgroups develop the group-as-a-whole.

In forming the systems-centered group, therapists use a sequenced and replicable series of methods and techniques to modify the defenses that restrain the driving forces that are directed toward the goals of therapy. SCT goals are operationalized in terms of a vectoring, or directing energy toward system goals—through the methods and techniques of functional subgrouping, boundarying, and defense modification, in the context of the phases of group development.

The goal of SCT is to enable patients to use their own common sense to manage their everyday lives. In SCT common sense is understood as the product of a good relationship between two parts (or subsystems) in the self: comprehension and apprehension. Comprehension is the cognitive knowledge arrived at through thinking and imagination; it is the world that is already known through words. Apprehension is the knowledge that comes from intuition; it is affective, not cognitive, and has to be translated into words. The SCT goal is to make the boundary permeable between apprehensive and comprehensive knowledge (Agazarian, 1996). This goal is reached when the knowledge gained in therapy is not merely comprehended (as it is in intellectual insight, which enables people to explain their dynamics in words) but also apprehended (thus yielding an insight that comes from experiencing and understanding what was unknown). Apprehensive insight changes people's lives. The first step in reaching this goal is learning to discriminate between thinking and feeling. And, indeed, this is the first fork-in-the-road in the journey one undertakes in SCT, a journey that involves exploring experience rather than explaining it. At this fork, SCT patients take their first step in learning the differences between experience as they know it and the unknown levels of their experience they have entered therapy to discover. The fork-in-the-road is one of the most important of the techniques in SCT which makes operational the principle of discrimination and integration. The patient makes incremental discriminations of differences by exploring and subsequently integrating the experiences they discover at each fork-in-the-road.

DEFINING LIVING HUMAN SYSTEMS

A theory of living human systems defines a hierarchy of isomorphic systems that are energy organizing, goal directed, and self-correcting. The three systems defined for the practice of group and individual psychotherapy are the member, the subgroup, and the "group-as-a-whole." The practice of SCT is based on the following ideas about systems and how they change and progress:

Systems give and take. Systems exist in a hierarchy of give-and-take (output and input). Systems keep themselves stable and in balance by giving no more than they can afford and taking no more than they can integrate.

Systems open and close their boundaries. Systems manage the flow of give-and-take by opening and closing their boundaries. This, in systems-centered language, is called "boundary permeability." Similarities and differences in a living system hierarchy are communicated across the system's boundaries. System boundaries open to similarities and close to differences. Similarities are already familiar to the system's internal organization and thus do not introduce the system to much that is new. Systems let in the familiar with little difficulty. Integrating similarities does not require the system to change. Differences that are too different, however, do require change.

Systems stay stable and survive by integrating similarities. The give-and-take of familiar information between the system and its environment maintains the system in a good relationship with its inner and outer world, keeps the system stable, and increases the probability that it will survive in the short run. Too much similarity and not enough difference, however, introduces redundancy and rigidity, which in the long run will threaten system survival.

Systems close boundaries to differences. Systems have difficulty with differences. Differences introduce new information into the system. Both the new information and the existing system have to be reorganized before the new information can be integrated. Differences create "noise" in the system while the system changes sufficiently to integrate them.

Systems change and transform by integrating differences. The give-and-take of unfamiliar information between the system and its environment require both the system and its environment to develop the ability to change. Differences make for bad relationships within the system and between the system and its environment in the short run, but integrating differences is what enables systems to change and transform in the long run.

Systems organize differences in two ways. When differences are not too different, the system can do the work of integration without too much difficulty and can change from simple to complex without too many growing pains. When differences are too different, however, the system either closes its boundaries and keeps the differences out or lets the differences in as a split-off part of the system, that does not communicate with the rest of the system. Sometimes the system maintains the split, and whatever developmental potential would have developed from integrating the difference is lost permanently. At other times, as the system develops greater complexity, the difference can be taken in and integrated. Functional subgrouping (described in Chapter 2) is the SCT method for managing the challenges in integrating differences.

In SCT we deliberately and actively structure each system to potentiate the system functions expressed in the following statements:

Systems are energy organizing. Energy, in the theory of living human systems, is defined as the ability to do work (Rothman, 1992) or, more specifically for SCT, the ability to work toward the goals of therapy. Energy also means communication. Communication is understood in terms of the transfer of energy across the system's boundaries (boundaries are the structure within which information is located in space and time) (Miller, 1978). In SCT the technique of boundarying reduces the noise in communication so that boundaries can remain permeable to information.

Systems are goal-directed. The goals of a system are survival, development, and transformation of the system. These are the primary goals of SCT, the secondary goals being the solving of problems in the environment. Vectoring is the process by which information is directed across boundaries in space and time and toward goals.

Systems are self-correcting. Systems stay stable in the context of an ever-changing world by receiving, containing, and integrating information. Conflictual (noisy) communications destabilize the system. Systems restabilize through conflict resolution, either by splitting off differences that disrupt the existing integration (avoiding change) or by delaying and containing conflict until differences can be integrated. Functional subgrouping is the conflict resolution method of containing conflict through the change process until differences in the apparently similar are recognized and similarities in the apparently different can be discovered and integrated. Systems survive through the ability to approach and solve the problems that lie on the path to the goal.

THE THEORY AND ITS DEFINITIONS

A theory of living human systems approaches all living things, as small as a cell and as large as or larger than society, by defining them as systems that are similar in structure, function, and dynamics. This then sets up a hierarchy of classes of living systems whereby each class, and every member in it, has a set of factors common to all classes in the hierarchy. Yet each class, and every member of each class, is unique unto itself. The advantage of keeping the isomorphism of all systems in mind is that what one learns about the dynamics of any one system says something about the dynamics of all the other systems in the hierarchy (Agazarian, 1989d).

As with all theories, the bridge between the theory of living human systems and reality is made by developing operational definitions. For the theory of living human systems on which SCT is based, connections have been made from the constructs of the theory, through the definitions of those constructs, to the methods that form the blueprint for practice. Each systems-centered intervention can therefore be thought of as a hypothesis that tests the reliability and validity of the ideas that lie behind it. Since the theory behind SCT is necessarily abstract and has its own terminology, a glossary is presented at the back of the book for the reader's convenience. Readers may find themselves consulting the glossary frequently while reading the early chapters of this book. Later, the definitions will seem almost self-evident.

SCT uses three major methods: subgrouping, vectoring, and boundarying. These methods, which are described in detail in Section I of this book, relate both to the definition of the theory of living systems on the one hand, and to the techniques that characterize systems-centered therapy on the other (see Table 1.1).

Hierarchy

Every system in the hierarchy exists in the environment above it and is the environment of the system below it. To visualize a concrete hierarchical system, imagine a set of nested Russian dolls: Each doll exists in the "environment" of the doll above it and is the environment for the doll below it. The practical implications that can be drawn from this image (or map) is that communication is most direct between dolls that are next to each other. SCT defines the hierarchy of a group as the member, the subgroup, and the "group-as-a-whole." The subgroup exists in the environment of the group-as-a-whole and is the environment for its members. The subgroup shares its boundaries with both the member and the group-as-a-whole. Therefore, the most efficient intervention is usually to the subgroup.

That the subgroup and not the individual member is the basic unit of the group is a new idea to the field of group psychotherapy and introduces a systems-centered orientation to the existing leader-centered, member-centered, and group-as-a-whole orientations to group psychotherapy. This systems-centered focus in SCT discriminates between the *self-centered system* (that exists for the person who is aware of themselves as their context) and the *systems-centered system* (that exists for the person who is aware both of themselves and of themselves in a hierarchy of con-

TABLE 1.1. Isomorphy: Definitions of Theory, Methods, and Techniques

Isomorphy: Systems are similar in structure and function and different in different contexts. There is an interdependent relationship between function and structure.

Definitions

Function	*Energy*	*Structure*
Systems-centered systems survive, develop, and transform through the process of discriminating and integrating differences	Systems-centered systems organize and direct information (energy) toward primary and secondary goals	Systems-centered structure defines boundaries in the context of space, time, reality, and role

Operational methods

Subgrouping	*Vectoring*	*Boundarying*
Methods for containing and managing conflicts in communication around differences and the unknown	Methods for directing communication toward the goals	Methods for managing the permeability of boundaries to information across the boundaries by reducing "noise" in communication

Techniques

Functional subgrouping	*"Fork-in-the-road"*	*The hierarchy of defense modification*
"Containing" "Resonating" Self-system observation of contexts from four systems Perspectives: changing from self-centered to systems-centered	Weakening the restraining forces Redirecting flight, fight, and pairing toward work goals	Determining what to communicate and how to communicate in the context of time, space, reality, role, and phase of system development

texts). The steps in this process are discussed later in this chapter (see Table 1.3).

The impact of hierarchical system development in an SCT group is well illustrated by the difference in perception and experience when group members take something "just personally" as compared to when their awareness extends to their roles in relation to the systems-centered contexts. The context for the person in the systems-oriented "member role" is the subgroup, whereas the context for the subgroup is the group-as-a-whole. Understanding how the context changes as roles change opens the door to seeing the world from more than one perspective. Enabling group members to recognize the differences in perception and experience as the context changes is one of the tasks of SCT practice. Every participant of an SCT group increases his or her potential to access different levels of experience.

The term *hierarchy* also refers to the systematic hierarchy of strategies used in SCT for effecting change. Whereas in most disciplines the path to the treatment goals is intuited rather than spelled out, in SCT the path is explicitly mapped and the methods and techniques are specifically developed from a systematic application of the theory. What the next step is for a patient can always be determined by where he or she is on the map.

All systems develop from simple to complex. This basic principle underlies the methods of SCT defense modification. A specific hierarchy of defenses is defined, and each defense is then modified in sequence. The modification of the simplest defense can (and does) have a complex impact. For example, the first modification in SCT involves defensive intellectualization. The patient is introduced immediately to the fork-in-the-road between exploring and explaining. The technique of the fork-in-the-road puts into practice the SCT concept that change comes through the process of first discriminating and then integrating. Thus, rather than taking the more usual path of explaining their problems and symptoms to the therapist, SCT patients are required to explore the conflict that is generating their problems. This simple modification has a complex effect on the whole course of therapy, for it discourages interpretations by both patient and therapist, enables a focus on the unknown instead of the known, and bypasses typical resistances (since SCT patients work at the fork-in-the-road between exploring their experience and acting it out).

Isomorphy

All systems in the hierarchy of living human systems are isomorphic in that they are similar in structure and function and are different in different contexts. The hierarchy of nesting Russian dolls is a good example of iso-morphy. Although the size of each doll is different from the others, according to its context, the dolls have the same structure and function (to nest). Moreover, if you influence one system, you influence them all. It is the isomorphy between the self-centered and systems-centered systems that enables therapeutic change at any level of the system hierarchy to potentiate change in the individual.

Structure and function are interdependent: Structure influences function and function influences structure. Just as a river bank influences the flow of the river, so the river itself shapes the bank. A good demonstration of how structure and function are interdependent occurs at the beginning of every SCT group. As soon as the group begins, members immediately move their chairs in relationship to each other so that every member can see every other member. The structure that results not only forms the geographical boundary of the group (a boundary that marks the difference between outside the group and inside it) but also makes it possible for each member to meet the eyes of every other member. It is through the technique of eye contact that SCT members deliberately shift their attention ("vector their energy") across the boundary between the distractions outside the group and the responsibilities of membership inside the group. This shifting of attention structures the group in space and time. It is also through eye contact that members take their first step into subgrouping, the method by which the basic principle of systems-centered function is put into operation.

FUNCTION

All living human systems are similar in function in that each system survives, develops from simple to complex, and transforms through discriminating and integrating similarities and differences—both differences in the apparently similar and similarities in the apparently different.

Managing System Function by Subgrouping

Subgrouping in the SCT group is the method that puts into practice the system's developmental process of discrimination and integration. Subgroups are used deliberately to split the two different sides of the conflict, so that each side can be contained and understood separately as a discrimination step toward developing whatever ability the system needs in order to accept and integrate the conflictual differences (Agazarian, 1989b). Conflict resolution through functional subgrouping is successfully applied to all living human systems, not just to group psychotherapy. It is through discriminating and integrating differences that systems develop from simple to complex. Thus, the group-as-a-whole develops from simple to complex by splitting into subgroups around differences, which the larger system of the environment contains until the differences are integrated.

The method of functional subgrouping is used to address conflicts and process problems in a group so that they can be contained, explored, and managed. Managing conflict is the major challenge in all groups. In every meeting of every group, subgroups come together around similarities and separate on differences. However, whereas groups typically stereotype or scapegoat differences, in SCT work the natural tendency to subgroup is actively directed into functional subgrouping and away from stereotype subgrouping. The differences between stereotype subgroups and functional subgroups pertain both to how the group splits and to how those splits are worked through.

Stereotype subgroups form around obvious differences: men and women, black and white, yeas and nays, and so forth. Stereotype subgroups manage conflict by denying that it exists, by explaining why it should not exist, or by behaving as if it should not exist. Stereotype subgroups scapegoat on the basis of differences; functional subgroups explore them.

Functional subgroups form around conflicts. In functional subgrouping, members form a subgroup by vectoring their energy toward the similarities, rather than the differences, between themselves and others. They then focus all their energy on discovering more about their own similarities. The conflict is thus contained in the group-as-a-whole in working subgroups. As each subgroup explores its own side of the conflict, differences (that are not too different) are discovered in what was apparently similar. As differences are discovered and integrated, differentiation in each subgroup increases. As differentiation increases within each subgroup, so does the potential for discovering similarities between the subgroups. It is at this point that integration occurs in the group-as-a-whole and information is spontaneously transferred without the conflicts of the original communication. The developmental process of the SCT group is to split, contain, integrate, reintegrate, and transform, all at ever-increasing levels of sophistication and complexity.

Through this process, functional subgrouping increases the probability that splits will be contained at the group-as-a-whole level, rather than displaced into stereotype-containing roles (Agazarian, 1992a). SCT encourages the confrontation of conflict and discourages escape into ambivalence, passive withdrawal, depression, or other solitary defenses. Subgrouping helps all members to experience both sides of their conflict and to acknowledge and accept both their internal similarities and differences. Stereotype subgroups assign stereotype roles like the identified patient or the scapegoat. These roles then serve as separated subsystems for unacceptable differences that are denied and externalized. In SCT the very act of subgrouping integrates the splits that inherent differences cause (which is the obverse of solving the conflict through projection and projective identification).

STRUCTURE

All living human systems are similar in structure in that each system is defined by its boundaries in space, time, and reality. The structure of a group determines not only how it reaches its goals but also if it can reach its goals. The structure of an SCT group is defined by its boundaries—its boundaries in real space and time and its boundaries in psychological space and time. Boundaries contain the potential work energy for the group. It is by communication across the boundaries within, between, and among subsystems in the group's hierarchy that systems transform from simple to complex. Both individual and group boundaries open and close to information. How permeable boundaries are depends upon how well new information fits with the current store of information. How each group and individual develops is determined by what information crosses the boundary and how it is organized. System structure is managed by the methods and techniques of *boundarying* and *vectoring* (defined below; for more on boundarying, see Chapter 3).

Boundaries in Space and Time

Groups exist in space and time. It is important for the group to know where and when to meet. The group that is clear about its starting and stopping time can do its work in the real world and not be distracted by the fantasy that time is forever. For a group to exist its members must also be present psychologically. Unlike reality space and time boundaries, which structure the group by geography and clock time, psychological boundaries structure the group in the mind. The mind does not recognize boundaries, and members roam through space and time unless psychological boundaries are established in the group.

The first psychological boundary to cross is from the world outside the group to the world inside. One of the goals of SCT therapy is to develop a consciousness in members of when they cross psychological time and space boundaries in the service of *flight* from difficulties in the here-and-now of the group and when they turn to their memories of the past or their thoughts about the present and future as a *resource* to help them in the present. Learning to recognize when psychological time boundaries have been crossed begins with the first simple act of recognizing the difference between the here-and-now experience of the present and the fears and preoccupations that prevent this experience. SCT members are encouraged to redirect their energy away from intrusive thoughts (one fork-in-the-road) and toward the experience that they are now defending against (the other fork-in-the-road). They learn that boundaries in the here-and-now contain the available energy in the group for work.

In SCT, *trust* is defined as "tested expectations." Members need to test their expectations against reality outcomes and to take this journey over and over again. SCT members come to trust that learning how to deal with the intrapersonal and interpersonal issues in the here-and-now of the group helps them not only deal better with parallel issues in their environment outside the group but also deal differently with their relationships from the past. Taking flight from a present problem to one that easily associates to it in the past substitutes the pain of the past for the unresolved conflict in the present. When members turn to the problems of the present instead, they nearly always discover that the abilities they have now, compared to their abilities in the past, make solving their problems in present reality much less difficult than they anticipated.

Reality Boundaries

The boundary between reality and irreality marks the threshold between the fantasies of the group—the wishes, fears, hopes, and aspirations of its members—and the real facts of group life, which constitute the context within which the group must solve its problems. Cognitive misinterpretations and misconstructions generated by defensive explanations of experience are contrasted with reality-tested and self-validated information acquired by exploring experience. Solving the problems that misconstructions of reality cause requires undoing the defenses that created these problems; only then can the original real-world problems (that were defended against) be identified and addressed. SCT insists on developing a communication climate in which reality testing is taken for granted; members are encouraged to test in the group the reality of their fears of what others are thinking rather than associate to those fears. This is both hard and courageous work. However, there is great reward: Many of the symptoms that bring people into therapy are secondary, rather than primary, problems, and such symptoms change quickly when defenses are modified.

Role Boundaries

Roles are subsystems that have boundaries and function in relationship to a goal. "Member," "subgroup," "group-as-a-whole," and "person" are all roles in an SCT therapy group. So, at another level of abstraction, is the role of leader. Roles are defined by behavior. If the person in the role of leader behaved like an identified patient, he or she would be out of role (actually, out of one role and into another!). Roles are not the same as the people in them. Roles are typically interactive: Many group members volunteer for the role of hero, victim, identified patient, mascot, or scapegoat, but few are chosen. Nor are roles necessarily confined to a single person: Usually, we see only one identified patient or scapegoat but many caretakers or scapegoaters. Roles have different meanings in different contexts. The role of the identified patient, for example, has one meaning for the member who has volunteered for the role (the import of an old role into a new setting), another meaning for the people who are caring for the identified patient (projecting onto another the part of themselves they cannot care for), and yet another meaning for the group-as-a-whole (that of containing the group conflict around dependency by splitting it into subgroups of "caregetters" and "caregivers"). Understanding their personal experience in terms of being "in role" in these different contexts prevents members from taking things "just personally." When a person takes things just personally, they exist only in the context of the self. Their boundaries are impermeable to any information, from inside themselves or outside, that is different from the way they think already. Their boundaries have become barriers.

In sum, the work of SCT members is to learn the skills of vectoring or directing energy across the boundaries from outside to inside, from the past and future to the present, from irreality to reality, and across the boundaries that define their roles in the context of the member system, subgroup system, and the system of the group-as-a-whole.

Boundarying

The nondefensive communication climate that is characteristic of an SCT group is a result of "boundarying" techniques, which filter out defensive communications before they cross the boundaries and cause problems in the group. Techniques for vectoring, or guiding, group energy across relevant boundaries are quite specific and rely on recognizing the location of the defensive communication and modifying it at the boundary (by weakening the restraining forces at the boundary). The SCT therapist focuses on the transactions across the boundaries between, within, and among systems. Modifying the restraining forces to communication increases the probability that the system will reach its goals.

More specifically, boundarying is used to filter out defensive "noise" in communication. How much noise there is determines how permeable boundaries are to the information in the communication. In SCT, defensive behavior (whether verbal or nonverbal) is understood to function like noise in a communication channel and makes it difficult to get the message across.

For SCT, noise is defined in terms of ambiguous, contradictory, or redundant communication. Too much ambiguity, as when the group speculates in vague and obscure and meandering ways, will flood the group. Too much redundancy, as when the group says the same thing over and over again, will stall the group. Too much contradiction—even socially acceptable contradictions like "Yes, but . . . " or "Don't you really think . . . ?" or "I know you won't . . ."—will irritate the group. Once an ambiguous, redundant, or contradictory climate is imported into the group, both the stress it arouses and the impact it has on the ability of the group to solve problems has to be managed. In other words, the way the group is communicating preempts what is being communicated and has to be managed if it is not to seriously impair both the climate for work and the ability to work. It makes good sense, therefore, to stop trouble before it starts. SCT leaders intervene to reduce the noise in communications at the boundaries, within the person, between the members and subgroups, and in the group-as-a-whole.

A major difference between SCT and psychodynamic therapies is the management of boundaries. In most psychodynamic therapies, free associations serve both work and flight from work. Patients associate to the present, the past, and the future; to fantasies, wishes, and fears; and to speculations and interpretations of reality. Interpretations of projections and motivation generate anxiety as well as insight. Defensive communications are not filtered as they cross the boundaries. In short, psychodynamic therapists pay attention to all communications, whether they increase or decrease symptomatology; SCT therapists do not.

An SCT group climate is developed by filtering out as much defensiveness and anxiety as possible before it enters the group and by developing communication norms within the group that are low on explanations and high on exploration, that is, low on interpretations and critical judgments and high on reality testing.

Vectoring Energy

Vectoring in SCT is the management of energy as it is directed toward a goal. The SCT method of vectoring introduces techniques that make it possible for SCT group members to direct their energy away from their defenses and toward the goals of therapy. At each fork-in-the-road, members direct their energy toward the alternative of solving problems rather than the alternative of defending against them. A vector can be visualized as a moving arrow that has a direction, a force, and a target (goal). Shifting energy from one part of the system to another is like changing the direction of this arrow and redirecting its energy. Vectoring enables individuals to cross the boundaries from all their many roles outside the group and into the role of group member in the context of this particular group system.

By thinking in terms of the vectoring of energy, SCT group members learn to recognize when they are avoiding their here-and-now reality and emigrating across the boundaries of space and time. Group members emigrate in two ways: in physical reality, by changing locations or by ignoring clock time, and in psychological reality, by turning their thoughts and emotions toward the past or the future or by leaving the here-and-now experience and living in the reality created by their thoughts.

In SCT, energy is deliberately vectored; that is, it is directed by conscious choice. Members are sensitized to notice when they are shifting their attention from their relationship to the here-and-now of the group to thoughts of a relationship that takes them to some other place in space and time.

All group therapies have methods for resolving conflicts and vectoring the work energy of the group. What is different in the SCT approach is that the methods and techniques for managing both activities are introduced from the first few moments of a group (in a step-by-step hierarchy from the simplest and easiest to the more complex and difficult). Subgrouping provides the method for containing the conflicts and problems that lie on the path to the goal, thus allowing them to be addressed in a way that reduces them rather than increases them. Boundarying provides the methods for managing noise, which would otherwise disrupt the system, by reducing the restraining forces of ambiguity, contradiction, and redundancy. Vectoring directs the driving forces so that both the primary and secondary goals (see below) lie in the same direction.

The Force Field

A force field of equal and opposite driving and restraining forces defines the level of equilibrium of a system. The restraining forces maintain the status quo of the system whereas the driving forces are vectored toward change. Whether or not boundaries are permeable to change is determined by whether or not the driving forces are stronger than the

TABLE 1.2. A Map of the Boundary between Reality and Irreality

Force field[a]

Driving forces ——>	<—— Restraining forces
Explore ——>	<—— Explain
Checking out whether someone is thinking what you think they think ——>	<—— Mind reading
Collecting data about what you know about the future and discriminating the present from the past ——>	<—— Negative predictions

[a]Adapted from Kurt Lewin's concept of a field of force to illustrate SCT boundarying.

restraining forces. Reducing restraining forces is always easier than increasing the driving forces.

SCT methods are designed to consistently weaken the restraining forces so that the drive within all living human systems can be vectored toward goals of change. Using the force field model makes it easier to understand the interaction of the driving and restraining forces. For example, the force field in Table 1.2 demonstrates how, when they are translated into driving and restraining forces, communication behaviors become relatively easy to modify by using SCT techniques.

Every force field defines the condition of the system's boundaries. The force field in Table 1.2 depicts the reality boundary, which is crossed as members shift from their social roles to their member roles. By encouraging members to pause at the fork-in-the-road between exploring (a driving force) and explaining (a restraining force) and by reminding them that explaining takes them into the world they know already ("irreality") whereas exploring takes them into their experience (reality) and into the unknown ("future reality") (see Table 3.1), the SCT therapist increases the choices of SCT group members and enhances their potential for reality testing.

GOALS

Primary goals are those that relate directly to the system: survival, development, and transformation. Secondary goals are the explicit goals that are stated for the group. Provided they both lie in the same direction, all is well. Since energy cannot be efficiently vectored in two different directions at once, primary goals will take precedence over secondary ones when primary and secondary goals lie in opposite directions. The primary goal in an SCT group is not to solve problems! It is to develop a problem-solving system. This is done by reducing the restraining forces in the communications across system boundaries and by increasing the ability to discriminate and integrate communications within the system. All secondary system goals can only be reached when they are brought into line with the primary system goals of system survival and development.

CONTEXT AND CONTEXTUALIZING

In systems-centered language, *contextualizing* means "being able to see more than one context." From a theoretical perspective, context changes as the system environment changes (and so do the roles and the relationship between roles and goals). Context has two dimensions: One dimension of context is the way it serves as the environment of the system. For example, when SCT therapists discuss their work, they first identify the phase of development as the context or "environment" in which the work of the group is taking place. Each phase of development is a different environment for work and, as such, is the context that determines which defenses in the hierarchy of defenses are appropriate to modify.

The second dimension of context is a systems hierarchical dimension that changes conceptually, in a quantum leap, as the system develops from simple to complex. This process begins as group members develop the capacity to observe themselves and ends when they can access the systems-centered context. It is the observing system (the "eye" of the systems-centered self) that comes to recognize the difference between the self-centered system (the self as the context) and the systems-centered system (the self-centered system-in-a-system context).

THE BLUEPRINT FOR CONSTRUCTING
A SYSTEMS-CENTERED GROUP

The blueprint from which an SCT group is built includes the methods and techniques that bring alive the hierarchy of the self-centered system, observing self-system, member system, and group-as-a-whole system (see Table 1.3).

Words connect ideas to reality. The words *person, member, subgroup,* and *group-as-a-whole* refer both to real people in the world of reality on the one hand, and to the world of theory on the other. The hierarchy of the individual, subgroup, and group-as-a-whole systems is an abstraction. It is the methods used to develop a systems-centered group that brings the realistic implications of these constructs into a person's experience.

Subgrouping, boundarying, vectoring (and contextualizing) are not only independent activities in the practice of SCT but, taken together are the blueprint for building an SCT group. All people enter an SCT group in their individual self-centered system. As they develop their member role, a bridge is built between their individual system and the group system, and the potential for subgroup membership comes into being. Subgroup membership develops subgroup systems, and subgroup systems develop the systems-centered group-as-a-whole. This changes the context of experience for group members from the self-

---

TABLE 1.3. Hierarchy: Definitions of Theory, Methods, and Techniques

---

Hierarchy: Every system exists in the environment of the system above it and is the environment for the system below it. The hierarchy of isomorphic systems defined for group and individual therapy are the member system, the subgroup system, the group-as-a-whole system.

Definition

The systems-centered hierarchy

Self-centered system: intrapersonal personality and character, the source of potential energy for developing the systems-centered hierarchy
Observing system: discriminates between thinking (comprehension) and emotion (apprehension) in the self-centered system
Member system: contains self-centered system energy and vectors it into a subgroup
Subgroup system: discriminates, contains splitting and integrates differences
Group-as-a-whole system: contains subgroup systems and vectors energy toward primary and secondary goals

Operational method

Creating the systems-centered group by contextualizing, boundarying, subgrouping, vectoring

Techniques

Observation of the hierarchy of system contexts
Functional subgrouping
The fork-in-the-road
Hierarchy of defense modification

---

centered system to the self-centered system in the systems-centered context. The steps in this process are discussed below.

Step One: Structuring the Observing System from the Self-Centered System

The *observing system* is the "eye" of the self-centered system. The person who enters an SCT group begins the transformation from being a person who relates to himself or herself as an individual to being a person who relates both to the self and to the group. The person's first task is to learn how to observe the self objectively from a systems-centered perspective; an observing system is eventually created through the process of discriminating between thinking and feeling. This is the first step toward the goal of SCT, which is to access and differentiate between comprehensive and apprehensive (intuitive) knowledge. In SCT language, this entails structuring a permeable boundary between comprehensive and apprehensive sources of knowledge. For some people this is easy to do, for others nearly impossible. However hard it is and however long it takes, differentiating between comprehension and apprehension is essential if people are to learn to tell the difference between their direct emotional responses to reality and the emotional responses that are generated by their interpretations (and misinterpretations) of reality.

The goals of the observing system are both similar to and different from those of the observing ego (A. Freud, 1936; S. Freud, 1937). Like the observing ego, the observing system functions to get a bird's-eye view of the self in context and an increased capacity to discriminate and integrate both comprehensive and apprehensive information. Unlike the observing ego, it has the explicit goals of discriminating between self-centered and systems-centered contexts and of enabling role transitions in relation to the changing goals of different contexts.

Step Two: Structuring the Member System from the Observing System

The observing system is also required to make basic discriminations between intrasystem and intersystem boundaries. With the ability to self-observe, SCT participants are able to (1) bring their *member system* into being by vectoring energy toward the emotional (apprehensive) part of the self and (2) contain the energy while they experience resonance, first with themselves and then with a subgroup. Increasing the ability to resonate with both the subgroups in themselves and in the group is the goal of the member role.

Step Three: Structuring the Subgroup System from the Member System

The functional subgroup is the basic unit of an SCT group. Until functional subgrouping is practiced in the group, there is no systems-centered group. The boundary between the member system and the *subgroup system* begins when people become attuned to the resonance between their own emotions and others' emotions. This attunement is the first step in recognizing that experience changes as context changes (and a step along the way to recognizing that as the context changes, so do goals and so does one's role).

This attunement is also an extremely important step in the building of the subgroups that make up an SCT group in that it focuses attention on the similarities between the self and the other rather than on differences. The technique of *containing* (i.e., of maintaining potential energy within a relaxed state of focused alertness and readiness without discharging, binding, or constricting it) requires members to increase their sense of self by staying in resonance with themselves until they can resonate with others. Resonating with others brings members into contact with their potential subgroup. Subgrouping techniques introduce the structure that encourages people to stay connected with themselves (individuated) and connected (related) to their subgroup no matter what else is happening in the group. This structure, in turn, creates the boundaries of the subgroup.

The subgroup system increases members' awareness of the social role responsibilities in the subgroup and also of the role the subgroup is playing for the group-as-a-whole. The increasing freedom to have different personal experiences as one shifts from one context to another increases one's recognition that taking things "just personally" is a sentence to solitary confinement in a self-centered world.

Step Four: Structuring the Group-as-a-Whole System from the Subgroup System

Just as the observing system is the bridge between the person system and member system, so the functional subgroup system is the bridge between the member system and the group-as-a-whole. The concept of these bridges is simple; the implications are profound.

The group-as-a-whole system, as a containing environment for subgroup systems, is brought into being by the process of subgrouping. In this process, conflict is transferred from the individual systems (i.e., from the individual group members) and is contained in the group-as-a-whole, where the integration of information takes place. On the one hand, members work in the comparatively conflict-free resonance between themselves and their subgroups. On the other hand, they are also working in a group environment that explores and integrates the differences that cause conflict, rather than splitting them off and rejecting them (as most groups do most of the time).

This final step in systems-centered work is the first step toward transformation from self-centered to systems-centered: This step involves being continually aware of (1) the context in which one is living and (2) the fact that it is the context that governs what one can and cannot accomplish in reality at any one time.

It is through apprehension (the nonlinear understanding not limited by space and time) that human beings become able to grasp the interdependence of the coexisting contexts in the hierarchy of living human systems. Change for the person who sees the self in a member role, in a subgroup, and in the group-as-a-whole is a change in his or her way of thinking. This new way of thinking is like looking out of different windows of the mind. As the view changes, it is the internal perceptions and experiences of the person that change, not the outside world. However, as perceptions change internally, the behavior of the person will probably change externally. In that sense, a purely conceptual change in SCT group members may well reflect in their behavior. Changes in system behavior will, in turn, influence environmental change and relationships to the real world.

DEFENSE MODIFICATION IN THE PHASES OF GROUP DEVELOPMENT

In SCT, defenses are modified in a predetermined sequence in the context of the phases of group development. This sequence of defense modifications is divided into discrete modules. The interdependence between the hierarchy of defense modification and the phases of group development (see Table 4.3) has made it possible to develop a generic blueprint that provides a basic structure for all systems-centered treatment, that is, for both individual and group psychotherapy.

Developing the SCT approach to managing the phases of group development has been a long journey, both in theory and in practice. As noted in the Introduction, my first and greatest debt is to Lewin's field theory, which is essentially a systems concept that lends itself to illustrating the isomorphic and hierarchical relationship of systems and subsystems. Lewin's concept of life space (a life space is like a map that traces the path of least resistance to the system's goal) has been most useful in understanding the relationship between defense modification and the phases of group development. Applying the life space model to phases of group development makes it possible to create a map that identifies the path of least resistance that an SCT group can travel toward its goal. Each phase of development has its own life space map, as does each subphase (Agazarian, 1986). Each phase and subphase also has inherent goals, namely, survival, development, and transformation.

Boundaries exist at all levels. Each boundary marks the threshold of transformation between one phase or subphase and another. What determines whether or not a boundary will be a barrier or a threshold is how permeable it is to the energy of the driving force toward the goal. The energy available to the driving forces is increased to the extent that restraining forces are reduced. It is the *easiest* restraining force that is always reduced first. In the SCT group, the method by which the forces that restrain the drive are reduced, within each phase and between each phase, is defense modification. Defense modification systematically and sequentially weakens the forces that generate resistance to change.

In the 1940s, Wilfred Bion (1959) observed that the group-as-a-whole had a life of its own that seemed to be independent of its members. He noted that all groups behaved as if driven by forces of flight/fight, dependency, and pairing. In the 1950s, Bennis and Shepard (1956), who were behavioral scientists teaching classes in group dynamics by the method of T-grouping (training groups), built on Bion's work and developed a theory of group development. They observed not only that groups appeared to be driven by underlying forces but that these forces manifested themselves in a predictable sequence. Flight led to fight, and fight led to the "barometric event" of scapegoating the leader, an event that served as the transition between the first phase of group development (oriented around issues of authority) and the second (oriented around intimacy issues).

In the 1960s, Simon and Agazarian (1965), using the SAVI instrument developed as a method for the sequential analysis of verbal interaction, coded communication within each of the phases described by Bennis and Shepard and found that there were discrete and predictable communication patterns characteristic of each phase (e.g., defensive social communications and intellectualizations characterized the initial stages of flight).

In the 1980s, in the process of translating a theory of living human systems into systems-centered practice, Agazarian (1989a, 1993) used the SAVI communication patterns to generate a force field for each developmental phase. Each force field identified the specific defenses that served as the restraining forces to the developmental tasks inherent to the phase. The behaviors that defined the driving and restraining forces were identified through empirical observation of the characteristic member, subgroup, and group-as-a-whole responses.

A study of these force fields made it clear that defenses occurred in a predictable sequence and that when they were modified in sequence, events taken for granted as generic to group development did not occur! In fact, many familiar group events (such as the creation of the identified patient and the scapegoating of members and the therapist) not only were not generic but were in fact iatrogenic: They were the consequences of acting out the underlying forces that Bion originally identified in his "basic assumptions" of flight/fight and pairing. In other words, the very process of SCT defense modification allowed the impulses that were being defended against to be experienced and explored instead of acted out.

Once charted, the hierarchy of defense modification (Agazarian, 1991) was formalized and defined in terms of five discrete and sequential modules. With a clearly apparent synchronicity between defense and phase, it became possible to define guidelines for developing an SCT group, guidelines for modifying defenses in a systematic progression. This in turn led to developing methods and techniques that are specific to the character of each defense. The final result is a blueprint for practice that takes into account the synchronicity between the systematic, sequential SCT modification of defenses, and the progression of an SCT group through the phases of group development.

Each intervention in an SCT group is a hypothesis that checks out the validity and reliability of the theory and its practice, and each change in behavior of the people involved in therapy determines whether or not they have reached the outcome criteria for the phase of treatment they are in. In SCT, a patient either is able to modify a defense or is not. Until patients are able to modify a defense in the containment of the therapeutic situation, they are not ready to modify the next defense in the sequence. And until they can contain for themselves the impulse they are defending against, they are not ready to move from one phase of system development to the next.

There are five modules that define the hierarchy of defense modification. Each module provides guidelines for treatment within each phase of development. The overall map of the life space of the phases of development thus serves as a treatment plan that can be carried out within the boundaries of real space and time. The life space of the phases of group development serves as the SCT therapist's blueprint for what defenses to weaken and when in order to follow the path to the goals of therapy. Boundaries define the different phases of work, and specific outcome criteria enable the therapist to judge the readiness of the group and its members to take the next step in their therapy.

In contrast to most therapies that encourage the therapist to respect the person's defenses, SCT claims that respecting defenses is often at the expense of respecting the person. Rather, the SCT approach requires therapists to immediately bring defenses to their patients' attention while simultaneously teaching them the skills they need in order to modify the identified defenses. This requires careful and systematic sequencing. The defense that is brought to the patient's attention is the defense that the patient can modify. Each new skill that the patient learns relates directly to the structure of the defense that is being modified.

SCT therapists do all of the following: humanize, normalize, legitimize, and depathologize defenses; help patients learn to state the obvious, use common sense, discover reality, and contain the potential work energy in frustration rather than discharge it or constrict it; and ensure that patients always recognize the fork-in-the-road and understand the choices available to them. SCT methods reframe and contextualize rather than interpret; they orient patients to their relationship to themselves as a system that exists only in the context of the here-and-now environment. SCT is a therapy that provides a treatment plan that is both inductive and deductive.

STRUCTURE OF THE BOOK

Each major defense, and the manner in which it is modified within the context of its particular phase and subphase of development, is addressed in its own chapter, as shown in the Table of Contents. Chapters 2 and 3 introduce the SCT methods for modifying the defenses in the phases and subphases of group development. Functional subgrouping (Chapter 2) introduces new methods for containing and exploring the conflicts in the group process. Boundarying (Chapter 3) actualizes the group's potential work energy in relation to the goals of each phase of the developing group. Chapter 4 traces the SCT group through its phases of development and outlines the specific sequence of defense modification within each phase and subphase so that the underlying forces that threaten group equilibrium can be explored rather than acted out.

In Section II, Chapters 5 through 13 further describe the defenses associated with the five modules of defense modification. Chapter 5 introduces the social defenses against communication. In Chapter 6, guidelines are given for how to undo the cognitive distortions caused by negative predictions and mind reading, together with techniques for undoing the anxiety they generate. Chapter 7 discusses the etiology of the straightjacket of tension and introduces some important criteria for determining when to decondition the patient's somatic symptoms before attempting any further defense modification. Chapter 8 introduces the defenses against the retaliatory impulse. This is an important chapter, as it describes the fork-in-the-road between depression and sadism. Depression is illustrated clinically as a defense that automatically targets the self instead of others. By acquiring the techniques for undoing the depressive, masochistic defense, the group becomes able to access the sadistic fantasies and impulses that depression defends against. Chapter 9 outlines the steps in the process of detoxifying sadism: decoding and integrating progressively deeper levels of projective identification until there is the breakthrough into the primary experience of aggression. Apprehending (intuiting) the innate aggression of living human systems enables SCT members to begin the work of containing their retaliatory impulse without turning it back on themselves in depression and without discharging it into rage and diatribes, hostility, sadistic bullying, or violence. Chapters 8 and 9 cover a very important transition in systems-centered therapy, namely, the transition from the subphase of flight into the subphase of fight and the transition from Module 1 defenses into Module 2. Completing Module 1 of defense modification completes the *triad of symptomatic defenses*, so called because they generate four of the major symptoms that bring people into therapy: (1) anxiety generated by cognitive distortions, (2) somatizing, (3) depression, and (4) hostile acting out.

The shift from Module 1 to Module 2 defenses also marks the transition from intrapersonal defenses to interpersonal defenses, which play out in the "role-locks" of repetitive one-up–one-down reciprocal relationships. Chapter 10 describes the management of these Module 2 role-locks in the subphase of fight. Chapter 11 describes another transition: from developmental conflicts with authority to developmental conflicts with intimacy. This chapter is devoted to the major resistances to change of Module 3: scapegoating the therapist in a crisis of hatred and the stubborn, defensive resistances to giving or taking authority. Chapter 12 describes the two basic defenses against separation and individuation in the phase of intimacy (Phase Two): (1) enchantment and blind trust and (2) despair and blind mistrust. Chapter 13 describes the defenses against the comprehensive and apprehensive knowledge of reality (i.e., the defenses against outer and inner reality) and is the transition module between therapy and everyday life. The book ends with a Glossary.

Subgrouping

*T*he subgroup, not the individual member, is the basic unit of an SCT group. It is the introduction of functional subgrouping that begins the transformation of a non-SCT group into an SCT group.

All living human systems survive, develop, and transform from simple to complex through an ongoing process of recognizing differences and integrating them. SCT is a method that capitalizes on this principle by deliberately introducing functional subgrouping to do the work of discrimination. As the subgroups communicate their perceptions not only of differences in the apparently similar but of similarities in the apparently different, integration takes place in the group-as-a-whole.

All groups naturally come together around similarities and separate on differences. People typically move away from the different and form groups around the similar. Subgrouping around obvious similarities between members of a group tends to split the group along stereotype lines: male or female, black or white, young or old, high status or low status. Although stereotyping solves one problem, namely, how to contain differences, it creates another. Rarely is stereotyping the best way to divide up the resources that are needed to do the therapy work that people have come together to do. Functional subgrouping introduces an alternative to stereotype subgrouping, an alternative that increases the probability that differences will be used in the service of the work of therapy.

SCT introduces the technique of functional subgrouping to resolve the conflicts that differences cause in groups. Instead of automatically splitting around differences and stereotyping them, SCT groups deliberately subgroup around differences and explore them. Functional subgrouping influences each phase of group development; contains regressions; weakens resistances to change; and increases the forces that drive the system toward its goals of survival, development, and transformation.

This chapter explains how SCT group members learn to subgroup functionally. It describes the difference between functional subgrouping and stereotype subgrouping and discusses the advantages of functional subgrouping. It also focuses on the skills required of SCT leaders and the specific techniques used by SCT group members to join and maintain their subgroups. All stereotypical responses move toward the known; the purpose of the SCT approach is to explore the unknown.

FUNCTIONAL VERSUS STEREOTYPE SUBGROUPING

In all kinds of groups, people have a greater tolerance for the differences (already established as acceptably similar) between members in their own subgroup than for the differences (already established as unacceptably different) between themselves and the members of other subgroups. It is a common human tendency to manage differences by denying them or by splitting them off and projecting them out. In SCT it is a given that no living human system can contain conflict without splitting and projecting. *Containing* these splits, so that the differences can be integrated later, is always desired, but in most groups there is no structure in place to contain them, let alone integrate them. In SCT terms, "containing" means maintaining potential energy within a related state of focused alertness and readiness, without allowing it to be discharged, bound, or constricted.

The simpler the system, the simpler the method of splitting around difference and the less likely there is to be a future integration. The simplest way to manage the discomfort of containing two conflicting sides of an issue at once is to get rid of one. The traditional example of this function is the biblical scapegoat, which is driven off into the desert along with all the unacceptable differences society has projected onto it. A less simple solution, but almost as effective, is to encapsulate differences and contain them within the system behind impermeable boundaries: The scapegoat, kept in the group as a target for attack, is a version of splitting away from differences. The less obvious "encapsulating" role of the identified patient, discussed in Chapter 4, serves a similar function.

In sum, living human systems defend against difference and maintain the status quo (resist change) either by stereotyping around similarity or by splitting off, rejecting, or persecuting deviance.

Stereotype Subgrouping

Stereotyping maintains stability in the SCT system-as-a-whole but slows down the rate of change. Stereotype subgrouping, the simplest level of subgrouping (Agazarian, 1992a), serves an important function by contributing to the stability of the group in the short run. But the danger is that the group may fail to develop the ability to reintegrate what was originally split off in the service of stability; thus, stereotyping may threaten group survival and development in the long run. Inability to integrate splits is the difference between groups that fixate permanently at a stage in their development and those that do not.

Consider, for example, the predictable process in a therapy group that has a particular "identified patient" to turn to whenever the group gets stuck. The group, and sometimes even the therapist, may have the illusion of doing therapy—until it is seen that neither the group nor the patient changes. Another stereotypical process in groups is scapegoating, which may keep a group involved for weeks, or even months. Of the two, it is the scapegoat role that is reintegrated into the group more often than the role of identified patient. Scapegoating is only one of many acceptable stereotypical ways that members act out their hostility. Curing the identified patient, on the other hand, is the easiest way of acting out the wish to be vicariously cured.

Functional Subgrouping

In SCT groups, conflicts are managed by channeling the group's tendency to form subgroups on the basis of stereotypical differences into creating functional subgroups instead. Functional subgrouping provides a structure within which the splits in a group can be contained in a way that enables the group to work toward integrating those splits. For example, explicitly encouraging the group to do functional subgroup work around conflicting impulses, like the impulses to be an identified patient or help an identified patient, or to be a scapegoat or to attack a scapegoat, makes it more likely that those impulses will be explored within different subgroups and contained in the group-as-a-whole.

The method of functional subgrouping keeps therapy groups stable both in the short run and in the long run. In contrast to stereotype subgrouping, functional subgrouping simultaneously contributes to the survival *and* development of the group by developing an increased potential in group members for recognizing and integrating differences, first in subgroups and then in the group-as-a-whole. Table 2.1 below contrasts functional and stereotype subgrouping.

Splitting conflicts into two opposing forces is deliberately promoted in an SCT group so that each member can choose to work one side of his or her conflict in one subgroup and trust the other subgroup to work the other side. This bypasses ambivalence, the manifestation of the experience of being pulled two ways. By intentionally locating each side of a split in a separate subgroup, the therapist allows the split to be contained within the group-as-a-whole, rather than within the individual members.

TABLE 2.1. Functional versus Stereotype Subgroups

Functional subgroups	Stereotype subgroups
All subgroups join around similarities and split around differences.	All subgroups join around similarities and split around differences.
Functional subgroups contain and explore differences instead of stereotyping and scapegoating them.	Stereotype subgroups discriminate differences and won't integrate them.
Functional subgroups join around similarities and split differences between them so that all conflict is contained within the group-as-a-whole.	Stereotype subgroups come together around obvious similarities like black and white, male and female, them and us.
Each subgroup discovers new differences by exploring the similarities within them. So each subgroup discovers new similarities by exploring the differences between them.	Everybody knows how to make stereotype subgroups.
When the differences within each subgroup join with the similarities between each subgroup, the group-as-a-whole transforms into a new group able to work differently from the old group.	Everybody knows what to do and what to say to make top dogs, underdogs, and little dogs.
	Everybody knows how to keep the ups up and the downs down.
	Everybody knows how to keep the ins in and the outs out.
Reintegrating around similarities after deliberately splitting around differences moves the group-as-a-whole along the path to its goal.	Everybody knows how to make scapegoats of each other.
Functional subgrouping upsets the social order by making a place for everyone and letting everyone find their place to make the social system work.	Stereotype subgrouping manages the hatred and fear that is aroused by differences by creating a social pecking order, which has a place for everyone and keeps everyone in their place to make the social system stable.

SCT therapists encourage functional subgrouping by identifying one side of a conflict that has arisen in a group session and explicitly calling for formation of a subgroup. For example, an SCT therapist might say: "Anyone else feeling like that?" or "Is anyone resonating with what Mary said?" or "Who else is in this subgroup?" or "Is anyone wanting to explore the other side of this issue?" By working one side at a time, individuals experience each half of their conflict sequentially instead of denying, projecting, or acting out in the struggle to contain both at once. Having chosen one side of the conflict, members explore it in the supportive context of the subgroup.

The therapist encourages the members to learn to recognize when they are ready to work, either because they have an impulse to start some new work or because they have an impulse to join others who are already working. This is exactly the opposite of feeling compelled to join because one "ought to" or thinks one "should"—or even because one is tired of the waiting and containing that is necessary until one knows which way one wants to go. Joining for any of these reasons means joining with the false self and, as SCT members learn, subgrouping works much better when its members are authentic.

When members are resonating with each other's similarities, it is easier to work together and to accept and integrate small differences. Integrating differences increases the complexity in the subgroup. As the opposing subgroups increase in complexity, the ways in which they are similar to each other become apparent, and the process of recognizing similarities in what was apparently different begins between the subgroups. With similarities recognized, integration takes place. Each integration develops greater complexity in the group-as-a-whole, and with greater complexity comes the ability to differentiate and integrate still more complexity. Functional subgrouping creates a climate of confidence in the group's ability to integrate differences, resolve conflicts, and solve problems.

A practical example is the management of the popular defense of "Yes, but. . . ." SCT leaders encourage group members to subgroup around either the "yes" or the "but." There is information in both positions, and when this fact is legitimized, resources are not lost. As members gain experience in functional subgrouping, they increasingly tend to look for similarities instead of reacting to differences as a standard response to conflict in the group-as-a-whole.

Subgroup members build on each other's explorations, and the work often acquires a rhythm of member following member into new recognitions of their experience. Each subgroup actively works until it reaches a temporary hiatus. The hiatus of one subgroup makes space for the other. Members of whichever subgroup is not actively working maintain their membership in that subgroup by maintaining nonverbal contact, resonating with each other while the other subgroup works. In this way, subgroup boundaries are preserved and differences are contained in discrete subgroups. For example, members who are waiting to explore their impulse to help "identified patients" will be less likely to be distracted by the issues being explored by the "helped" members if they maintain eye contact with each other. Each time a new subgroup takes a turn, members in the now-inactive subgroup get more experience in keeping their energy vectored, or channeled. Maintaining resonance with the self inside, in spite of different resonances outside, mirrors the process of separation and individuation.

Applying the principle of discriminating differences in the apparently similar and recognizing similarities in the apparently different is a useful way for therapists to tailor their interventions to the context in the group. For example, when a group is too cohesive, as it sometimes is in the phase of enchantment, pointing out differences in the apparently similar helps the members to split into subgroups and continue working toward goals. And in the contentious fight subphase, pointing out similarities in the apparently different serves the same purpose.

ADVANTAGES OF FUNCTIONAL SUBGROUPING

The conditions of functional subgrouping include several group dynamic variables that are directly connected to successful goal achievement. Subgroups come together around similarity, which increases cohesiveness. The task of each subgroup is clear. The working methods are simple and familiar. There is intense work energy, focused over a relatively short period of time, toward a clear goal in an environment of high cohesiveness. Thus, the probability of positive outcomes for members who join and work within functional subgrouping norms is high. A member's subjective experience of subgrouping includes, on the one hand, the comfort of attunement and mirroring and, on the other, the intensity of involvement in a self-reinforcing activity. Work in a subgroup is a process that gradually increases the depth of the actual experience members have joined the subgroup to explore.

Subgroup support. Functional subgroups ensure that no member has to work alone. It is the task of the functional subgroup, not the individual, to identify, explore, understand, and either resolve or accept the conflicts of the group and the individual. When individuals encounter difficulty working, they are not expected to struggle with the resistance. Rather, they are encouraged to call for a fellow subgroup member to carry on. In this way, a member can rest while the group works and can rejoin the subgroup's work when he or she is ready. Every step a member takes is for himself or herself, as well as for the subgroup and the group-as-a-whole.

Exploration of conflict. Functional subgroups ensure that conflicts are dealt with directly. Both intrapersonal conflicts and conflicts within a group arouse strong feelings that have to be managed. The usual group responses to conflict are frustration, anxiety, tension, and irritability. SCT frames these as defensive responses and modifies defenses instead of treating them as problems in themselves. The SCT methods for modifying defenses bring awareness to group members of the difference between the defenses against experiencing a conflict and the realities of the conflictual experience itself. When one has the support of a subgroup, it is easier to turn one's attention away from symptoms and defenses in order to explore the conflict one is defending against. This subgroup support is also one of the advantages that systems-centered group therapy has over systems-centered individual therapy.

Functional subgroups also reduce the potential for acting out by providing a containing structure within which to explore the conflicts that inevitably arise as the therapeutic system is being developed. In all groups, conflicts can be avoided by silence or acted out in fight or flight. This is particularly true when "role-lock" relationships with the therapist develop which have strong elements of transference. (This is discussed at length in Chapter 10.) Subgrouping increases the probability that conflicts will be contained and explored at the level of the phase of group development that is appropriate.

Integration of splits. Rather than maintaining differences based on unintegrated splits, functional subgrouping promotes integration. Most groups emphasize difference, which is a way for people to stay safe and separate from the issues at hand. In an SCT group, differences are contained and explored, not resolved superficially or fought over. Subgroups maintain the opposing sides of the conflict while the group-as-a-whole develops methods of integrating them. Thus, discrimination and integration at the group level potentiates separation and individuation at the level of the individual.

Promotion of separation–individuation. The skills that members acquire in the process of learning how to subgroup mirror the skills that occur during the process of separating and individuating. Through learning how to communicate nondefensively, members learn to let their true selves speak. Through staying loyal to their subgroup, members learn how to stay separate from others in spite of the temptation to join or rebel every time they hear a different member speak. When members have learned to keep their energy vectored in their own subgroup and can stay centered (whether or not they also pay attention to other subgroups), then they can individuate by deciding for themselves when their work in their chosen subgroup is finished and it is time to move on to another. The work of staying separate (different yet related) is learned through maintaining eye contact with others in one's subgroup. The work of individuating is accomplished through learning both how to center and how to resonate with one's self and others. The joy with which a member experiences a new ability to stay related, but separate while at the same time resolving his or her conflicts is a moving experience for all members of the group.

Management of regression. The method of subgrouping requires keeping communications in balance. It is this aspect of the process of functional subgrouping that also contains and titrates regression in SCT groups. "Containing" in subgroups monitors the flooding of earlier experience by requiring members to go no deeper than their subgroup goes in exploring an issue. Being able to depend on the support of a subgroup makes it less likely that a member will be flooded by, for example, the yearning to be dependent. Exploring the issues in dependency will eventually lead to the disappointment that underlies the defenses against dependency. However, by the time this level is reached, discriminations between different aspects of the experience will already have been made. What would have been overwhelmingly undifferentiated is now differentiated and contained. It becomes possible to make the important discrimination between the deeply satisfying experience of yearning and the pain of disappointment. Pain has not gone, but it is identified with disappointment, not with yearning. It is also differentiated from the pain generated by the process of sliding into a chaotic experience of dedifferentiation.

INTRODUCING FUNCTIONAL SUBGROUPING INTO A THERAPY GROUP

There are two ways to introduce functional subgrouping into a therapy group. The first and easiest way is to introduce it from the very beginning. However, for an ongoing group that is already working well (but in which the technique of functional subgrouping has not yet been used), it is probably wiser to introduce new methods gradually rather than to attempt a sudden change in group style. In this section, therefore, non-SCT therapists are introduced to ways of identifying functional subgrouping (both functional and stereotype subgrouping exists in every ongoing group) so that the phenomenon may be brought to the group's attention.

Every group subgroups, both stereotypically and functionally. Stereotype subgroups, which form spontaneously around obvious similarities, are explicit and easy to see. Unlike stereotype subgroups, subgroups that spontaneously form around resonance are implicit and are not so easy to see with an untrained eye. Before introducing functional subgrouping, the therapist must first have a sense of the dynamics of the group-as-a-whole and must be able to recognize and differentiate between the subgroups that are spontaneously functioning as driving forces in relationship to the group work and those that are serving as restraining forces. From an SCT point of view, this is what Bion (1959) did when he observed the forces of flight/fight and of work in the group-as-a-whole. It is the functional subgroups that do the work in the group, either implicitly or explicitly. It is the defensive and stereotype subgroups that form around the fears and chaos that are generated while the group works. The interplay between these opposing subgroups determines how the group masters each developmental phase and what overall problem-solving styles it develops for reaching its goals.

Different from SCT subgroups that are deliberately developed for work, implicit subgroups emerge, disappear, and reemerge as different resonances occur in the group. Both explicit and implicit subgroups perform the function of keeping the group stable by splitting and containing differences that the group cannot integrate. Whether they are functional or not will depend upon whether the group develops sufficient maturity of reintegrate these split-off differences later. Explicit subgroups tend to maintain the splits in the group. Given that implicit subgroups form around resonance, there is good potential for using them functionally if they are recognized and harnessed. Once the group recognizes that it is already subgrouping spontaneously, it is easier to formally introduce the SCT method of functional subgrouping.

Using implicit subgroups in the work of a therapy group requires making them explicit to the group. For example, let us suppose that a non-SCT therapist recognizes that group members who fight are in the same subgroup. Thinking in terms of systems, the therapist will then assume that the fighting subgroup is one half of a split and will look for how the other half of the split is manifested in the group-as-a-whole (perhaps it will implicitly balance the group's fight/flight response). Such a therapist is on the way to recognizing dynamics that are being acted out in the group. This example is a good one for the therapist who is learning to use subgrouping, as it demonstrates how to make explicit subgroups out of implicit ones in the context of group dynamics. The therapist can draw the group's attention to this implicit subgrouping by pointing out that one part of the group is carrying the ability to fight over differences while the other part (nonfighting subgroup) is carrying the reluctance to take sides. The therapist then might encourage members to explore their experience with other members who have made the same kind of choice: to fight or to watch. This would be useful work in any therapy group.

Implicit subgroups often have a silent impact on what happens in groups. Until they are made explicit, their impact cannot be harnessed explicitly for work. For example, research in group dynamics (Cartwright & Zander, 1960) showed that low-status members tend to talk to high-status members and that high-status members talk to each other. It was found that authority is delegated in the group by the way the members communicate, whether the high-status members have the resources for the work or not. If the group ignores this communication pattern, it is unlikely that the resources of the low-status members will be made available to the group.

Every subgroup performs a particular function for the group. Implicit subgroups tend to keep certain issues out of the group unless they are made explicit. Since titular authority rarely corresponds to the hierarchy of resources in a group, much of the working power of this group is unavailable for group work as long as the status issue goes unacknowledged. Whether or not it would be wise for the leader to make this explicit to group members depends whether the group is ready to contain its competition and delegate authority on the basis of expertise and resources rather than status. It is important to bring implicit subgroups to light *in context.* Context is all important. For example, most therapists find it easier to work in a context of open aggression than in one of compliance. Unaddressed anger in a compliant group often leaves the group dead in the water, heavy and hard to steer! However, a group has to be ready to manage its aggression before it can be directed into conflict resolution. Thus, in the flight subphase of Phase One, one subgroup, heavy with compliance, may be managing the group as best it can while the silent defiant subgroup is containing the aggression that the group-as-a-whole will not be ready to use until the group develops further and enters into the subphase of fight.

For the therapist new to subgrouping, there are two ways to address the issue of implicit subgroups. One is to change what is being contained in subgroups; that is, the therapist might encourage group members who have spontaneously subgrouped around status to subgroup around resources instead. The other is to make implicit subgroups explicit and leave it to the group-as-a-whole to make the change. For example, the therapist might bring to the group's attention the fact that fighting members belong in one subgroup while those watching the fight belong in another and leave it up to the group to choose whether or not to explore both halves of itself. Making the implicit explicit is an example of a major SCT tool, namely, the releasing of driving forces by weakening the restraining forces. Sometimes it is easy to get groups to notice how their implicit subgroups are serving as a restraining force. It makes a difference, however, how the information is brought into the group. An important SCT technique, reframing, may well be very useful here.

Reframing

In SCT, reframing is the rewording of a description of an event or experience in such a way that it is related to general human dynamics rather than to members' personal issues. This has the effect of legitimizing what is, in reality, a common human experience rather than questioning whether an individual's experience is normal or not. Reframing dynamics at the group-as-a-whole level makes it less likely that members will feel singled out and more likely that they will be able to put their own experiences into context. Seeing themselves in context also makes it less likely that members will be humiliated or shamed when implicit group issues they were unwittingly involved in are made explicit. SCT uses the reframing technique to avoid unnecessary pain in the work of its members and to make it less likely that hurt feelings will precipitate a "barrier alert," that is, a cognitive disruption or a sudden intense somatic response that occurs when there is a threat of breaching the barrier, or disconnection, that exists between a person's thoughts, sensations, and feelings in a certain area. For example, reframing by changing the expressions of *slow talker* and *fast talker* to *ten seconder* and *two seconder* is a blueprint for a simple group change. Group members who talk easily and often are also fast on the draw and are able to enter the group whenever they wish; those who take a little longer to form their words often lose their opportunity. Exploring the two sides of this issue in the group makes it relatively easy for members to learn more about both communication styles. It also offers a simple solution to the problem of slow talkers being less active group members. Slowing down or speeding up by seconds makes room for everyone. It is useful to a group to recognize what it costs the group and its members to act out the particular developmental dynamic before the reframing technique was used. It is, for example, a potentially powerful intervention to make clear that there is a cost to a group that does not take time to hear all its members. Framing costs carefully will make a big difference to how the information is received in the group.

TRAINING SCT GROUPS TO SUBGROUP FUNCTIONALLY

SCT therapists not only learn the ideas that frame systems-centered thinking but also learn the skills that bring systems-centered techniques into practice in the therapy group. SCT therapists learn how to influence the containment of intrapersonal conflicts by taking the conflict out of the individual and containing it in the group-as-a-whole, through the formation of subgroups, thus enabling individual members to work with only one side of their conflict at a time.

From the beginning of the very first group session, the goal of the SCT therapist is to train group members to become systems centered. This will be an unexpected experience for new members (unless they have already been prepared for systems-centered methods before entering the group). Learning how to become a systems-centered member means putting into practice the SCT methods. It is the SCT leader's responsibility to help members learn how to subgroup. The first step is to introduce the idea that the work of subgrouping is to build on what others in the subgroup say by sharing what is similar in one's own resonating experience and that this response will deepen the exploration of the issue that is at the heart of the subgroup. This is in direct opposition to members' tendency to emphasize their differences.

There are three major tasks that are required in the first few minutes of an SCT group that determine how the group will develop. The first is drawing the boundaries that will define the group. The second is collecting the energy from outside the group into the group and focusing it on the goals. The third is developing systems-centered members, subgroups and the systems-centered group-as-a-whole which will introduce the way of working that characterizes an SCT group. All of these goals can be met by following the guidelines for developing an SCT group and using the techniques that have been developed to implement them. Members of new groups will inevitably have to be slowed down so that they can master each step before applying the techniques to solve problems. The experienced group, whose members have already learned how to navigate the steps, will not only apply these techniques to issues of greater complexity but will apply them in more complex ways. There is an interdependence between interpersonal issues and group developmental issues. Each phase of development in the group-as-a-whole is in isomorphic resonance with the corresponding phase of individual development in the group members. SCT leaders monitor both the pace and the process, both of which build steadily from simplicity to increasing complexity.

Maintaining Eye Contact

Subgroup members help each other to stay connected and to keep their energy in the subgroup by remaining in eye contact with each other. This is called "maintaining roving eye contact." By looking around and meeting each other's eyes, members take responsibility for staying joined with their subgroup. At the same time, each subgroup member's eye-contact-seeking behavior encourages others to stay present in the subgroup. This is particularly important when the other subgroup is actively working.

Communicating Nondefensively

Subgroup support encourages members to give information nonambiguously, clearly and audibly, and to deepen the experience they are subgrouping around. Communicating nondefensively means avoiding automatic social chatter (see Chapter 5). It means avoiding the many ways that one makes noise instead of communicating: talking for the sake of talking, saying something out of a sense of obligation or out of fear of looking bad in remaining silent; and talking to be heard rather than to communicate.

Resonating

SCT members are told to resonate with themselves and each other. This instruction often bewilders members until they experience what it means. Resonating is not as simple to define as eye contact or nondefensive communication, for it is a matter of experience rather than behavior. Resonating is being in tune with oneself or with another person; feeling a synchronicity between one's thoughts and one's feelings, between the words and the music. The goal for SCT members is first of all to learn to wait until they resonate with themselves and to join a subgroup only when they resonate with it. Every person in a subgroup brings a unique texture and richness to that particular subgroup. Resonating with one's subgroup yields a personal experience that is new and different, one born in the context of the existential moment.

One member described resonance in a group as follows: "It's like fireflies. First one, then another will glow, and then more and more will glow until they are glowing and pulsating together. This is when the subgroup is working. Then, suddenly that subgroup of fireflies dims, and different fireflies start to glow in the group. This is what happens when one subgroup rests and the other subgroup starts working. It's like a dance of fireflies, signaling each other, joining together and lighting the group, and then hovering until it is their turn again."

In learning how to resonate, it is helpful to discriminate what it is not. Resonance is not sympathy, which attempts to duplicate another's experience by feeling what one imagines the other is feeling. It is not projection or knowing how one would feel if one were the other person. It is not empathy, which is understanding the other person's experience from his or her perspective and not necessarily one's own. Resonance is an undefended experience that is generated within the self and triggered in response to oneself or another. Resonance is most like attunement (Stern, 1985).

SCT work demands two responses to resonance: The first is the discipline of *centering* (discussed in detail in the following paragraphs), which puts one in contact with one's own resonance; the second is checking whether the communion one feels with another is, in reality, a mutual experience rather than a projection. The skills of checking reality are learned early in SCT groups (see Chapter 3). It is important at all times in subgrouping to work with one's feet on the ground and not to romanticize. This is particularly important in the enchantment subphase of Phase Two of group development, when the work of developing intimacy could be confused with fusion.

Centering

Every SCT group session opens with the therapist asking the members to center themselves. Centering is the experience of making permeable the boundary between the apprehensive and comprehensive selves. It is what SCT calls "the way to insight."

Centering is quite easy to observe from the outside. When group members who are working to undo their defenses suddenly experience a breakthrough to their apprehensive experience, they know intuitively what it is all about. Their whole relationship to their physical, emotional, and mental self changes. They look unmistakably centered: solid in the chair, energized, potent, present, and "all of a piece." This is when centering happens spontaneously.

When centering does not happen spontaneously, it takes discipline and work to attain the insight. To make it easier, SCT group members sit straight, squarely in contact with the seat of the chair, their knees apart. This is a posture that comes more easily to men than to women (particularly if the woman is wearing a short skirt). SCT group members can look stiff—and, indeed, are—if they are uncomfortable or self-conscious or if their energy is not flowing freely. Pitfalls along the way to learning how to center include confusing it with trance, with the hypnagogic state, with self-focused meditation, with religion, or simply with sitting up straight. Centering is none of these. It is a focused awareness at the edge of the unknown, an openness to the wisdom of the moment in all of the many contexts of inner and outer experience. Knowing through centering moves one toward wisdom, toward what Huang (1988) calls "that particular emergence from your own spontaneity of an identification with what you know of the universe around you." His *Embrace the Tiger* is the best book I know for communicating what SCT means by centering, and Tai Ji is the most helpful form for practicing it.

THE LANGUAGE OF SUBGROUPING

Most modification of social communication is done in the process of boundarying (which is discussed in detail in Chapter 3). However, in learning how to subgroup, SCT members have to learn that different kinds of communication affect the group's work in different ways.

In teaching members the kinds of communications that help and hinder subgrouping, SCT therapists often use the analogy of rowing a boat. Members learn that there is a difference between (1) pushing someone's boat out to sea, (2) waving from the shore, and (3) getting into the boat and rowing too. They learn not to "push" by learning to avoid questions about what another member is saying or feeling. Questions are distancing communications; they push people away by requiring them to say more about themselves without getting anything in return. The alternative to questions is giving something from oneself in return. By asking questions one is actually controlling the direction of the other person's conversation and keeping him or her on one's own agenda. Following questions by making encouraging sounds keeps people talking without knowing whether anyone is listening. Thus, "uh-huhs" and "me toos," though meant to be supportive, are little more than a wave from the shore. These are social reinforcements, that keep someone else talking and keep oneself out of the conversation. One can say "uh-huh" at the same time as one is thinking about what to have for dinner!

The doggerel below is a brief introduction to the guidelines of what to do and what not to do to make a subgroup work. It is followed by some examples of pushes and waves and rows.

Asking "Why are you saying that?"
or "Tell me more about that!"
is a little like giving another member's boat a push out to sea.

Saying "I'm in your subgroup"
is like an encouraging wave from the shore.

Working as a member in your subgroup
is more than pushing another member's boat out to sea
or waving encouragingly from the shore.

Working in a subgroup
is getting into the boat and rowing, too!

What this verse communicates with a light touch is actually the significant SCT requirement to shift one's spontaneous way of warding off differences with defensive communication and to move directly to authentic communication instead. The art of subgrouping is keeping communication balanced, that is, putting into one's side of the scale a balancing communication of equal or slightly more weight than the communication one has just received. Unbalanced communication tips the scale too far up or too far down and disequilibrates the subgroup. Subgrouping has a significant impact on the communication climate in the whole group; it weakens the restraining forces of criticism, contention, and interpretation and makes space for the driving forces of descriptive communication of both thought and feeling.

Pushes and Waves

Responses that "wave" while another is working, or actually "push another member's boat out to sea" include the following:

Encouraging Uh-huhs

Responding with polite phrases or encouraging sounds ("Go on" or "Tell me more about that") invites people to continue in the direction they are going—while one stays safely behind and watches. Watching another person work and encouraging them to go deeper into psychological issues is like encouraging them out of the boat and into the water for a deep-sea dive. Making a personal contribution of equal weight to another person's words would be like getting into the boat and rowing, too. When members share the rowing, subgroups get formed around similarities and the climate is created for deepening the therapeutic experience.

Questions

Questions such as "Why do you feel that way?" or "What else happened?" or "What happened next?" or "So how did you feel?" are distancing behaviors; they push a group member's words into a monologue rather than create a dialogue. The SCT substitution for questioning others about their experience is to share one's own experience with others (i.e., to help them row their boat).

Interpretations

Another distancing behavior is interpretation: "I know you were really mad, that's why you got so upset." or "You're just saying that because I remind you of your mother!" Unsolicited interpretations are, in fact, opinions that invite a one-up–one-down relationship. Interpretations are actually a sophisticated way of indicating that you can read another's mind. Moreover, they often give the impression that you think you know something about others that they do not know themselves. One SCT substitute for making an interpretation is to reframe the interpretation as a hypothesis and to disclose the data that led you to your opinion. This invites the other person to see his or her situation through your eyes and to then decide about the fit between the hypothesis you offered and his or her own experience.

Mind Reading

Reading people's minds–for example, "I know that you think I've made a mistake"; "I can't say it, I'll only hurt your feelings"; "I know you think this is silly, but . . ."; or "You wouldn't want to know"—makes for double distance. It not only puts distance between you and the person whose mind you claim to be reading but also puts distance between you and yourself by projecting out of yourself whatever intrapersonal or interpersonal conflict you are experiencing. Mind reading is one of the first defenses given up in the work of crossing the boundary in SCT groups.

Pushing Dialogue

At first sight, the dialogue below looks like a perfectly ordinary interaction between a person who is distressed and others who are interested in knowing more about that person. A second reading, however, reveals that the effect of the "why" questions is to keep the focus on one person, who is encouraged to continue to give personal information without learning anything personal about the others in return. When members or therapists use this pushing communication pattern, the identified patient role is created.

A: I'm feeling a little anxious. (*Others nod.*)

B: Why do you feel so anxious?

A: I don't know. I mean, this is a new group. I think it's because I don't really know what to do.

B: Oh, really? I'm sorry to hear that you are so anxious. I don't think there is any reason to be anxious.

C: Does it really bother you when someone doesn't tell you what to do?

A: Yes, I mean, I look around and here we are. I am really beginning to feel more anxious.

C: That's too bad. Hmm can you tell me more about it?

A: Well, I find it hard to talk.

C: Have you always had this problem talking when you don't know what to do?

B: Yes, do you always feel anxious and tongue-tied?

A: Well, I feel anxious a lot, and sometimes when I'm in school a whole class will go by and I haven't said anything.

D: Boy, that must be embarrassing.

C: Were you the nervous type as a child?

A: Well, yes, I remember feeling like this, all shaky and everything.

D: That must have been just awful.

B: Yes, it really must be hard for you, always feeling anxious and trying to do what other people want you to do.

A: Well, it is, and I sometimes do. It's like it was when I was a kid and had to go off to school.

D: Oh, you've had this problem for a long time? With the nervousness, I mean.

C: You must have had a hard time leaving home. Were your parents strict? Did they always tell you what to do?

Launching and Waving Dialogue

Dialogues that launch people out to sea and wave them on their way do not end in resonance. Many "launchers" genuinely intend to be supportive and think they are joining the person who is talking about his or her experience. A closer look reveals that there is token joining rather than actual resonance on the part of the launcher.

A: I am feeling a little out on a limb and a little anxious.

B: I'm in your subgroup.

C: Me, too.

A: I feel vulnerable talking about myself in front of so many people.

D: Oh, I know just what you mean.

B: Yeah, I was out on a limb just the other day.

A: It makes me sort of anxious not knowing what they are thinking about me.

D: Sure.

C: Yeah, I'm in that boat, too.

A: I am feeling more and more anxious as time goes on.

D: I know just what you mean. I used to feel just like that before I went into therapy. I don't feel that way anymore, but I used to be in that boat.

B: Yeah, I sometimes get really nervous, too.

A: I feel more and more uncomfortable.

D: Hmm.

C: Hmm. I'm not anxious now, but I can really see why you would be. I would be, too, if I were you.

Rowing

"Rowing" is what keeps communications balanced. Rowing requires putting one's oar in at the same pace, rhythm, and depth as the others in the boat. Monitoring communication so that members can row together effectively in subgroups very quickly results in increasingly authentic communication. Authenticity makes members more vulnerable and also increases the meaning and pleasure in the connections they make with each other and within themselves.

Rowing Dialogue

In the dialogue below, the anxious member is joined by other members who have the same experience:

A: I'm feeling a little anxious. (*Others nod.*)

B: I am feeling a little out on a limb and a little anxious.

C: I'll join the anxious subgroup. It's good to know I'm not the only one.

A: Yeah, and I'm not quite so anxious as I was. I'm beginning to feel a little irritated.

D: Me, too. I feel irritated and have sort of an agitation.

A: Yeah, it's like a mixture of frustration and irritation for me. I have this energy that wants to move forward, to get on with it.

B: Every time the leader says something, my irritation goes up.

C: I am beginning to feel angry.

A: Me, too. It's a real energy, a heat moving up and down.

D: Yeah, a heat. I'm not agitated as much as excited.

A: As a matter of fact, I'm beginning to feel quite powerful. It's sort of exciting.

SUBGROUPING AND BOUNDARYING

In all established SCT groups, boundarying precedes subgrouping. A brand-new group is an important exception in which subgrouping

always precedes boundarying. In new SCT groups, subgrouping is introduced first so that a supportive climate is established before any defense
modification work is done. It is easier for members who have had the
positive experience of learning how to subgroup together, and who now
share a supportive climate of similarity, to work on modifying defenses
than it is for individuals to work alone on such tasks.

Introducing a brand-new SCT group to subgrouping, before anything else is accomplished, achieves several systems-centered goals at
once. Staying in balance with other members of a subgroup ensures that
a member is more likely to be able to integrate the work being done and
is much less likely to be flooded by emotion or to "do a deep-sea dive."
Not only does subgrouping contain the group communication process
and vector it toward the SCT goals of exploration, discovery, and integration, but it also carries with it almost immediate gratification—by
greatly reducing the stress that is naturally aroused in the members of
every new group by the unknown. Being alone in the unknown is one
thing, being in the unknown in the company of others is quite another.
Because the very act of subgrouping requires members to talk in resonance with each other, defenses against communication and anxiety are
aroused and can be modified at the same time.

As soon as a new group can recognize the difference between a row,
a push, and a wave and has had a successful experience of meaningful
exploration, the group should be introduced to boundarying.
Boundarying, in contrast to subgrouping, is done in a one-on-one with
the therapist. (The boundarying technique is called the "distraction
exercise"—see Chapter 3.) The steady discipline of the distraction exercise makes for hard, and often threatening, therapeutic work. It is important not to bypass this next step in SCT skill acquisition, because it is in
this work that members learn the techniques for keeping defensive criticality out of the group. Criticizing oneself and others is the most significant and destructive of all social defenses against communication. In an
SCT group, criticality is modified as members learn to separate facts
from feelings and to use the descriptive language of the distraction exercise. Boundarying makes an excellent springboard into subgrouping. It
creates a resonance around common issues, such as the cost of defenses
already developed in the group. It is the interaction between the work of
boundarying and the work of subgrouping that makes for the clear goal
focus and good climate of interpersonal support that is characteristic of
SCT groups.

The first rule of subgrouping is to join with those who have a similar
experience. As individual members work their way across the boundary
from defensive to authentic communication in a one-on-one with the
therapist, other members silently work along. At this transition between

boundarying and subgrouping, it is important for therapists to differentiate between subgrouping around content and subgrouping around
feeling. When subgrouping around content happens (as it inevitably
does), it is easy to help group members switch channels by asking them
which direction the content is taking them (i.e., in or out of the group)
and by inviting them to contrast what happens when there is subgrouping around feelings instead. Of course, the more experienced the group,
the more sophisticated the work that gets done in the initial stage of
crossing the boundary.

SUBGROUPING: FROM SIMPLE TO COMPLEX

Subgrouping itself develops from simple to complex in the course of a
group's development. The task of members in the subgroup is to explore
their own fork-in-the-road between the defense and the impulse. As the
group develops and subgrouping increases in complexity, the focus is no
longer merely the struggle with social defenses but the different relationships that surface around the issue of authority, and, later, around
intimacy. Thus, group members explore the boundaries within the inner
self as well as the boundaries between the self and others.

If ever there is any doubt that subgrouping contains the issues that
are relevant to each phase of group development, observing the difference in the focus and depth of group members' work at different phases
will dispel it. For example, there will be an *acknowledgment* by group
members of different aspects of the difficulty in making eye contact in
the first phase of group development, but there will not be an *exploration*
of the actual difficulty of experiences until the second phase. In the first
phase good subgroup work is often done with relative ease around the
embarrassment of checking out one's ideas of reality with the group.
Since the task of the whole group in the first phase is to develop a reality-
testing climate, members easily recognize their contribution to the
group task and the work becomes more important than the embarrassment. This is not true for the work around shame, which is addressed
later in the group's development. It is unlikely that the group will be able
to do much more than acknowledge shame as a painful and inhibiting
experience until further defense modification work has been done.

C h a p t e r   3

Boundarying

B oundaries are the containers of the energy that gives every system life. Boundaries determine system survival and development and also are the parameters that determine the
limitations of system transformation. The permeability of its
boundaries determines how energy can be used in the group.

The structure of a system is defined by its boundaries. Structure
gives a group its shape, and boundaries are the imaginary lines that keep
the group in that shape. Each time a boundary is crossed, something
changes. Boundaries of space, time, reality, and role define the difference between outside and inside the group; between the past, the present, and the future; between wishes and fears and the living reality; and
between realities that change and realities that do not. Boundaries make
it possible to stand at the fork-in-the-road, to contain the energy in the
system, and to direct it toward the goals.

A working group is a system that is structured to meet goals. Every
different style of therapy influences the kind of structure that develops
in the group. The structure, in turn, defines the therapy. SCT therapists
influence structure from the first minute of every group session by managing the boundaries of the group-as-a-whole, its subgroups, and its
members. By monitoring the direction and validity of communications
across the boundaries, the SCT therapist discourages stereotype subgrouping, encourages functional subgrouping, moderates pathologiz-
ing, and alerts the group to the containing function of roles.

TURBULENCE AT THE BOUNDARY

Every boundary is a threshold between the known and the unknown, a
feature that requires group members to make new discriminations or
new integrations. Each boundary crossing is a small system transformation. There is always turbulence at the boundary. It is impossible for
someone to cross a boundary without directing attention away from one
side and toward the other. Sometimes the eagerness to cross is so great

that the turbulence is hardly noticed; at other times resistance is so great that the boundary becomes a barrier.

Among its contributions, SCT frames common human experience into SCT terms. In this case, discomfort at the threshold of change is reframed simply as "turbulence at the boundary." For example, shyness, or apprehension at the edge of the unknown (as when one is not quite sure what to do or say next) is not experienced as a major difficulty when it is framed simply as turbulence at crossing a boundary that is new or difficult. This reframing is important clinically because it vectors energy away from making apprehension or shyness into a symptom or a problem and encourages those who are shy to vector their attention to *how* to say what they want to say, in spite of their shyness (or apprehension), so that they can get their message across the boundary.

BOUNDARYING AND VECTORING IN SPACE AND TIME

Part of the SCT leader's job is to clarify the boundaries that exist in space and time. When boundaries are clear, SCT members can locate themselves in both real and psychological space and time. When SCT members become aware of how they come and go across psychological as well as real-world boundaries in space and time, they can judge whether or not they have retreated from the working present. The work of locating the group and its members in space and time is called *boundarying.*

There is a direct relationship between being clear about whether the group and its members are in the past, present, or future and being able to deliberately direct the work energy from one place to another. The word *vectoring* means deliberately directing energy (information and energy are interchangeable in SCT theory) across the boundaries. Boundarying and vectoring are inseparable activities in SCT work: Boundarying draws the map of the boundaries of the system in space and time, and vectoring determines the direction in which the system travels through space and time. The clarity of the SCT leader's awareness of a group's boundaries in both reality and psychological space and time has a significant impact on the group. For example, when an SCT leader states that the group is "crossing the time boundary" in both real and psychological time, he or she is not only reminding the group of the specified starting and stopping time for work but also clarifying a group goal and urging members to center themselves and vector their energy; in other words, the leader is orienting group members to the realities of the context within which they will work to reach their goals.

Boundarying and vectoring are used in conjunction with subgrouping (discussed in detail in Chapter 2) to help SCT group members manage the conflicts and problems that occur on the path to their goals.

BOUNDARY PERMEABILITY AND COMMUNICATION

Whether or not information gets across a boundary depends on whether the boundary is permeable or not. How permeable a boundary is to information depends on how much noise there is in the communication. *What* is communicated is determined by *how* it is communicated. The concepts of noise and defensiveness are interchangeable. It is the defensiveness in communications across boundaries that distorts the message and creates a defensive climate—both in interpersonal communication between group members and in intrapersonal communication within the self. The task of the SCT leader is to reduce noise by "consulting to the communications at the boundaries" at all levels of the system. (As long as boundary interventions are congruent with system goals and membership, the principles of "consulting to boundaries" apply to all change interventions—in the private and public sectors as well as in therapy.) SCT therapists do this by reducing defensiveness in verbal and nonverbal communications by a systematic sequence of defense modifications at each of the boundaries between the past, present, and future in the context of the developmental phases of the group. For example, if in the first phase of group development a member says, "People have always hurt me," the boundary between the past and present is addressed by asking, "Are you being hurt by people right now?" If, on the other hand, the member says, "People will always hurt me," the boundary between the future and the present is addressed by asking, "Do you believe that you know your future?" And if the member says, "People always hurt me," the boundary between irreality and reality is addressed by asking, "Would you please look around the group and see who you think is going to hurt you." The SCT leader poses these questions in a way that is appropriate for the phase of development the group is in. For example, if any of the aforementioned statements about being hurt by others is made when the group is in the second phase of development, the SCT leader will draw the group's attention to the ways it is closing itself off from intimacy.

How the group moves through the phases of its development determines what mechanisms it develops for survival, development, and transformation. These are the group's primary goals—always the primary driving force in all groups. Secondary goals are different in different kinds of groups. Primary goals take precedence over the secondary environmental goals. The amount of unconflicted energy directed toward the primary goals determines how much group energy is available for secondary goals. There are different ways a group can meet its survival, development, and transformation goals, and every different way results in a different kind of group system. The major difference between SCT and other approaches lies in the ways of managing the noise that is aroused by differences in the group, before those differences are integrated. The SCT techniques for managing noise are boundarying, vectoring, and subgrouping: reducing the noise at the boundary by modifying defenses, directing the energy into the here-and-now; and managing conflict by splitting it in two and locating each side in separate subsystems of the group-as-a-whole.

Boundary permeability functions to control information input and output across boundaries. Permeability of boundaries between an SCT group's subsystems (its subgroups) determines what can be openly talked about and what has to be talked about covertly, indirectly, or not at all. Boundary permeability between subgroups also determines how deviants, like scapegoats, heroes, leaders, and identified patients, are created to contain issues that the group is closed to. It is the function of internal boundary permeability to equilibrate the system and keep it stable enough to organize itself. Boundary permeability between the system and its external environment determines what problems the group solves, what problems it avoids, and what path it chooses in its movement toward its goal. One way a group survives its internal differences is to split off and separate from that which is too different. The rest of this chapter describes the SCT methods for managing boundaries and keeping them permeable to new information.

BOUNDARIES IN SPACE AND TIME

Managing group boundaries in real space and time is a powerful intervention in a group. The validity of this statement has been confirmed again and again. For example, on an inpatient psychiatric unit for drugs and alcohol—where the routine of group psychotherapy was neither popular with the patients nor respected by the staff—introduction of time boundaries by a new SCT therapist turned out to be more than just a training experience of putting SCT theory into practice. To her colleagues the new therapist stressed how important it was to the group's identity that they respect its time limits: "How can you have a group that doesn't begin and end on time?" "Why would the patients take group seriously if they get pulled out of group all the time?" To everyone's surprise (particularly the new therapist's), within a week groups not only started and stopped on time with full cooperation from the patients but were not interrupted by the staff. Within a month, in spite of a revolving population, the patients themselves prepared the circle of chairs before the group began—and it was the therapists, not the patients, who were in danger of being late.

Geographical space boundaries are crossed when members join the circle of the group. Clock-time boundaries are crossed when the group starts. However, there are also psychological space and time boundaries, which are sometimes not crossed at all. When that is the case, the potential energy of a group is never actualized for work. When members are only half-present, there is less than half the potential energy available for work in the group. Therefore, at the beginning of each SCT session, all members of the system (both therapist and patients) bring themselves into the group across the boundaries of psychological space and time so that their energy is available for work toward the goals.

The simple activity of crossing this boundary at the beginning of each group session sets the tone for the day's work. The defenses that have to be undone before people can cross the boundary are typically the defenses whose modification is appropriate to the phase of development the group is in. This is particularly well illustrated by the distraction exercise (to be discussed later), which spontaneously mirrors the defenses that are relevant to each phase of the group.

Space Boundaries

In the inpatient unit example above, the act of placing the chairs in a circle established a boundary in space. When the patients pushed their chairs into place, the space boundary thus created also became a functional boundary, that is, one that improves group function. Making structure functional makes it easier for systems to reach their working goals. As SCT group members sit down, they ask each other to adjust their chairs so that everyone can see everyone easily, without having either to lean forward or sit back. When this happens, a geographical boundary is transformed into a functional boundary that potentiates subgrouping.

When members adjust the circle at the beginning of a group session, so that every member can see every other member, they experience the interdependent exercise of influencing and being influenced. This exercise, which brings into immediate and public focus the individual difficulties that exist in relation to influencing and being influenced, in and of itself can easily provide subgroup work for those who have difficulty with these issues. Adjusting the placement of chairs has the extra benefit of diverting energy from the more usual tendency for group members to make judgments or feel critical about themselves or others at the beginning of group. As with all systems-centered work, this experience is live, that is, available for immediate exploration, and what is learned from it can be generalized by each member as a way of solving problems in everyday life.

Crossing from "outside" to "inside" a group also entails crossing from outside social roles into one's systems-centered member role. It is at the initial boundarying of the group that the therapist actively discourages social role behavior. Social roles are stereotype roles that maintain the status quo; member roles, however, require authentic communications. (Role boundaries are discussed in detail later in this chapter.)

Information is the raw material for all group work. There is a predictable tendency among new group members to withhold risky information. For this reason, systems-centered leaders alert members early to an easily ignored fact of group life: that they are responsible for the effect on the group of what they don't say, but that they cannot take reponsibility for the effect on the group of what they do say. For example, every group member has the experience of saying something at one time and being completely ignored and saying the same thing at a different time in the group and being heard. The message is the same, but the context is different. The group hears a member's communication only when it is ready to respond to the issue being raised.

Time Boundaries

Time boundaries mark the coming and going of the system in reality; they mark the phoenix-like quality of the life of ongoing groups. Time boundaries are among the most important boundaries, yet they tend to be neglected. The group that starts and stops on time has a working quality that is never present in a group whose starting and stopping times are blurred.

Psychological Time Boundaries

One of the greatest differences between the psychodynamic and systems-centered group approaches is the response to psychological time boundaries. In psychodynamic groups serious attention is paid to whatever is said, whether it is about the past, the present, or the future. In contrast, in SCT groups the question is always whether or not the change in the time dimension functions as a driving or a defensive (restraining) force to the work in the present. In all groups there is a tendency to take flight from the present into the relative safety of the past or the future. Crossing time boundaries is likely to result in the creation of a world of "irreality" in the group that serves to insulate people from checking out their fears in reality. The cognitive misinterpretations and misconstructions of reality (of the past, present, and future) that are generated from defensive perceptions of experience differ, often greatly, from the reality-tested and self-validated information generated from the act of exploring experience (see Table 3.1).

Crossing from the Past into the Present

Groups tend to retreat across the boundaries into the past whenever the present gets tough. Escaping the present across the boundary into the past results in living the present as if it were the past. Unfortunately, members may even come to believe that recreating the pain of the past in the group *is* the work of therapy. However, when problems that were not solved in the past are addressed in the here-and-now experience of the group present, the experience of both the present *and* the past is changed. Asking members to talk about the differences in the present as compared to the past helps to make current boundaries less permeable to the past.

Crossing from the Future into the Present

The group tendency to take flight away from the present and into the future—and to make negative predictions about anything that is unknown—involves crossing another boundary into an "as if" world. Work energy now becomes consumed by pessimism and anxiety. Negative predictions about what will happen in the group, how other members will react, and what other members will think and feel about

TABLE 3.1. Map of the Boundaries in Space, Time, and Reality

	Past	Present	Future
Explaining experience (irreality)	Interpreting of memories	Interpreting on the basis of wishes and fears	Making negative and positive predictions
Exploring experience (reality)	Exploring past experience	Exploring present experience Common sense Reality testing	Making plans and goals

Note. This is an elaboration of Lewin's (1957) Map of Reality and Irreality in the Past, Present, and the Future.

them keep the focus of attention out of the here-and-now of the group. Negative (and positive!) predictions function as restraining forces. They generate a barrier experience by setting up boundaries that are impermeable to any information that does not support the prediction. When boundaries serve as barriers to differences between predictions of the future and perceptions in the present, both common sense and intuition are lost, and so is the ability to collect data and generate hypotheses, an ability essential to making reality-oriented plans and goals.

REALITY–IRREALITY BOUNDARIES

Refocusing attention away from the world of explanations, mind reading, and negative predictions requires crossing yet another boundary: the boundary between irreality and reality. The world of "should" and "if" and "maybe" creates a reality that never needs to be tested. Mind reading creates relationships that have no existence except in the mind. The boundaries between past and present and future irreality and reality are thresholds between the fantasies of the group and the real facts of group life. As will be discussed later in this chapter, the major skill necessary for a group member to negotiate the boundary into here-and-now reality is the ability to check out his or her fantasies and fears about what others are thinking by asking a question that can be answered with a yes or a no. Here-and-now reality is the only context within which group problems can be solved.

Exploring and Explaining Reality

The goals of explanation and exploration lead in different directions. Explanations organize what is already known and keep the world comfortably familiar; exploration requires experiencing the unknown. SCT emphasizes exploring experience rather than explaining or interpreting it. When explaining is used defensively, it not only keeps the picture of the world comfortably familiar but also makes it more difficult to explore for different worlds. Exploring makes it possible to see the same event from different contexts and to recognize that different contexts yield different explanations. This ability to see oneself and the world from different contexts is another skill that is built into the work of crossing the boundary. Crossing the boundary between irreality and reality requires exploring and experiencing *before* any explaining is done. For this reason, SCT therapists focus most of their energy on weakening the defenses at the boundaries and spend very little time interpreting what is going on.

ROLE BOUNDARIES

Roles are usually thought about in terms of people. In SCT, roles are conceptualized as systems that have an existence quite independent of people. Thinking about roles as systems requires defining each role in terms of its boundaries, function, and goal. When group members take on a role, therefore, they take on a role function that requires them to use behaviors that are appropriate to the context and goal of the role. Even traditional roles in everyday life require people to use behaviors that differ according to context. For example, behavior in the parent role in general is any behavior that will move the parent system toward the goal of bringing up children, but which parental behavior is appropriate to the moment depends on the context of the moment. Appropriate bedtime behavior is different from mealtime behavior and different again from playtime behavior.

A person's appropriate behaviors also change with the role being played. For example, appropriate role behaviors connected to the goal of parenting are quite different from those connected to making decisions about marriage. Much marital tension disappears when partners understand that the conflicts arising from mixed roles are relatively easy to avoid. For example, when partners meet each other in the context of the same role system, they avoid the kinds of frustrations that arise when one partner is oriented toward, say, doing the budget (husband and wife roles) while the other wants to make love (man and woman roles). Unfortunately, crossing the boundaries between roles often requires explicit and open negotiating skills. These skills cannot become consciously available until the individual has learned to discriminate between the personal experience of the role and the impersonal requirement of the role context. One of SCT's major contributions has been to bring role consciousness and a system's orientation into couples, marriage, and family therapy.

In an SCT group people can speak for themselves in their person role; behave within the norms of the group in their member role; explore one side of a split in their subgroup role; and speak for the group as a voice of the group-as-a-whole. With each role shift, there is a shift in context and the potential for a different perspective for the same event. This can be a confusing and disconfirming experience, even a threat to one's own sense of reality, until or unless the individual understands that although he or she may say the same thing, the meaning carried by his or her words depends on the boundaries of the system they are framed within.

There is always more than one way of hearing a communication, and taking something personally is the most familiar. Taking roles personally is taking one's experience out of context. The personal *experience* of one's role is only part of the story, the part that has to do with personal dynamics and history. The full story takes into account the social context, namely, the group dynamics and the group history. Social forces have at least as much to do with how members experience themselves in groups as their personal dynamics do; often they are more important than personal dynamics. When members recognize that their role, the goal, and their experience change as the context changes, they are better able to avoid taking things "just personally."

All members do better if they can understand their group role impersonally and observe their behavior as it serves a function for the group-as-a-whole and as it relates to the goals. This aspect of group life is emphasized early in SCT groups. "Don't take things *just* personally" reminds group members that the role one thinks one is playing and the way the group is using the role are rarely the same.

All group roles serve a containing function for the group. The hero or the villain leader, the scapegoat, the identified patient—all are ways a group stores information in a subsystem until the group-as-a-whole can integrate it. Thus, the hero leader today may be tomorrow's villain; today's scapegoat may be tomorrow's pathfinder. Remembering the function of the different SCT roles makes it easier for members to cross the intrapersonal boundary into the group in spite of the turbulence of shyness, uneasiness, or some other discomfort.

THE INTERNAL BOUNDARIES
OF A SYSTEMS-CENTERED GROUP

There are three internal boundaries in a systems-centered group that mark the beginning, middle, and end of the group. Every SCT group starts with the work of crossing the boundary into the group: not only in real space and time, but also in psychological space and time. The SCT method of encouraging this transition is the distraction exercise, which is described following these paragraphs.

Initial boundarying has several goals. It vectors the person's working energy into the group and requires the person to meet other people by looking around. It requires people to use descriptive language in order to filter out the major kinds of defensive communication, like critical opinions and vague generalizations. It requires people to discriminate between thinking and feeling. Discrimination is the prerequisite for systems-centered therapy and the precursor for integration and system transformation. Discrimination requires self-observation, which in turn allows people to explore their thoughts and feelings "as if" they were working in internal subgroups. Initial boundarying work is isomorphic to the work of SCT therapy, and is vectored towards the therapeutic goal of discriminating and integrating ever-deepening levels of comprehensive and apprehensive knowledge.

It is not until after people have crossed the boundary and entered into the middle phase of group, that they meet the criteria for taking up systems-centered membership. Once they have activated the ability to observe their emotional self, they are able to take up the "containing" position, sit at the edge of the unknown, and to join a functional subgroup when they experience resonance. A systems-centered group is not established functionally until its members can subgroup. As soon as subgrouping is established, the group manages its phases of development as systems-centered work. Modification of individual, subgroup, and group-as-a-whole defenses is synchronized with the developmental context the group is working in, individual regressions are contained within the subgroup, and subgroup regressions are contained in the group-as-as-whole.

The boundary at the end of each SCT group marks the transition from apprehensive to comprehensive experience and prepares people to change out of their SCT member roles and back into their everyday social roles. The SCT method for this transition is to call for "surprises, satisfactions, dissatisfactions, discoveries, and learnings" fifteen minutes before the end of the session. The feeling of surprise signals that something unexpected and unfamiliar has occurred. "Thus, surprises indicate what are new data for the individual, and their occurrence represents a step in the development of the group-as-a-whole. Surprises are apprehensive, and encouraging members to put them into words crosses the boundary into comprehension. Satisfactions and dissatisfactions are driving and restraining forces, which enable people to note what they want to do more of, or less of, in their work. Discoveries are the raw material for learning, and learnings are the generalizations into the everyday self.

All systems-centered groups end each therapy session with a period of review of the process. It is always difficult to change roles and cross boundaries, whether one is entering the group or leaving it. At the end of the therapy session, it is particularly difficult for patients to change from the deeply experiencing part of the self to the part that reviews the experience. However, if this shift is not made successfully at the end of a therapy session, group members are in danger of exporting their patient role into their everyday world. SCT sees the role of patient appropriate only to the context of the therapy; it is considered a barrier experience when it is taken out of a therapeutic context.

BOUNDARYING TECHNIQUES

The Distraction Exercise

Boundarying involves defining the boundaries of the systems as well as vectoring the energy inside the boundaries so that it can be directed toward system goals. The distraction exercise is the SCT method for managing the initial boundarying work of the group by modifying defensive communication *before* it enters the group.

Defensive communication is modified at the boundaries at the beginning of each therapy session for all groups, both new and old. All people who "come in from outside" will bring into the group the self they are on the outside. Formally crossing the boundary helps them make the transition from their outside roles to their systems-centered role. New groups will take much more training before the skills of nondefensive communication are acquired. Experienced groups have the advantage of taking "turbulence at the boundary" as a matter of course and of being prepared for the experience of both the frustration and the apprehension at the edge of the unknown. Therefore, experienced members intuitively adjust their boundary crossings to build a bridge between their life outside and their work in the current group context.

The very first question in an SCT session is whether anyone is distracted by anything that is keeping his or her energy out of the group. With this question, the distraction exercise is launched and the major work of the systems-centered group has begun. It is unlikely that untrained members will be able to report a distraction in factual language. It is through learning how to state the distraction in factual language and how to discriminate between facts and feelings that a major part of the early work in defense modification is done.

Independent of both the content and the intention, how someone says something, not what they say, signals whether it is a thought or a feeling. For example, "I feel that this group is too big" is an opinion and therefore a thought; substituting the word *feel* for *think* does not change a cognitive process into an affective one. In SCT work, people are encouraged to validate their experience before they interpret it. This leads to discovering an inner world that is often quite different from what they thought it was. For example, when people explore their experience of frustration, many discover that they are actually experiencing arousal and energy, and when they explore the experience they have labeled anxiety, they often discover that they are actually feeling excited.

The task of describing experience, instead of explaining it or mislabeling it, is an opportunity for discrimination work to be done. The discrimination between thoughts *about* feelings and the *experience* of feeling is made first. Discrimination *between* feelings and anxiety comes second. It is in the distraction exercise that members first learn that in an SCT group anxiety is immediately modified. In SCT, anxiety is framed as a restraining force that interferes with one's access to one's resources. It is immediately modified by relating it to its source: thoughts, sensations, or apprehension at the edge of the unknown. When the source is a cognitive distortion, the distortion is immediately undone: Negative predictions are brought into the context of the present, and mind reading is validated directly with the member whose mind is being read.

When the source of anxiety is sensations, it is important to discriminate between the primary feelings (i.e., emotion) and the frame for those feelings. In SCT it is important to discriminate between emotions, which are connected directly to a nonverbal emotional experience (e.g., rage or grief), and the words used to communicate the experience. There are two kinds of such verbal communication. One kind *labels* the primary emotion; for example, one labels the experience of rage with the word *rage*. The other kind of verbal communication *interprets* or *explains* the feelings. "I feel abused," or "I feel abandoned" is a frame and will have to be decoded to access the primary emotion contained within the frame.

"Doing distractions"—that is, exploring whatever is keeping a member's energy out of the group—is an example of a simple exercise that contains the potential for complex work. This exercise provides the opportunity from the first few moments of group life to undo social defenses—and to undo the more obvious cognitive distortions in the process. Using factual, descriptive language and stating facts before feelings automatically undoes the defensive aspects of social communications. What is more, the work of formulating the context of the distraction and separating the thoughts from the feelings automatically interferes with the characteristic ways (e.g., histrionic or obsessive) people play out their repetitive roles and signal others to respond to them in reciprocating ways. Thus the distraction exercise also moderates the character defenses. Encouraging patients to monitor their tendency to be histrionic or obsessive in the way they present themselves is the first step towards separating out the defensive from the nondefensive self. The technique of the distraction exercise both discourages role repetitions and modifies defensive communications at the boundary of every group.

Making eye contact in the distraction exercise is a stimulus for exploring issues in separation and individuation. It is also a precursor for separation and individuation work in subgrouping.

Steps in the Distraction Exercise

Step One: Focusing Attention

The exercise begins when the group leader asks, "Is anything distracting anyone?"

The question encourages members to identify any distractions that are keeping energy out of the group. The goal of this question is to encourage members to vector their energy away from their preoccupations with the outside world and into the work of the group. If their energy is to be brought into the group and made available for work, it must be brought across the boundaries into the here-and-now. The immediate framing of outside preoccupations as distractions from the here-and-now work discourages the use of the typical social defenses that prevent members from exploring the unknown context of a new present, namely, the group here-and-now.

Step Two: Separating Facts from Feelings

Once a group member acknowledges the presence of a distraction, the leader urges him or her to "state the facts first, feelings second." This requires the member to define the context of the experience explicitly, separating out facts from feelings. Describing the context factually is not as easy as it sounds. It requires learning a major skill: the skill of description. Communication that is vague, general, and intellectual is the primary defense used at the beginning of group life. Such communication introduces ambiguity, contradictions, and redundancy into the group and maintains old roles. Clear, descriptive communication undoes this initial defense and makes it easier to establish a reality-testing communication pattern. At the same time, it negatively reinforces evaluative, pejorative, self-deprecating, or critical language.

The leader's goal is to have the distraction described clearly enough so that other members do not get curious and distract themselves trying to fill in the blanks and succinctly enough so that other members do not get distracted by the story. If the person with the distraction states the context in a vague, generalized, abstract, or nonspecific way, the therapist might say, "Your description is general and will leave people filling in the blanks" or "Will you please give the facts of your distraction so that people know just enough to know what is distracting you?" or "Would you please translate that into specifics?" or even "Just the bare facts, please! What's the bottom line?"

If the person states a feeling before the facts, the leader will say, "Please give facts first and how you feel second." This is a very important step. If feelings are communicated before the context, the person's defenses may color his or her description of the distraction. When the person is urged to describe the context first, his or her feelings can be clearly related to the context and not to the defenses against the context.

If the person's feeling is a discharge, the group leader might say, "You are full of feeling; will you please tell us the facts first, so that we know what you are feeling so strongly about, and share your feelings second" or "You are full of feeling, but we don't yet know what it is about; please describe the context, that is, give us the facts first." This step in the technique is particularly important when someone enters the group flooded with emotion. The SCT management of flooding is through discriminating the differences in the emotion that is flooding the person's intrapersonal system. By containing the person in the relationship while his or her attention is focused on the facts of the situation associated with the emotion, the first containment of the flooding is managed. If the person is in fact recalling and responding to an event that was experienced as a trauma, collecting the sequence of step-by-step facts in that event brings the facts from the nonspecific mixture of thoughts and feelings into reality, where the episode is then normalized by the group as one of the "bad experiences in real life." This technique is particularly useful for hysteria. The activity of stating the facts of the situation that is generating the hysteria lowers both the anxiety and the affective discharge.

Step Three: Feeling the Feelings

The goal is to have the person feel the feeling that the experience of the distraction arouses. As soon as the facts of the distraction are stated, the leader asks, "How do you *feel* about the facts?" It is important to differentiate between feelings and thoughts. For example, *happy, joyful, sad,* and *angry* are words that label emotions (the physical experience that feeling words identify) whereas *lonely, abandoned, deprived,* and *left out* are frames for the emotions, not the emotions themselves. Often, it is in stating the facts that it first becomes clear to a group member that the feelings are being generated from a constructed reality rather than from their true experience. Work is then immediately done to undo the negative predictions or mind reading that is causing the distress; as the distress is relieved by reality, the contrast is reinforced between feelings that are generated by thoughts and feelings that are responses to reality.

When a group member does not know what he or she is feeling about the facts of the distraction, another road to the goal is for the leader to ask, "How do you feel for yourself in the situation?" For example, in response to a group member who has presented as a distraction the recent experience of waiting 15 extra minutes for a bus, the leader could say, "The facts of your distraction are that you waited for a bus for 15 minutes and you don't know how you feel about those facts. How do you feel for yourself that you had to wait 15 minutes longer than you had expected to?" If the person still does not know what the feeling is, the leader can ask, "If I told you that I had to wait for the bus for 15 extra minutes when I was in a hurry, how would you feel for me?" Typically, such people will be able to have a feeling for another person even though they cannot feel for themselves. This is then worth pointing out: "Do you see that you seem to have feelings missing for yourself that you are able to have toward others?" The work of differentiating between feelings that are generated by thoughts and those that are generated by direct experience is one of the building blocks of defense modification. By requiring members to state the facts before expressing their feelings, the SCT leader helps members clarify the source of their feelings.

Anxiety is often presented as a feeling. In SCT, anxiety is understood not as a feeling but as a "false alarm" generated by anxiety-provoking thoughts about internal or external reality. This is in contrast to the reaction of fear to real danger that potentiates a fight or flight response. Group members often report anxiety as the feeling they have about the facts of their distraction when it is actually the negative predictions they are making about the facts, not the facts themselves, that are generating the anxiety. When these negative predictions are undone, anxiety disappears, making it possible for the person to access the feeling that was buried under the anxiety. In SCT, members discover that the anxiety (natural apprehension) they experience at the edge of the unknown becomes a qualitatively different experience when their curiosity is aroused.

When a group member is generating anxiety from anxiety-provoking thoughts, the leader responds by asking a specific series of questions. (The management of anxiety is discussed more fully in Chapter 6.)

> "You say you are anxious. Are you thinking anything that would frighten you?"
>
> "Do you see that you are reading people's minds when you think that way, that you are making an interpretation of what is going on in their heads?"
>
> "How do you feel when you think that people are thinking like that about you?"
>
> "You say you feel bad. Do you see that your feeling bad comes from the way you are thinking and that you do not actually know in reality whether people are thinking that way or not?"

"Will you please check that out with group members and ask them
if they are thinking what you think they are thinking."

"How do you feel now that you have checked out your anxiety-
provoking thoughts?"

"So, you had thoughts that we call mind reading, and when you
checked them out you found that people were not thinking what
you were afraid they were thinking. Do you see that your bad feelings were coming from the way you were thinking and not from
your experience of the real world?"

"You have discovered a fork-in-the-road. One road takes you to the
feelings that are generated by the way you think, and the other
road takes you to feelings that are generated by your experience."

"Do you see that as your thoughts change, your feelings change?"

"Do you see that when you discover that your experience of the
world is different from your thoughts about the world, your feelings change to match your experience?"

"Do you think that next time you feel bad because you are reading
people's minds, you will check the reality so that your feelings
come from your experience and not from the way you interpret
reality?"

The distraction exercise is an excellent container for anxiety, both
at the individual and the group-as-a-whole level (there are few things
more reassuring than watching someone overwhelmed by anxiety regain
color, presence of mind, and a sense of self). The distraction exercise
performs a dual function: It contributes to boundarying by vectoring
energy into the group, and it also operationalizes the SCT theory of
function, namely, that systems transform through the process of discriminating and integrating differences. Learning to distinguish feelings
that are generated by thoughts from feelings that are responses to experience is a fundamentally important task in SCT.

Step Four: Bringing Feelings into Relationships

Bringing feelings across the boundary and into contact with the group
and its members brings members into the group. The leader ends the
distraction exercise by asking members to "Look around the group.
Meet people's eyes. Bring your feelings about your distraction into your
relationship with each person." Thus the person's distraction is left "outside the group," but his or her feeling is brought "inside the group."
Many people cannot do this initially, and this is the power of the distraction exercise. It requires the capacity to separate experience in outside
contexts from experience in the context of the here-and-now, as well as

the capacity to recognize that experience changes when it is communicated to others. It is fundamental to a group member's success in SCT to acquire the ability to distinguish between the intrasystem boundary work of the self-system and the interpersonal systems-centered boundary work. The goal is to reinforce members' ability to bring feelings into relationship with others. This is also the first step in subgrouping, in helping group members acquire the ability to resonate and connect while maintaining their own experience when it is different from that of others.

Step Five: Verifying

The group leader's final task in the distraction exercise is to check whether or not the exercise has worked and to make explicit the locus of the person's energy. Thus, the leader says to the distracted member, "After meeting people's eyes, check back with yourself and see if your energy is more in the group, less in the group, or the same as it was before." By framing the description of the distraction as the "context" that generates the feelings (see Step Two above), it is easier for the leader to draw the member's attention to how feelings change as the context changes. When a group member talks about events outside the group, the group's attention is drawn to the outside context. When he or she talks to the group about his or her feelings in the here-and-now, the boundaries of his or her self-system are opened to resonance. This enables the group to subgroup around experiences that involve similar feelings (but different content) and enables the shift from the context of the self-system to a systems-centered context.

Frequently, members find their feelings changed by the very act of focusing on the interpersonal experience of communicating. The content of the communication remains the same, but the experience of it does not. This is easy to understand when the boundary crossing requires the testing in reality of mind reading or negative predictions. Less obvious, but equally true, is the change in experience across the boundaries from there-and-then to the here-and-now.

Eye Contact

SCT requires eye contact between people. Meeting each other's eyes is the first-fork-in-the-road between intimacy and alienation. The conflict is whether to *be* behind one's eyes when one meets another or to *hide* behind one's eyes. The eye contact exercise confronts this issue at the very beginning of the group when each distracted member looks around the group and meets the gaze of each of the other members. In this way, closeness and distance are tested at the very beginning of an SCT group.

The nonverbal resonance achieved through making eye contact precedes the verbal resonance that characterizes the SCT group. Thus, making eye contact is generic to the work of the group as each person crosses the necessary boundaries into systems-centered group membership. As the SCT group proceeds through different phases of its development, different issues are aroused for each group member as each formally crosses the boundaries into the group and meets the others' eyes. In this way, eye contact brings into the group the individual developmental issues that are stimulated by the dynamics of the developing group. In the context of resonance and subgrouping, these issues are then explored and integrated within the containment of the group-as-a-whole in a process of transformation that both matures the group and the person. Making authentic eye contact requires making authentic contact with the self before one attempts to make contact with another. Parenthetically, the training of SCT therapists begins with an analysis of whatever restraining forces prevent them from being fully behind their own eyes. In SCT work, therapists are expected to work toward an authentic relationship both with their patients and with their own self. The first clue to a countertransference response in SCT practitioners is the moment when they find it difficult to be fully behind their eyes as they look into the eyes of the people they are working with.

Eye contact is the single most powerful driving force in containing people in the here-and-now. Meeting another's eyes and maintaining the contact makes it impossible to withdraw in the familiar ways people use to disconnect their feelings from one another, whether those feelings be pain, grief, joy, or rage. Making eye contact is a powerful driving force—but one that also arouses powerful resistances.

Too Close or Too Far

For some members, almost any eye contact is too intense, and arouses fears of being too close. For others, there is never enough connection, and unsatisfied hungers are aroused. The underlying dynamics of "too close" or "too far" reach deeply into the history of each person's experience. As these issues are explored in subgroups, experiences of mirroring and of being dropped, failures in attunement, and the many ways of being recontained or uncontained are addressed. It has been emphasized that one of the major strengths of subgrouping is the structuring of regression that the method manages. Thus, each member's work is contained in the pace and rhythm that arises between subgroup members in the here-and-now developmental phase of the group. In this way, the containment by the subgroup of members' wishes for and fears of fusion lays the substructure for the later work with annihilation anxiety.

Breaking Eye Contact

At the beginning of every group session, the developmental issue that is aroused is not only how to make eye contact but also how to break it. When these issues are explored in subgroups, members deal with their fear of not being "met" if they *do* look into another's eyes; with the sometimes overwhelming experience of bonding when their gazes do meet; and with the great difficulty of breaking eye contact with the first person to make contact with the next person.

Eye Contact and Mind Reading

The power of checking out mind reading with another group member by asking for yes/no answers to specific questions is not just in the words one uses. It is also in one's relationship with the other person, which is maintained in the eye contact, while the questions are being asked and answered. This is particularly important psychodynamically. Meeting another's eyes when checking out mind reading is bringing across the boundary the suspicious part of the self, which may be linked to a profound mistrust. Voicing suspicion is also the first step in learning how to test reality! The onus is on both parties to be honest with each other. It is just as important for the answer to *confirm* the mind read—if it is correct—as it is to disconfirm it. Reality is always a relief, even when it confirms one's worst fears. It is just as important for the questioner to be honest when asked whether or not he or she believes the answer the other person has given.

Checking out mind reading is a small task that may well make the difference between a group's ability to contain and explore the various layers of paranoid reality which exist in every group, and members' need to collude in defense against them. It is also one of the foundation exercises that lays the groundwork for working with intimacy much later on in group development, when distrust links with despair. Thus, again, work in the first phase of group development lays the foundation for work in the second phase. The guidelines are the same, but they serve a more complex purpose.

Eye Contact and Separation–Individuation

The systems-centered goal of having members meet each other's eyes as they look around the group is to bring both their own and the other members' energy into the group. Whenever there is an energized contact, a resonance has occurred and there is potential for functional pairing. Functional pairing is, on the one hand, a step toward functional subgrouping; on the other hand, it is a temptation to bond by drawing pair boundaries and excluding all others. Here again the methods required for SCT group membership increase the probability that the foundations for the work on intimacy will be laid.

The act of making eye contact is not complicated, but it involves extremely complex issues. Making eye contact involves managing the annihilation, separation, and social anxieties that are aroused in crossing the boundaries between the irrealities and realities of the past, the present, and the future. The experience will be different for each individual who puts it into practice. The differences idiosyncratic to each individual signal the developmental issues that will be the work of that individual in the group.

CONCLUSION

In SCT, individuals are required to enter the group with communications that not only discourage their characteristic defenses but which also encourage them to contribute to the group in the style of communication that is most likely to build the reality-testing climate that SCT relies on. By crossing the boundaries of time and space; by bringing their energy fully into the group; and by containing their experiences until there is subgroup resonance for work, group members are doing the work of becoming systems-centered members. The distraction exercise is a technique that synchronizes crossing these boundaries and creating an observing self-system. The observing self-system prepares the individual for subgrouping as a functioning SCT member. At the same time, it modifies the forces restraining the person's ability to communicate and helps the person discriminate between feelings generated by thoughts and feelings generated by experience. Developing the observing self-system thus requires members to observe two parts of themselves-the thinking part and the feeling part. Thinking leads to comprehension; feeling leads to emotion and apprehension. Thus from the very beginning, SCT members are learning to cross the boundary between their apprehensive and comprehensive selves.

It has been shown that the distraction exercise is an apparently simple technique that involves an ever-increasing complexity. Initially, it does little more than introduce people to the idea that feelings and thoughts not only are different, but also lead to different experiences. However, the issues that arise naturally in the distraction exercise performed at the beginning of each group session correspond to issues pertinent to the phase of development the group is in. For example, during the flight phase, the negative predictions of group members shift from vague fears at the group's inception to more specific fears of not being able to belong or to join. Later, critical thoughts toward other members or the leader emerge, a phenomenon that requires much more advanced work. If the norm that members must voice their distraction at the boundary is not established strongly enough at the beginning, the more difficult embarrassing, shaming, or humiliating disclosures may never be made at all. It is undoing the restraining forces to authentic communication between, among, and within all levels of the hierarchy of systems that makes for a successful systems-centered group.

Defense Modification in the Phases of Group Development

O ur behavior shapes the norms of the groups we live in, and group norms shape our behavior. Once group norms are set, it is difficult to change them. Yet group norms determine not only who each one of us can be in the group but also who each one of us can become. The challenge for group psychotherapy is to develop norms within the group that will enable members of the group to actualize their potential. Members will naturally import into the group the norms of the culture outside the group. The danger is that if the norms that develop in the group replicate the culture outside the group, members will repeat in the group the very things they have come to group to change; history will repeat itself before it has had a chance to be rewritten. The alternative is to modify behavior at the boundary— *before* it is imported into the group—and to shape behavior in the group so that the norms that develop will enable members to actualize the potential that was inhibited in the process of acculturation.

PSYCHODYNAMIC AND SCT GROUPS: SIMILARITIES AND DIFFERENCES

There are almost as many different ways of practicing group psychotherapy as there are group therapists. Systems-centered therapists differ from psychodynamic therapists not in their understanding of the dynamics themselves but in how they deal with them. SCT therapists follow a road map that indicates which dynamics should be addressed first and which should be avoided until after certain phases of group development have been mastered. In an SCT group, dynamics are framed in terms of the context, and the context is framed in terms of the driving and restraining forces that characterize it. Within the context of the work that is appropriate to the phase of development of the group, the SCT therapist works to identify and reduce the restraining forces in the developing group by modifying defenses in a systematic sequence.

It is important to note that many therapists do not conceptualize group development in terms of a predictable sequence of phases that have a predictable impact on the members of the group. This is particularly true for therapists who do not see the group-as-a-whole as dynamically different from the people in it. For those readers who fall into this category, it is particularly important to bring to this chapter a willing suspension of disbelief.

In psychodynamic therapy, therapeutic change occurs through uncovering, recovering, and understanding the past as it is relived in the unconscious transferences to the present. SCT takes a different path to the unconscious. Systems-centered techniques rely on the exploration and discovery of reality contained in the present. The aim of SCT is to reinforce the skills of reality testing and to develop a problem solving culture that will enable the unconscious to be slowly and deliberately made conscious, as each step toward regression is contained and integrated into the here-and now.

SCT therapists actively discourage group members from working with their past memories in the first phase of group development. There is an important rationale for this: Roles and relationships in the nuclear family are only addressed after group members can see things from more than one perspective, specifically, after they can see not only from the self-centered memories of the pain of childhood frustrations and disappointments but also from a systems-centered understanding of the roles in the family system. This transition does not occur until the group has moved through its preoccupations with authority figures and into the phase of intimacy, that is, until members have come to understand that their early memories have been filtered through the good/bad split. Thus, for SCT to work, it is necessary to establish, *before* the major dynamic issues of therapy are addressed, a depathologizing understanding of dynamics as common to all living human systems.

Transferences to the therapist are also worked through in context. Defense modification in the subphase of flight focuses on the simpler secondary transferences (those transference phenomena that are accessible to the conscious and preconscious experiences of members). In the beginning phase of group, the one-up–one-down nature of the secondary transferences are brought to the group's attention in the process of modifying the social defenses (postural signals), while the systematic, undoing of cognitive projections inhibits the emergence of the more pervasive and regressive primary transferences. As the group continues from the subphase of flight into the subphase of fight, members projec-

tions into the containing roles of identified patient and scapegoat surface, and still later, the underlying role suctions into victim and abuse.
This is the transition into the virulent negative transference on the therapist which has the potential to erupt into a crisis of hatred unless contained directly by the therapist.

The structure of the group is easy to influence in the beginning
stages of development. However, the longer the structure is left to itself,
the more likely it is to develop stereotypically, rather than functionally,
and the harder it will be to change. The explicit shaping of the structure
at the beginning of the group's development and at the beginning of
each group session is another significant difference between the psychodynamic and the SCT orientation. Typically, psychodynamic group therapists shape the structuring of the group by the simple request that
group members say everything that comes to mind and refrain from acting out, in or out of the group. Having set these norms, they tend not to
intervene in or interpret group process until after the group has developed its own structure. In contrast, systems-centered therapists intervene
in group process immediately, before the group can structure itself, so
that the group is shaped to SCT norms.

SCT DEFENSE MODIFICATION CONCEPTS

There is a lot for SCT group members to learn in the beginning phases of
group development—not just the new words that have come into use
along with SCT but new ways of understanding basic facts about their
world. The skills that are acquired in the beginning phase of group are the
basic tools that carry the group through to its maturity as an SCT group.
Members who are new to SCT work are asked to choose between explaining and exploring experience. This introduction to the concept of choice,
the fork-in-the-road, is the first of many SCT surprises. Another surprise is
the idea that one can deliberately direct and focus one's energy across
boundaries. Members learn that there are psychological boundaries that
structure mental reality, just as there are real boundaries in space and
time. Coming to recognize mental time and space boundaries introduces
members to the "time travel" of the mind. Another surprise for most new
members is SCT's assumption that there is always turbulence when one
crosses a boundary and that taking turbulence for granted, instead of worrying about it, saves a lot of energy for the crossing.

The distraction exercise (discussed in Chapter 3) brings the working energy of group members across the boundary at the beginning of
each group session and simultaneously reduces the noise in communication. The therapist begins each group by asking if any member is dis-

tracted by anything that is keeping his or her energy out of the group. This exercise ends with a research question to each distracted member: "Are you more here, less here, or the same?" This question tests whether the distraction exercise has achieved its purpose.

There is one exception to this rule. Working with members' distractions as they cross the boundary into the group is primarily individual work in the context of the group. However, no work is done with individuals in a brand-new SCT group until *after* the security and support of functional subgrouping is firmly established in the group-as-a-whole. Therefore, functional subgrouping is introduced first in a new group, and the distraction exercise is introduced later.

Subgrouping requires members to "row" with each other, instead of "waving" at each other from the shore or "pushing each other's boats out to sea" (see Chapter 2 for a detailed description of these terms). By rowing, members join each other around their similarities (before addressing their differences), instead of hiding behind the stereotypical "Yes–but" response. It does not take long to establish functional subgrouping in a new group, for members soon recognize that when the group manages conflict by functional subgrouping rather than by stereotype subgrouping, no one member will be put on the spot. Another advantage of starting a new group by functional subgrouping is that it is easier for members to tolerate the therapist's shaping interventions when they can subgroup around their reactions. It is in the context of this early subgrouping work that members learn that in an SCT group there is always a fork-in-the-road, with one way leading to discovering how they defend themselves against reality and the other leading to recognizing the emotions, impulses and conflicts that are being defended against.

Emotions and Feelings

Recent neurophysiological work on intelligence suggests two different kinds of intelligence: rational and emotional. According to Goleman (1995), "It is not I.Q. that matters but emotional intelligence." Without emotional intelligence, people have no common sense, that is, they cannot connect ideas and actions (Damasio, 1994).

In SCT it is understood that comprehension involves both cognitive and emotional information and that it is through the process of "feeling" that the nonverbal, intuitive world of emotion becomes comprehensible. Recall that in SCT the word *feeling* has a separate meaning from the word *emotion*. The latter is reserved for the combination of arousal, sensation, and motion that is always accompanied by an intention movement, that is, a movement that signals an impulse to action (Tinbergen, 1951). Each emotion prepares the body for a different response (Goleman,

1995). Intention movements are important in SCT work as indicators of states of being that may or may not be accessible to consciousness. SCT therapists check this out with members by asking questions like "Did you notice that you clenched your fist just then?" or "Did you have an experience or feeling that went with that gesture?" This gives the person an opportunity to see if he or she can bring the subliminal information into consciousness. The experience that accompanied the intention movement is not always available, however. In that case, the SCT therapist will reframe the question: "Your body knows something that you do not yet know. Are you curious?" In SCT, the major difference between the emotion and feeling is that emotion is an experience that has no words and feeling is the experience that occurs after emotion has been translated into words. Emotion is a primary, apprehensive (intuitive) process; feelings are a secondary, comprehensive process.

There is a difference, however, between translating our feelings into words and guessing, interpreting, or framing them. Descriptively reporting what we feel is different from saying what we think we feel or speculating about what we might be feeling. Interpreting or speculating is a complex activity that is subject to cognitive distortions, which will themselves, in turn, generate feelings. For example, negative predictions generate pessimism, positive predictions generate optimism, and worrying about what we feel generates anxiety. Unfortunately, whether their source is reality or distortions of reality, feelings feel the same. What is important in an SCT group is the ability to recognize what is generating the feeling—reality or thoughts about reality.

Understanding the difference between feeling and emotion in SCT is important in order to understand the sequence in which defenses are modified in the SCT group. Defense modification is done in a hierarchical sequence, starting with defenses that stereotype communication and thus reduce its functionality and continuing with defenses that interfere first with thinking, then with feeling, and then with the ability to contain and understand emotion.

Modifying Flooding at the Boundary

In flooding (discharge), all the shades and nuances of feeling are swept away in a tidal wave of emotion. This occurs either through regressive dedifferentiation of experience or because the ability to discriminate is still poorly developed. SCT manages flooding by requiring discrimination and integration. A deescalation and containment of flooding takes place when emotional members are required to describe (discriminate) rather than ventilate their feelings—even though ventilation may bring temporary relief.

Discrimination and integration techniques are also used when members are overwhelmed by feelings generated by a current event. Focus is on the recall of each fact of the event, in sequence and without omission. As each fact of the experience is described, it is linked to the emotion (not to the thoughts about the experience) that was aroused. In this way, there is discrimination between the different feelings about the experience. As the "noise" in the feeling is reduced in the process of discrimination, the information that the feeling contains becomes available to the person.

A different kind of flooding occurs when discharges of frustration and aggression happen too fast for a group to contain. The result is a disruption of work both for the member and for the group. If this occurs in a new group, all defense modification work stops until the member is either contained by the therapist, joined by a subgroup, or transferred to a more appropriate group (where he or she will not be deviant). Containment is work accomplished by the therapist directly with the member until he or she can make discriminations in the experience of discharging that are sufficient to enable him or her to resonate and subgroup with other members. Typically, the managing of hostile or aggressive discharge does not become a salient issue until after the earlier defenses are modified and the group has been through several stages of subgrouping. The work of learning how to contain hostility and aggression in a developing SCT group relies on earlier defense modification of anxiety, cognitive distortions, tension, and frustration.

Modifying Regression from Past to Present

When flooding is generated from past memories rather than current events, there is an intervening step to the process of discriminating the source of feelings. First, the boundary is drawn between the past and the present by discriminating the differences between the here-and-now context and the context in which the overwhelming experience originally occurred. Next, members are reminded that if they regress to the past, they will have only the resources that were available to them then. When the members are able to cross the boundary from the past back into the present, they are able to state the facts of the past using the resources of the present. It is then that the work of discriminating and integrating the facts can begin.

Modifying Anxiety at the Boundary

The SCT technique for modifying anxiety resides in three questions that introduce to the group the fact that anxiety does not come out of the blue but is generated from one of three sources: thoughts, emotions, or fear of the unknown. The first question asks whether or not the person is thinking something that is generating anxiety. If the person answers in the affirmative, the cognitive distortion is modified and the real source of conflict is identified. The second question asks whether there is an emotion or sensation that is generating the anxiety because it is either frustrating, forbidden, unfamiliar, or threatening in its intensity. The person is then encouraged to make space physically for the experience. The third question asks if the person is anxious in the face of the unknown. If the answer is yes, the therapist normalizes the response by saying something like, "Everyone is apprehensive at the edge of the unknown, and it helps to become curious."

Crossing every boundary is a shift from the known to the unknown. The natural apprehension that occurs is called turbulence at the boundary. Members deal with this turbulence whenever they translate their thoughts into words. When shyness, embarrassment, humiliation, or even shame is framed as turbulence at the boundary, it is easier to take it less seriously. It is also easier for members to accept the turbulence that results when a new or vulnerable part of the self is brought into the group when they see how many others join their subgroup.

The Five Modules of Defense Modification

In SCT it is understood that directing energy into defenses increases symptomatology. Furthermore, attending to symptoms—focusing on them, talking about them, associating to them, and interpreting them in therapy—becomes a defense in and of itself. In contrast, vectoring energy into reality by collecting descriptive, diagnostic data serves a deconditioning function. In SCT work, energy is always vectored toward reducing the defensive restraining forces that are maintaining the symptomatic status quo. It is characteristic of force field work that as one set of restraining forces is reduced, the strength of the corresponding driving force is increased, thus making more energy available for reducing the next set of restraining forces. Empirical application of this model results in the ordering of the five modules of defense modification presented in this book. The simple techniques that were developed to modify each set of restraining forces in sequence generate increasingly complex skills that can be applied to weakening the next, more complex, set of restraining forces one step higher in the hierarchy.

When the hierarchy of defenses are modified in sequence, they systematically reduce the restraining forces that inhibit the developmental drive in the hierarchy of living human systems. As each defense in the hierarchy is modified, so restraining forces that are generic to each subphase in each phase of development are weakened.

The therapeutic work of defense modification is divided into five modules as shown in Table 4.1.

Each module corresponds to a specific phase or subphase of group development (see Table 4.3). The goal of each module is twofold: to reduce a specific set of individual defenses and to simultaneously reduce the restraining forces inherent in the phase of group development that the module defenses represent. Defense modification manages defenses in a predetermined sequence that is correlated with a developing SCT group's capacity to benefit from the intervention. Defenses that have already been modified in sequence do, of course, emerge again and again. Each time they reappear, the appropriate modification techniques are reapplied—often with a greater sophistication and depth than the group was able to absorb at its first exposure to these techniques. Initiation into the techniques of SCT defense modification occurs each time members cross the boundaries into the group. The major work of understanding the defenses—how they work, what they cost, how to change them, and their connection to the phases of group development—is done in functional subgrouping within the phases and subphases of group development. Thus in SCT work, defense modification involves a systematic sequence of steps. Current work reinforces the

TABLE 4.1. The Five Modules of Defense Modification

Module 1.
    A. Social defenses against communication
    B. The triad of symptomatic defenses
        i. Cognitive defenses against anxiety
        ii. Tension defenses against emotion
        iii. Masochistic defense against the retaliatory impulse: depression
        iv. Sadistic defense against the retaliatory impulse: hostile acting out
Module 2.
    Role-lock defenses
        One-up–one-down pairing
Module 3.
    A. Resistance-to-change defenses
        i. Externalizing hatred onto authority
        ii. Stubborn resistance to reality
Module 4.
    A. Defenses against separation
    B. Defenses against individuation
Module 5.
    A. Defenses against knowledge
    B. Defenses against common sense

work that has gone before and prepares for the work that lies ahead. Successful SCT work depends on identifying the alternative choices in every fork-in-the-road so that exploration is always available as an alternative to acting out.

THE PHASES OF GROUP DEVELOPMENT

Three major phases of group development are defined for SCT work (Agazarian & Peters, 1981). The first phase is oriented around conflicts in giving and taking authority, and is marked by the presence of defenses against authority issues (Modules 1, 2, and 3 defenses). The second phase involves conflicts around intimacy and its characteristic defenses are those against separation and individuation (Module 4 defenses). The third phase of group development is oriented around the interdependence between roles and the goals of work, and the defenses common to this phase are those against knowledge and common sense (Module 5 defenses). (See Table 4.2.)

TABLE 4.2. Defense Modification in the Phases of Group Development

Phase One: Authority

Subphase of Flight
    Social defenses against communication
    Cognitive defenses against anxiety
    Tension defenses against emotion
    Depressive defense against the retaliatory impulse
Transitional Phase between Flight and Fight
    Sadistic defense against the retaliatory impulse
Subphase of Fight
    One-up–one-down role-lock defenses
Transitional Phase between Authority and Intimacy
    Externalizing hatred onto authority
    Resistance to reality

Phase Two: Intimacy

Subphase of Enchantment and Hope
    Defenses against separation
Subphase of Disenchantment and Despair
    Defenses against individuation

Phase Three: Interdependent Love, Work, and Play

    Defenses against knowledge
    Defenses against common sense

There are subphases within each phase. In the phase of authority, (Phase One), the two major subphases are flight and fight; in the phase of intimacy, (Phase Two), the two subphases are enchantment and despair (Bennis & Shepard, 1956). In Phase Three, the defenses against comprehensive and apprehensive knowledge and common sense are addressed. Defense modification in SCT weakens the restraining forces to the developmental drives of each phase.

Table 4.3 brings together the information in Tables 4.1 and 4.2. The relationship between the phases of group development and the developmental issues that are generic to each phase and subphase is shown in the first column. The middle column of Table 4.3 defines the five modules of defense modification and the specific restraints to development that they represent. The third column of Table 4.3 contains the symptoms that are generated by the defenses. These symptoms are automatically modified by the defense modification techniques of SCT. Each row in the table illustrates the interdependence between the developmental issues inherent to each phase and subphase and the defenses and symptoms that increase the probability that they will be acted out. In SCT, as the restraining defensive forces are systematically reduced, the potential for acting out is reduced and the inherent developmental drive in each of the phases and subphases of group development is released.

PHASE ONE: AUTHORITY

Phase One of group development is oriented around the issue of authority, that is, around (1) preoccupations with one-up–one-down relationships to authority figures and (2) the development of a status hierarchy that will provide members of the group with structure. The first three of the five modules of the SCT hierarchy of defense modification are addressed in this phase. The social defenses are modified from the very first moment of every systems-centered group. Module 1 also contains the triad of symptomatic defenses that defend against anxiety, tension and the retaliatory impulse. Cognitive defenses against anxiety and the somatic defenses generated by tension are modified in the flight phase, depression and hostile acting out are modified in the transitional phase between flight and fight. Module 2 defenses are called role-lock defenses, and these are modified in the fight phase, enabling the group to explore its retaliatory impulse instead of acting it out.

The Subphase of Flight

The major management issue in the initial flight subphase of all groups involves the group's tendency to create an identified patient. Invariably,

TABLE 4.3. SCT Modifications of Restraining Forces to Group Development

Subphase issues	Restraining forces modified	Symptoms modified
Phase One of group development: Authority		
Flight subphase: Creating the identified patient	*Social defenses* (Module1): Stereotypic social communication.	Inauthenticity
	The triad of symptomatic defenses (Module 1): 1. Cognitive-distortions and worrying that divert attention from reality testing.	Anxiety
	2. Tension-generating stress-related psychosomatic defenses, which avoid the experience of emotion.	Tension Psychosomatic symptoms
Transitional subphase between flight and fight: Indirect scapegoating	3. Defending against the retaliatory impulse by constricting it in depression or discharging it in hostile acting out.	Masochistic depression Sadistic and hostile acting out
Fight subphase: Scapegoating self and other	*Role-lock defenses* (Module 2): Creating one-up–one-down role relationships.	Reciprocal maladaptive role pairing
Transitional subphase between authority and intimacy: Scapegoating authority; negative transference	*Resistance-to-change defenses* (Module 3): 1. Externalizing conflicts with authority: defensive stubbornness and suspicion from the righteous and complaining position.	Role suction into victim and abuser roles
	2. Disowning authority: defensive stubbornness and suspicion of self that blames personal incompetence.	Crisis of hatred Resistance to reality

(cont.)

TABLE 4.3. (*cont.*)

Phase Two of group development: Intimacy

Enchantment and hope subphase: Cultism; idealized transference	*Defenses against separation* (Module 4): Enchantment, idealization, blind trust of others, merging and love addiction as defenses against differences.	Idealization Cultism Dependency at the expense of interdependence and exploitability
Disenchantment and despair subphase: Alienation; existential despair	*Defenses against individuation* (Module 4): Disenchantment and blind mistrust of self, others, and groups. Alienation, contempt, and despair as a defense against similarities.	Despair Independence at the expense of functional dependency and interdependence

Phase Three of group development: Interdependent love, work, and play

Ongoing phases of work in the experienced group: Interdependence	*Defenses against knowledge* (Module 5): Defenses against inner reality and comprehensive and apprehensive knowledge.	Impairment of decision-making and implementation abilities; loss of common sense and humor
	Defenses against common sense (Module 5): Defenses against outer reality and reality testing.	Self-centeredness at the expense of both self and the environment

---

a member of the group will present in a way that catches the group's attention, and the group will solicitously encourage the member to take on the role of patient. The therapist may join in or may preempt, observe, or interpret this event. Typically, in a psychodynamic group there is little for the therapist to do except to let the process run its course. This is one of the important occasions when the SCT method of subgrouping changes both the underlying dynamics as well as the way they are acted out. The therapist invites group members to subgroup around the two sides of the conflict and explore the underlying impulses by saying something like "Does anyone else besides John have an impulse to help Alice?" or "Who else is resonating with Alice's wish to be helped?" One subgroup explores the yearning to be taken care of and the experience of helplessness that goes with it. The other subgroup explores the strength of the impulse to respond to the weak and helpless and the bondage inherent in the role of helper—the long hours, the dedication, the cost to their own lives. Each subgroup gradually comes to recognize how the roles are reciprocal. Those who take on the role of helper understand how they project into the identified patient all their own wishes to be cared for; those who take on the role of "patient" understand how they project into the helpers all their own strength and autonomy. The subgroups recognize that each is the mirror image of the denied half of the other. When the group-as-a-whole has integrated this understanding, the group energy is freed to do the rest of the work of the flight subphase.

In these initial stages, the group is introduced to subgrouping and to the fork-in-the- road between *explaining* what is known and *exploring* what is unknown. These two techniques lay the foundation for all future defense modification in the phases of development. Subgrouping around explaining introduces members to their defenses and to methods for modifying them. Modifying defenses releases the energy that was bound up defensively. Members then feel much better. But feeling better is not a major goal for SCT; it is simply a step toward reaching the fork-in-the-road at the edge of the unknown and tempering foreboding with curiosity. The major SCT goal is to enable members to direct energy into an exploration of the unknown; rediscover the vitality in the undefended self, and access the basic emotions and impulses that were unavailable when energy was being misdirected into defenses and symptoms.

As soon as a new group knows how to subgroup, the SCT therapist introduces the distraction exercise (see Chapter 3) for modifying the social and character defenses exhibited by each member as he or she crosses the boundaries into the group.

Social Defenses against Communication (Module 1A)

Social defenses are the oil on the troubled waters of everyday life. They are the important social skills that enable people to interact socially. Social defenses also constitute a shorthand that signals status in the pecking order and lays down the rules of interpersonal relationships. Because breaking social rules is such a shaming experience and because social defenses are such a powerful influence in shaping the norms of a developing group, undoing social defenses is a crucial step toward enabling people to enter an SCT group in a role that is functional rather than automatic and stereotypical.

Modifying Social Stereotyping

Social defenses establish the status hierarchy by sending instant interpersonal signals. Those members who take up lower positions signal submission, rather like Tinbergen's (1951) chicks, an attitude that inhibits attack from those signaling higher positions. These defenses are more unconscious than conscious and more nonverbal than verbal.

Social defenses are stereotype defenses and, unless redirected, the group will structure a status hierarchy that replicates the social stereotypes that characterize the group members. This will increase the risk that the group will remain fixated in the subphase of flight.

Modifying Social Communication

Typically, people entering a group greet each other by name, talk about difficulties getting to the group session, tell jokes, catch up on gossip; in short, they are generally disarming and personable. At the same time, each person is sizing up the other members, gauging moods and climate, and locating himself or herself in relation to any new members. These behaviors are easily brought under voluntary control.

Essential to the SCT approach are methods that increase each member's range of choice before requiring choice. Each of the SCT techniques introduces alternative ways of managing problems. The distraction exercise is the technique that both introduces alternative ways of communicating and, at the same time, identifies patterns of socially defensive communication. The distraction exercise actively trains SCT members to talk descriptively (the language of reality testing) and to separate facts from feelings in order to assess whether the feelings reported are generated by defenses against the facts of experience or by the experience itself.

Modifying Social Character Defenses

Although the simplest work on character defenses begins informally as soon as the social defenses are addressed (which is in the first few moments of the flight subphase of group development) the formal modification of character defenses does not begin until the role-lock defenses of Module 2 are modified in the subphase of fight. Character defenses (an integrated constellation of defenses that are characteristic of the person and have the same interpersonal effect as the signal-

ing of preconscious intention movements) typically manifest as subliminal signals, that is, without conscious intent, through posture and
voice tone. They indicate how one wishes to treat and be treated and
what kinds of role relationships one wants to establish in the group.
Small changes in posture signal significant changes in role. For example, a shift in the tilt of the head—from looking up from under one's
eyebrows to looking down one's nose—signals a shift from submissive
to dominant; so does a shift from slumping forward with hands clasped
between the knees to leaning back with arms folded and legs stretched
out in front.

Early in the development of an SCT group, members are encouraged to test the difference between sitting "centered"—that is, as if
they are containing within themselves the potential energy of the here-
and-now before it is actualized—and sitting in ways that are more typical of their characteristic posture. Discovering the difference that
changing a characteristic posture makes in one's mood is one of the
first major surprises for many members in a systems-centered group. By
changing their posture, members can deliberately change their mood
from depressed or irritable to centered; they can change their experience of anxiety by relocating their center of gravity from the tension in
neck and shoulders to their center. Even a change of expression can
make a difference. There is a direct connection between how one looks
and how one feels (Ekman, 1984): Changing a frown into a smile or
smoothing the worried expression from one's face can modify one's
mood.

Members also have characteristic ways of managing their emotional
energy; some tend to constrict it whereas others tend to discharge it.
Controlling the energy of emotional response through constrictions of
energy is characteristic of what is clinically known as the obsessive
defenses; discharging it characterizes the hysterical defenses. The major
work in modifying both the obsessive and hysterical defenses is initiated
as members cross the boundaries into the group whereas the ongoing
modification of different aspects of the character defenses takes place in
subgroups.

The Triad of Symptomatic Defenses (Module 1B)

The triad of symptomatic defenses are defenses against anxiety, tension,
and irritability and include the cognitive defenses (discussed in Chapter
6), the psychosomatic defenses (discussed in Chapter 7), and the
masochistic and sadistic defenses against the retaliatory impulse (discussed in Chapters 8 and 9). This triad of defenses generates most of the
symptoms that bring people into therapy (see Table 4.4). The cognitive

TABLE 4.4. Triad of Symptomatic Defenses

Cognitive distortions and cognitive disruptions	Tension and psychosomatic defenses	Depressive and sadistic defenses
Mental maps that misrepresent reality and divert energy into explanations and away from primary experience: Cognitive distortions, mind reading, (painful interpretations about what others are thinking); gloomy thoughts, suspiciousness and obsessions; negative predictions; yes–buts; rationalizing; intellectualizing, externalizing (seeing the source of all problems as outside the self) *Cognitive defenses that discharge energy:* Cognitive disruptions, confusion, memory loss, becoming stupid, flooding, flushing, anxiety attacks	*Benign psychosomatic defenses that constrict and straightjacket energy:* Hysterical conversions, tension, muscle pain, stiff neck, tight chest or abdomen, cramp, nausea *Benign psychosomatic defenses that discharge energy:* The jitters, tics, tremor, anxiety attacks, dry heaves, diarrhea *Nonbenign psychosomatic defenses that misdirect energy into the body*:* Fainting, migraine, upper gastrointestinal or irritable bowel syndromes, etc.	*Depression defenses that constrict irritable energy and deny and bypass the retaliatory impulse:* Blaming and complaining, obsessive hate fantasies, anguished love fantasies, self-criticism, etc. *Sadistic defenses that discharge irritable energy and act out the retaliatory impulse:* Violence, hostility, diatribes, moral outrage, restlessness, manic behavior, tantrums, histrionics etc.

*Note: Decondition symptoms before modifying defenses against the following or increase of symptoms may occur.

defenses against anxiety generate more anxiety, not less, and result in pervasive and phobic anxiety as well as many forms of panic. The somatic defenses of tension create psychosomatic and somatic symptoms, which themselves increase stress. Both the cognitive and somatic defenses against irritability increase frustration, and increased frustration arouses the retaliatory impulse, which is typically defended against by depression or hostile acting out (responses that, in turn, create secondary problems not only in the self but also in the environment). Returning to the context of the frustrated impulse at the center of the problem restores the person's potential for containing the energy. When energy is contained, it can be directed toward discovering more about the intrasystem and the intersystem conflicts that arise.

Cognitive Defenses (Module 1Bi)

SCT owes much to Beck (1976) and Burns (1981) for the range and depth of their understanding of cognitive distortions, as defined in cognitive therapy. SCT technique differs from cognitive therapy in that undoing cognitive defenses is only one fork-in-the-road; discovering what conflict or impulse was defended against is the other.

Cognitive defenses enable the individual to avoid the conflicts in the here-and-now. Vectoring attention into foreboding, making negative predictions, and believing that others are thinking critical or embarrassing things about one, are all ways of diverting attention away from present conflicts or frustrations. Unfortunately, a defensive retreat into a substitute reality not only generates still more anxiety, tension, and irritability—but also produces secondary experiences like guilt, dread, and worrying. Thus, all the problems that existed in the first place are compounded by new problems generated by the imagination. A foundation for reality-testing is laid by establishing norms of communication that check out the reality of attempts at mind reading and negative predictions and that describe experience rather than interpret it. As SCT group members work at the fork-in-the-road between their conflicts on the one hand and their defenses and symptoms on the other, they may discover that the defenses themselves and the symptoms that the defenses generate are more disturbing than the conflicts they defend against.

Defensive Tension and Somatic Defenses (Module 1Bii)

As defensive thoughts, and the feelings they generate, are modified, the emotions that were originally defended against start to surface. People manage the impulse to act that goes with emotion in different ways. They may contain the energy that is aroused by emotion, constrict it, or discharge it. Tension is a defense that acts like a straightjacket: It constricts the sensations of arousal and emotion, inhibits action, and binds the impulse. When there is sufficient muscular tension, there is no longer even an awareness of the impulse or the emotion. People can no longer even guess what they feel.

The straightjacket of tension is modified by using simple SCT modification techniques, as long as conversion symptoms are not involved. SCT is in debt to Davanloo (1987), who did much of the pioneering work on identifying the nonverbal signals that telegraph the difference between stress that is being safely routed through striated muscle (via the central nervous system) and stress that is being routed dangerously into psychosomatic symptoms (via the autonomic nervous system).

Davanloo demonstrates in his videotaped clinical interviews that when stress shows as tension in the hands or as muscular twitches in the face, defense modification can be accomplished whereas when the patient has flaccid hands, turns white, or has an incipient attack of colitis, the therapist needs to decondition the symptom before any further work can be done (see Chapter 7).

When members of an SCT group successfully access the experience of the emotion that was being constricted by tension, they often discover that what they thought would be an unpleasant experience involves arousal, readiness, and energy and, in fact, leaves them feeling warm, good, and "full of themselves." When this happens, members have a direct experience of what being "centered" means.

Experiencing being centered is a fulcrum learning experience for SCT members. It is the discovery that one path of the fork-in-the-road leads to an experience of that part of the self that was unavailable while it was being defended against. This is a lesson that repeats itself for SCT group members each time an aspect of the self that has been split off, denied, or compromised is regained.

The Transitional Subphase between Flight and Fight

In the transitional subphase between flight and fight there are important discriminations for SCT group members to make. The experience of frustration must be differentiated from the irritability that often accompanies it, and irritability must, in turn, be differentiated from the impulse to retaliate against what is frustrating. This work is part of developing the ability to discriminate and integrate emotional experience so that it is available as emotional intelligence. As in all SCT work, tolerance of experience is increased by making two different kinds of discrimination: (1) one that separates the secondary experiences (generated by defenses against primary experience) from the experience of frustration itself and (2) one that differentiates between the different feelings in the experience.

In the process of discriminating, SCT group members learn that a large part of the discomfort they experience in frustration comes from the defensive attempts to constrict frustrated energy for fear it will otherwise explode. In SCT, increasing frustration tolerance is the same as—and is more commonly referred to as—increasing the ability to contain energy. As they learn to make more space for their experience, for example, by relaxing the diaphragm, group members increasingly discover a good experience of power, arousal, and readiness instead. Frustration often generates irritability in people. By exploring frustration and irritability separately, SCT group members discover (1) that frustration does not necessarily make people irritable and (2) that irritability is not necessarily related to hostility. These two discriminations are prerequisites for the discovery that the impulse to retaliate against the frustrating person, object, or thing is separate from, although often triggered by, frustration. With this work done, the group is ready to explore the retaliatory impulse itself and the two major defenses against it: depression and sadistic, or hostile, acting out.

Work with depression and hostility requires the patient to connect the irritability in frustration with the experience of irritable energy and to become familiar with the triggers that reroute the retaliatory impulse into depression or discharge it into hostile acting out. In group and sub-group work, members learn that impulses are under voluntary control by watching others and by experiencing containment themselves in the process of making choices about how fast and how much to experience. The therapist helps pace the work so that impulses are contained as consistently as possible rather than acted out. Containment is learning by not doing, in contrast to first learning by doing (i.e., by discharging the impulse first and then learning about the experience by retroactive exploration).

In the transitional subphase between flight and fight, SCT group members learn that righteous indignation and hostile diatribes are fueled by cognitive distortions (what may come as a surprise to the group is how much pleasure is experienced in these discharges of hostility). The group also learns that the discrimination technique, used to contain flooding, works just as well for containing emotional discharges into tantrums. The fork-in-the-road technique (i.e., identifying for a group member the point at which there is a choice to be made between alternative paths) works just as well when used to discriminate the different components in guilt over sadism (namely, a disapproving thought in conflict with an impulse) as it did when used to discriminate between a thought and a feeling. The bracketing technique that will be used in deconditioning the depressive response is an adaptation of the one used for undoing somatic symptoms. Each defense that is modified by SCT techniques leads to a deeper and more complex experience of emotion.

Until this point, members have often been half aware of the internal experiences they are discovering. When they discover that the retaliatory impulse is buried in depression, however, there is a descent into truly unconscious processes. Since the critical superego is consistently modified in SCT groups by the process of legitimizing, depathologizing, and normalizing common human unconscious processes, bringing the underlying retaliatory and sadistic impulses from the unconscious to the conscious level of knowing is often done without the trauma that might otherwise be expected.

Work around irritability starts when frustration rises towards the end of the flight subphase, and continues in the transition subphase between the flight and fight subphases, when the group discovers that depression is a defense against the retaliatory impulse. The group moves out of the transition subphase and into the subphase of fight when it is discovered that the fork-in-the-road away from masochistic depressions leads into the sadistic impulse to "do unto others that which was done unto you." This is only the second step in containing and exploring the retaliatory impulse, and the work is not completed until the "crisis of hatred," which occurs in the transitional phase between authority and intimacy (discussed later in this chapter and in detail in Chapter 11). The SCT leader's role throughout this process is to contain the various projective identifications that occur as the defenses against the retaliatory impulse are modified, until the projections can be surfaced and integrated into the group.

Masochistic Defenses against the Retaliatory Impulse: Depression (Module 1Biii)

In the work of undoing depression, group members must learn how to choose not to turn the retaliatory impulse back on the self (the masochistic defense). However, before this can occur, members first have to recognize consciously that there *is* a retaliatory impulse! Some members know this before others. Although a subgroup in the group is often fully aware of the impulse to target the therapist—and may even manage a token rebellion—it is unlikely that the group-as-a-whole will be ready. Subgrouping around hostility is not likely to last long before it is drowned out by a group-as-a-whole depressive defense. It is at this point that the group goes dead in the water—heavy, bored, and unable to work. This particular group-as-a-whole response is almost always a signal that the group is in a stalemate between the impulse to target the therapist and the depressive defense against it. Although psychodynamic groups certainly also enter this stalemate (and for the same reason), they have an alternative route for their irritability: They can act out their irritability by scapegoating a member, as an alternative to scapegoating the therapist. The therapist interrupts this impulse in SCT groups.

The undoing of the depression begins, first, when the group accepts that it is suffering not from boredom but from a depressive defense and, second, when it starts searching for an alternative. The SCT technique presented at this point to group members is called bracketing, the process of recalling events that occurred in the bracket of time between the last event remembered before the symptom (here, depression) started and the first signal of the symptom. Thus, group members learn from a careful itemizing of the events in this bracket of time that somewhere during this interval is the moment when the impulse to retaliate was aroused and was then either discounted or was quickly forgotten by them.

The group depressive defense is undone when there is access to the alternative work around the retaliatory impulse. Now the sadomasochistic and sadistic fantasies and impulses surface in the group. Subgrouping work is particularly important at this stage for containing members who are not yet able to resonate. It is through explorations in subgroups that the group-as-a-whole is educated to the facts of the retaliatory experience. Even though members may not be able to join the active subgroup, they do come to recognize the fork-in-the-road between depression and sadism in others and are alerted to look for the same in themselves.

The major management issue in all groups as the retaliatory impulse surfaces is scapegoating. Helping group members explore their projections, instead of acting them out on a scapegoat, is a more difficult task for the SCT therapist than was helping members repossess their hurt self from the identified patient. The more complex constellation of scapegoating is not so easily made conscious. Members of the group-as-a-whole (scapegoating is a group-as-a-whole phenomenon) are asked to explore their impulse to scapegoat for what it is in themselves that they are disowning. This entails recognition of the fact that there is a suspicious absence in group members of *any* similarities with the person being scapegoated. Functional subgrouping is of great help in noticing the absence in the self of the intolerable "differences" perceived in the other. Recognizing the function of sadism and exploring for, and undoing, the projective identification begins the really difficult work in the SCT group.

It is appropriate here to emphasize the importance of the techniques used for managing this aspect of the therapeutic work. Many of these techniques have been built directly on the foundation that Davanloo (1987) laid in his own clinical journey, which he makes available to other clinicians through his videotapes. Like many psychodynamic therapists, Davanloo takes for granted that a breakthrough into the dynamics of sadism will involve a guilt-laden journey into "the bloody charnel house of the unconscious," a journey often traumatic enough to overwhelm the ego and one that sometimes requires hospitalization of the patient. However, in contrast, we have found that as long as guilt is modified first (in SCT guilt is worked in the same way as any contradiction between a thought and reality) SCT methods for exploring sadism result in a contained experience that does not threaten to overwhelm the ego. SCT contains emotion by first decoding its complexity through a systematic and separate exploration of its contradictory components. This technique monitors regression by discriminating and integrating experience within the developmental capacity of the phase of group development in which it occurs.

Sadistic Defenses against the Retaliatory Impulse: Hostile Acting Out (Module 1Biii)

The group has learned through experience that depression is a defense that automatically targets the self (masochism) instead of others. The alternative task requires recognizing the sadism in the impulse to retaliate. There are two major, albeit contradictory, accompaniments to the sadistic impulse: sadistic pleasure and cringing horror. SCT deals with these as alternative paths in a fork-in-the-road, each leading to a different projective identification.

How Sadistic Triumph Transforms into Potency

The "sadistic pleasure" path leads first to a recognition of the thought "I will do unto others what they did to me," a thought that represents a transitional state between sadistic feelings toward others and a triumphant feeling of invulnerability ("No one will ever do that to me again"). This is the bridge between sadistic pleasure and primary energy which is in the service of the life force (primary aggression).

How Cringing Horror Transforms into Compassion

What is discovered in exploring the "cringing horror" path is not a reaction formation but an intuitive compassion for the human race in recognizing the cost to it of the many forms of defensive sadistic and masochistic acting out that occur when primary aggression is mistaken for sadism and is defended against, rather than experienced, contained, and consciously directed.

As the SCT group explores sadism, members recognize that there are alternatives to acting out frustration, turning the retaliatory impulse back on themselves, and discharging primary aggression as righteous indignation, hostility, sadistic bullying, or violence. When members access their primary aggression, they have a powerful experience of being "full of themselves" and an intuitive understanding of both the costs of their defenses and the hard work ahead.

The Subphase of Fight

With depression undone, the energy of the retaliatory impulse becomes available. The group changes from passive to active; it begins to "feel its oats." This is a transition point for the group, as it is for the SCT leader, who is required both to support the group's movement toward autonomy and to continue the boundarying work, so that the group has the requisite structure to continue developing. It is at this point—as the group slides fully into the fight subphase of Phase One of its development—that the therapist begins the process of transferring the management of the group to the group itself, a process that will come to a head in the "crisis of hatred" and that will be slowly resolved as the group does its work around separation and individuation in Phase Two, the phase of intimacy.

Role-Lock Defenses (Module 2)

There is a natural progression in the group from the different stages of sadism to the breakthrough into the experience of primary aggression, which is a deeper stage of the apprehensive (intuitive), centered experience. It is from the centered self that members become aware in a new way of their interpersonal relationships (pairing) with the other people in the group, as distinct from their experience of them as members and subgroup partners.

The difference between pairing and subgrouping highlights the concept of role-locks. Role-locks are the Module 2 defenses against role suction. It is at the point of the experience of primary aggression that members notice that some roles lock them into repetitive relationships with their own, other members', and their leader's authority. This recognition marks the full entry into the rivalry and competition that underlie the group process in the subphase of fight.

Subgrouping around compliant and defiant role-locks gives the group the structure to work with the interpersonal ramifications of the impulses that members are now discovering in themselves. The reciprocity of subgrouping helps members notice how they each unwittingly seek a partner who will act out old familiar roles with them. Subgrouping makes it easier to explore the compliant side of the self and makes possible the discovery that this compliance serves to defend against the impulse to take control or exert authority and is acted out in one-down roles (e.g., victim, martyr, and identified patient). Subgrouping also helps members explore their defiant side and discover that stubborn defiance makes it impossible for them to be influenced by others—or even to influence the self. This lesson is learned with particular poignancy as subgroups explore the multiple one-up roles of scapegoating, as savior, leader of moral outrage, bully, antagonist, rebel leader, and assassin. Integration takes place with surprising ease in this phase, as the group recognizes how each side of a role-lock mirrors the other and how both roles are necessary if each pair of role-locked individuals is to repeat in the present the old, familiar roles from the past.

The Transition between Phase One (Authority) and Phase Two (Intimacy)

Module 3 resistance to change defenses are modified in the transitional phase between authority and intimacy. This pivotal phase brings to a head the paranoid rage of the negative transference. Only when the defensive paranoia, is modified, can the fundamental issues in intimacy, separation, and individuation, be addressed.

Resistance-to-Change Defenses (Module 3)

There are two stages to the modification of a group's resistance to change. The first stage is oriented around the "crisis of hatred," in which the group externalizes the conflict, stubbornly defends against giving or taking authority from anyone, and scapegoats the therapist as the cause of its problems. The second stage is oriented around a crisis of personal stubbornness in which the group recognizes that the energy of change is within each individual but is imprisoned within the stubbornly resistant character defenses of that individual. There is a confrontation with the painful reality of the cost to the individual in maintaining these defenses and of the difficulty of bringing about and consolidating change. At the same time, group members recognize and develop respect for the power of these defenses that enabled social survival in the past but that are inhibiting further development and transformation in the present and future.

In both stages of the modification of the resistance-to-change defenses is the fork-in-the-road that leads to stubbornness on the one hand and courage and curiosity on the other. Stubbornness is first directed outward against all figures of authority. When the externalization defense is undone, the power struggle is directed inward against the stubborn self. Stubbornness has to transform into goal-oriented tenacity for the fight to be won. The courage, energy, curiosity—and also some humor at the human paradox—of the alternative path are easier to access in subgroups.

Externalizing: The Crisis of Hatred

The crisis of hatred is a developmental crisis for the group; it has all the recognizable characteristics of a virulent negative transference. How fully the members of any therapy group, whatever its leadership style, can explore their issues with authority will depend on the successful management of early incidents of scapegoating in the group. If, in spite of the therapist's best efforts, the designated scapegoat is injured or extruded and never reintegrated into the group, it is unlikely that the group will later be able to turn their scapegoating impulse toward the therapist. Similarly, if scapegoating has been avoided by a group—by fixing on maintaining an identified patient and an idealized therapist— then that group, the identified patient, and the therapist are all in a role-lock and have a long way to go before they can even approach the developmental crisis, let alone master it.

How well the SCT group is able to manage its own chaos in this transition phase will depend on how thoroughly the first two modules of defense modification have been mastered, how intensely the group is able to work in subgroups, and how seriously it is able to maintain its boundarying. It is, of course, essential for the leader to be prepared to contain the group hatred. This alone, however, is not enough. The leader must also have prepared the group to manage itself through the period of time when hatred is intense, for it is often too difficult for members to both accept help from the therapist (the representative of hated authority) and explore their hatred of the therapist at the same time.

It is also particularly important for the leader to maintain the group's structure throughout this time. Boundary breaks are always difficult for a group at any phase. In the Transitional Phase between Phase One and Phase Two, however, even a small boundary violation by the leader (being even a minute late for a session) can shake the containing relationship between the group and the leader.

It is in introducing functional subgrouping as a method for exploring hatred toward authority that SCT techniques have made a considerable contribution to the field of group psychotherapy. The negative transference, whether in group or individual therapy, is and has always been a traumatic part of therapy for both patient and therapist; it is the point at which the success of therapy most often hangs in the balance. Functional subgrouping has made a crucial difference to (1) the ability to contain the virulence with which the negative transference is experienced, (2) the potential for fixation in or regression from that transference, and (3) the depth with which it can be worked through.

There are two major factors to successfully delegating the work to subgroups in the crisis of hatred. The first factor is learning how to fight. At the earlier subphases of flight and fight in Phase One, leaders explicitly tell the group that SCT group members do not target each other until after the group has learned not to take feelings personally. Members are encouraged to bring their frustration, aggression, and sadism into the containing relationship with the leader instead of acting out on each other. It is in containing dyads—first with the therapist, later with volunteer members, and continually in subgroups—that members learn to stay in an authentic relationship in spite of the range of feelings (which include frustration, irritation, and flashes of hatred with each other as well as support, pleasure, and mutual satisfaction) that relationships arouse.

The second factor in preparing the group to work in subgroups through the crisis of hatred is the ability of SCT therapists to not only avoid taking members' work personally but also to recognize when subgroup work in a particular containing dyad is failing because they have become personally involved in a pairing role-lock with a group member. This is ongoing work throughout the training of SCT therapists and is equivalent to the psychodynamic work of managing the countertransference and working through projective identifications. It does not matter which phase of development a group is in; work will *always* fail if the therapist is in a role-lock with a member whose frustration and aggression the therapist is attempting to contain (or whose defenses are being modified). A major benefit of functional subgrouping is that it is always an available alternative any time the therapist recognizes that he or she is experiencing "role suction" with a group member.

Resistance to Reality: Stubbornness

An SCT group, unlike groups whose survival of the crisis of hatred catapults them into a phase of enchantment (Bennis & Shepard, 1956), faces an unexpected and painful period of work following the recognition that the hatred toward the therapist is in fact an externalization of the conflicts with authority that exist within the self. It is no longer so easy for members to disown responsibility for their conflicts. Instead, they are confronted with the cost to themselves of their externalizations. Most difficult of all is the realization that it is their own stubbornness that is the major factor in resisting change.

Members in the Transitional Phase confront this reality: One cannot have the relationships one wants, one can only have the relationships one can make. Relationships with authority figures have to do with work and interdependence, not with desires for approval and intimacy. The stubborn, self-centered stance in relationships is common to everyone, whether in authority or intimacy. We have all experienced that stubborn insistence on having our own way, as if our very life depended on it, even though we were being told to do exactly what we wanted! Subgrouping around this experience makes it easier to understand that being self-centered is the experience of being alone, imprisoned in the personal fort that was originally built to defend against enemies who seemed neither to understand nor care. Breaking free of the impasse requires a shift of focus away from the conflicts with others, away from the conviction that it is they who must change, and toward a recognition that change involves instead the internal conflicts one has with one's own personal authority and personal goals. When resistance to change is recognized as basically a conflict within the self, rather than between the self and external authorities and societal goals, therapy can begin!

PHASE TWO: INTIMACY

The major motivation in the phase of authority was to avoid pain; in the phase of intimacy, it is the search for the self. The self is found through the process of separation and individuation. This process must occur not only between self and other but also between the self and the self. The phase of intimacy addresses the Module 4 defenses against separation and individuation which are the major restraining forces to interpersonal intimacy. (These are discussed at length in Chapter 12.)

Separation and Individuation Defenses (Module 4)

SCT emphasizes the establishment of an authentic *intrapersonal* relationship as the foundation for establishing authentic *interpersonal* relationships. The major defense against separation is the denial of differences in relationships. Difficulties in discriminating and integrating differences leads to enchantment, idealization, and blind trust in others, self, and groups; the most common symptoms of such defenses are love addiction (Pennov, 1978) and exploitability.

   The major defense against individuation is the denial of similarities between the self and others. Difficulties in discriminating and integrating similarities leads to disenchantment, cynicism, contempt, and blind mistrust of self, others, and groups. The most common symptoms are despair and alienation.

   To the extent that these defenses are undone, individuals can endure the tidal rhythm of closeness and distance in intimate relationships and tolerate the individual differences in themselves and others. The work in this phase requires being able to separate and individuate without losing the self or the other. The discriminations that are required in this process are not available to consciousness in the way that Phase One discriminations were; their source is not verbal or even consciously preverbal, but intuitive. Up to now, the group has been basically engaged in a resocializing process: Now it is at the threshold of a transformational process; a new form of life is emerging.

The first experiences of the human infant are split between good or bad. When things are good, there is no bad; when things are bad, there is no good. This is not a function of denial, which represses experience that cannot be integrated, but a function of an as-yet-undeveloped capacity to integrate. As the child's integrative capacity develops from simple to complex, the child becomes able to accept mixed feelings—mixtures of good and bad, of love and hate—rather than experience these as separate worlds. Given sufficient stress, all living human systems, however sophisticated their functioning, can regress past the point of integration and back to one side or the other of the primary split. When this happens to patients, they cannot experience, or even remember, the existence of the other side.

The major therapeutic task in Phase Two of SCT group development is the management of regression. Those therapists who have witnessed uncontrolled regression in groups know what primitive anxieties can be aroused: terror of fusion and loss of identity in enchantment; despair, suspicion, isolation, and suicidal ideation in disenchantment. The deeper and more serious the difficulties in these areas, the more difficult it is for the individual to modify his or her typical ways of defending against terror and anguish. In SCT, the discriminatory process of subgrouping automatically differentiates the undifferentiated flood of feelings. The group-as-a-whole contains the split, subgroup work manages the pace and depth of the regression within each side of the split, and both the group-as-a-whole and individual members develop an increased capacity for integration. To discover and struggle with addictive love, shame, and the impulse to consume or be consumed, within the containment of a subgroup, or to explore isolation and existential despair together, is a very different experience from confronting these issues alone.

PHASE THREE: LOVE, WORK, AND PLAY

The work of moderating Module 5 defenses marks the transition into the final work of therapy, which is ongoing for the rest of one's life and is the primary source of continued development, maturity, and transformation.

Module 5 defenses are the defenses against knowledge, common sense and existential humor, that are the major restraints in work, love, and play. (These are discussed at length in Chapter 13). This final module consolidates the therapeutic work that has enabled individual group members, subgroups, and the group-as-a-whole to meet the challenges inherent in each phase of group development. The group has learned how to identify and integrate the splits that occur naturally when human beings attempt to manage frustrations and solve the problems of everyday life. The mature group has a history upon which it can draw. It can recognize characteristics of earlier phases when they recur. It has a memory of successful methods of defense modification and the experience of previous mastery of problems and vicissitudes in development. It has the ability to support and facilitate the work of an individual member when that member has to do personal work so that he or she can again function at the group level. Most important of all, at every group session, all members get support and encouragement to continue the work of weakening the defenses when they are evoked, so that they can redirect their energy toward the knowledge that comes from access to the authentic self.

In the earlier phases, the modification of defenses was taken in sequence and corresponded to predictable difficulties in group development that were specific to each developmental phase. In the experienced group, predictability gives way to the experiences that come when the group can work at the edge of the unknown and can turn, for knowledge, to both comprehensive and apprehensive experience. Comprehension requires being able to discriminate and integrate the information about the world one lives in and at the same time remain open to the apprehensive knowledge that little of what is possible in one's creative vision can be translated into reality. Defending against the existential pain of this realization results in impairment of the ability to make life-potentiating decisions and to implement them.

Defenses against Knowledge and Common Sense (Module 5)

The first four modules of defense modification are the necessary preparation for addressing the defenses against knowledge of the inner and outer realities of human existence. Modification of the defenses against inner reality involves continually seeking to make available to the person the full strength of his or her primary emotions, so that energy can be vectored into the roles that are appropriate to the person's goals. Modification of the defenses against outer reality enables the person to determine what roles and goals are appropriate to the context (common sense). When the defenses against knowledge are stronger than the driving forces, comprehension becomes increasingly constricted and people lose touch with themselves. When the driving forces are stronger than the restraining forces, common sense and a cosmic sense of humor make the task of knowing the boundaries of inner and outer reality a matter of joy as well as pain.

The goal of SCT is to make the boundary permeable between apprehensive knowledge and comprehensive knowledge. This goal is achieved by making emotional intelligence available both apprehensively and comprehensively. Throughout the developmental phases of the SCT group, defenses against recognizing and integrating the two kinds of knowledge are addressed. The challenge in experienced groups is to enable members to continue to sit at the edge of the unknown and discover the many dimensions of reality. With two kinds of knowing and understanding—comprehension and apprehension—now permanently available to them, SCT group members can go on to achieve ever-deeper knowledge of themselves, others, and the world. It is, however, the access to emotional intelligence that makes it possible to apply the apprehensive and comprehensive knowledge practically to the challenges of everyday life—with the common sense it takes to find one's way through reality to the everyday goals of work and love and play.

SYSTEMS-CENTERED PRACTICE

Phase One:
The Authority Issue

Chapter 5

Social Defenses

*I*n all systems-centered therapy, defenses are addressed in a hierarchical sequence that starts with the simplest and easiest defense to modify and progresses to ever more complex modifications. In group therapy, defense modification paces the phases of group development. In individual therapy, it paces the development of the interaction that unfolds between therapist and patient (which follows the same sequence as the phases in group development). The modification that takes place at each level of defense is a consolidation of the work that has led up to it and is a preparation for the work to come.

Although SCT modifies defenses one at a time and in sequence, defenses do not occur one at a time. The successful modification of social defenses requires knowledge of both what social defenses are and what they are not. This enables SCT therapists to help patients discriminate between a defensive communication and the specific defenses against anxiety, tension, and irritability, which are also aroused in the beginning stages of therapy. Social defenses are the first of the defenses to be addressed in Module 1 of the five modules of defense modification (see Table 4.1).

Defense modification begins as soon as therapy begins. This is true for all SCT therapy—whether it be group therapy, individual therapy, family therapy, couple therapy, or the initial diagnostic interview. In SCT it is important to begin in the way one wishes to continue. This is particularly relevant to the initial interview (the management of the social defenses in the initial interview is addressed later in this chapter).

THE NATURE OF SOCIAL DEFENSES

Social defenses are the first, and the easiest, of the defenses to modify. They are the defenses behind the stereotypical social interactions that maintain the status quo and that are as much a frustration as they are a relief. Social defenses against communication enable people to moderate their interactions so that they have as much freedom as possible from the social anxieties and irritations that inevitably arise when one person tries to relate to another. Unfortunately, these social defenses are also the prison that prevents people from having authentic relationships when they want to.

The first module in the hierarchy of SCT defense modification teaches group members how to recognize and bypass the social defenses and introduces the triad of symptomatic defenses (the cognitive defenses, the somatic defenses, and the masochistic and sadistic defenses). Social defenses are like a ritual dance, and most people know the steps. These defenses keep people safe from relating to each other (or to themselves) but may also make it impossible for them to focus on the real task at hand. Social defenses are also the shorthand that signals status in the pecking order and establishes the rules of relationship. Subtle but quite clear to those in the know, they are a source of shame and humiliation to those who are not. Indeed people will give up a lot of personal freedom to avoid experiencing that shame and humiliation.

Social defenses are the common automatic defenses that maintain the boundary between the self and the everyday world. They are generated from the use of such higher-order ego mechanisms of defense as intellectualization and rationalization. As first-level defenses, social defenses successfully block the input of new information so that the social system is defended against change. When first-level defenses fail, information that requires discrimination and integration crosses the boundary and destabilizes the system, arousing dissonance and frustration. Frustration arouses anxiety, tension, and irritability, which in turn elicit defensiveness. When the defenses come into play, the system is no longer primarily maintaining its boundaries but is instead concerned with maintaining its equilibrium.

Social Transference

Social transference is the transfer from the past into the present of ways of behaving that keep within the social norms. The social self is maintained by automatic social defenses, which are tactics available to keep appropriate social distance and to manage one's social life.

Social defenses exist an SCT in the group system as well as in the system of each individual in the group. The interpersonal aspect of social defenses is as important as the intrapersonal. The former relate not only to general stereotypical social behavior but also to the normative stereotype role behavior of group members in relation to each other and to the therapist. There is an important difference between the functional role of patient and therapist (which has to do with their responsibilities in solving the problems that lie along the path to goals) and the stereotype behaviors that define the role but not the function. For example, the dominant–submissive role relationship between doctor and patient is stereotypical of a fixating dependency, which differs from the functional dependency necessary in a role relationship based on differential responsibilities and resources. Luckily, social defenses are mainly context driven and are therefore relatively easy to modify in context.

BOUNDARY MANAGEMENT

Social defenses are the automatic social responses that maintain the boundary between the self and the everyday world. Social "talk" avoids transferring personal or factual information. Social defenses can be heard in the language of social flight: in answering a question with a question; in changing the subject, interrupting a speaker, and discounting information; in insinuations, sarcasm, and gossip; in funny stories as well as victimizing jokes; and in monologues and know-it-all pontification. These are all defensive communications that transfer little information and make few demands for discrimination and integration.

A system in conflict is not in an appropriate state to take in information that requires discrimination and integration. People in conflict defend against receiving (as well as giving) information by relying on automatic behaviors that require little investment of energy. Thus, the person's system remains stable through the use of familiar automatic social tactical defenses. When these work, the system boundaries remain relatively impermeable to exchanges of information and the internal equilibrium of the system is not further disrupted. When these defenses fail, however, there is a demand on the already overloaded system to discriminate and integrate. The result is anxiety and tension.

In an SCT group, social defenses are first modified by the very process of recognizing them. Once recognized, they are reduced in significance during the work of crossing the boundaries into the group and in the subgroup work of becoming more comfortable and less tense and anxious in a difficult new situation. They are made ego-alien when members recognize that social defenses cost them intimacy and authenticity in the group. This recognition begins the work of shifting stereotypical role-locks toward the functional role relationships needed for cooperative work toward the goals of therapy. This work can be relatively low-key. For example, the SCT leader might respond to a defensive member by saying:

> "Do you notice that when you talk of something difficult you look away? But if you remove yourself from contact with the group when you are trying to work on something difficult, you will be working

alone. This may well be the way you have learned how to work on difficult things, but will working alone be as efficient as working together and tackling the difficulties that arise as we work together? So let us both be alert for any of our automatic socially acceptable ways that, on the one hand, get us to feel more comfortable but, on the other hand, will cost us in that they will get in the way of addressing why we are working together here."

Because breaking social rules can be such a shaming experience and because social rules are such a powerful influence on what one does and does not do, it is extremely important to build a group culture that encourages functional relationships (i.e., relationships that relate to the goal or purpose of being together) rather than relationships that reinforce the stereotypes of status, gender, age, race, color, or creed. It is for this reason that SCT leaders pay particular attention to the communication pattern that develops in therapy. Once again, it is less what people say than how they say it that determines how a communication will be heard. Communication patterns reflect the state of the system and become the environment that influences both the way people experience the system and how they behave in it. It is therefore particularly important for the therapist to address and manage how people in the group communicate from the very beginning, before communication patterns are built that recreate and reinforce the very difficulties therapy is expected to resolve.

BREAKING SOCIAL TABOOS

One of the features of SCT that make learning to be a therapist difficult is that many of the behaviors that make SCT effective break social taboos. We have discussed in the Introduction and again in Chapter 4 some of the differences in technique between nondirective and directive therapy and the difficulty that nondirective therapists have in breaking the explicit therapeutic taboos. In this chapter we address the more subtle violations of the unwritten rules of nondirective therapy.

Traditionally, therapists are taught to hear, associate, think about, and interpret verbal communication—but not necessarily to observe nonverbal communication. Traditionally trained therapists are encouraged to hear and to think about what their patients communicate rather than to look and to see. Neurolinguistic programming studies (Bandler & Grindler, 1979), for example, have alerted therapists to the importance of such diagnostic clues as a patient's skin color and eye movements. Systems-centered therapists rely heavily on the nonverbal cues SCT group members send that signal their relationship to themselves and others (SCT calls these intention movements). For some therapists this reliance violates not only the unwritten rule that they should ignore what they see but also the rule that they should behave as if they do not know. Yet when therapists follow these unwritten rules, their responses to the patient's intention movements are no longer directly connected to the reality of the moment. (This is particularly true if the information in the moment is connected to transference and countertransference.) For some therapists (and for many of us in our everyday social life), denial of what we know and feel has become so successful that we actually have no awareness of, or feelings about, what we "should not know." It is particularly important for SCT therapists to recognize this phenomenon since SCT places a heavy emphasis on common sense, and common sense depends on the connection between reality, thought, and emotion.

The SCT emphasis on common sense and observations of reality in the here-and-now is a significant challenge for therapists who rely on other sources of information to guide them in their work. However, therapists who do not use observation of the here-and-now as a primary source of information are deprived of their everyday common sense, which makes use of all information available in all contexts.

Nonverbal communication is one of the richest sources of information, with good potential for increasing the permeability of the boundary between apprehension and comprehension in systems-centered therapy. It is not only systems-centered therapists but also SCT group members who must be encouraged to break the social taboos against recognizing and feeling what they "should not know." Patients often lack awareness of both arousal and sensations. The experience of arousal—warmth in the body signals arousal and cold signals defense—is common to all emotion, but what differentiate one emotion from another are the accompanying sensations. Sensations are reflected in our language: We say that our bowels move with compassion, that we see red, we melt, we fill up. We say that rage is hot, and, in fact, heat *does* accompany anger. We say that our heart is heavy or that it is bursting; we *do* feel a pressure or a fullness or an ache in our chest when we grieve. In extremes of emotion, there is little difficulty recognizing the sensations of the emotion. However, when people inhibit or deny emotion, they require considerable focusing of attention to become once more aware of the full experience of feeling.

Intention Movements

Helping patients regain the ability to once again experience full feelings, without defending against them, is one of the major goals in SCT. Successfully modifying the social taboos against recognizing the signals of intention movements takes a giant step toward that goal. Using the information contained in intention movements is a primary feature of reality testing in SCT, both for patient and therapist. The ability to use this information greatly increases the capacity to maintain a link between introspection and common sense.

There are two kinds of information available in an intention movement: There is the sensory information about the primary impulse that is generating the movement; this is experienced apprehensively (intuitively) as emotion. There is also the signal of the emotion, that is, the intention movement (e.g., clenched fist, eye movements, a smile, a frown) or a physiological change (e.g., a change in skin color, muscular tension, or posture). However, when the patient does not have access to the apprehensive self, the information in these signals is only available to the therapist (provided he or she observes them!).

Overt intention movements constitute useful information from the very beginning of therapy; both therapist and patient can observe them. Even when patients cannot make the connection between the signal and the experience, it is not difficult for them to accept that the apprehensive self has information that they are not yet ready to comprehend. Eye movements and changes in skin color and muscle tension, which only the therapist observes, on the other hand, cannot be usefully brought to the patient's attention at the beginning of therapy without risking an experience of dehumanization. Nevertheless, these psychophysiological changes provide essential diagnostic information that alerts the therapist to how available the patient is for continued defense modification. Later in the course of therapy, this information can be useful to the patient in increasing self-awareness.

The information in a person's intention movements is essentially species specific, that is, comprehensible to all human beings and available as apprehensive experience. People perceive each other's intention movements as both unique and universal. If SCT therapists keep in mind the meaning of the species signal at the same time they are attending to the individual, they can understand both the systems-centered and the self-centered context for the signal. Thus, from the species perspective, the clenched fist is a manifestation of a fight impulse—of which the individual who is clenching the fist may be totally unaware. From the individual perspective, that clenched fist may be a personal gesture that signals a defensive role-lock or resonance with the work of a subgroup or both, or it may signal latent aggression in the group-as-a-whole.

COMMUNICATION PATTERNS

Another source of information for the SCT leader is the communication patterns that signal the many system relationships to authority and intimacy. We have already discussed in the Introduction the use of SAVI to identify the patterns of flight or fight for the individual or for the group. A number of force fields (based on the approach–avoidance verbal behaviors identified by SAVI) of some of the most frequent socially defensive communications are discussed in the following paragraphs. These kinds of communications are caught and filtered at the boundary of the group by several of the SCT methods: the explore–explain junction, the distraction exercise, and subgrouping.

"As If" Talk

"As if" talk is the most popular of the social defenses in communication. In this pattern a whole conversation can take place without the exchange of any information. The as-if communication pattern is high on ambiguity, redundancy, and the safe contradictions of "yes–but" statements. Such a pattern is useful when people want to sound involved but want to avoid taking the risk that what they say can be held against them later. The pattern is relatively easy to change by reducing the number of statements characterized by the presence of restraining forces and increasing the number of statements representing the driving forces (see Table 5.1).

Emotional One-Downmanship

In emotional one-downmanship the person elevates the other and puts the self down in a communication pattern that discounts the self either explicitly or implicitly. People who use this way of talking set themselves up in the role of victim and issue an invitation to others to respond either by trying to talk them out of their one-down position or by taking advantage of it (see Table 5.2). This is one of the cases where it is difficult to change the communication pattern without explicitly introducing the driving forces of reality testing.

TABLE 5.1. "As If" Talk

Driving forces	Restraining forces
Facts, figures, a clear question with a pause for the answer, answering a question, owning a subject change, etc.	Intellectualizations, vagueness, answering a question with a question, nonanswers, changing the subject, concealed contradictions in the form of "yes–but," etc.

TABLE 5.2. Emotional One-Downmanship: Fighting for One's Place

Driving forces	Restraining forces
Checking out mind reading, checking out negative and positive predictions, owning triumphs, etc.	Unchecked mind reading, negative predictions about self, discounting oneself, complaining (and directly blaming) from the role of victim about what "they" did. Gallows humor. Volunteering as the identified patient.

Emotional One-Upmanship

Emotional one-upmanship (see Table 5.3) establishes dominance either subtly (by inviting the other into the role of subordinate or identified patient) or overtly (by making explicit devaluations of the other and by using threatening, hostile, or scapegoating communications). The first step for the SCT leader in weakening the restraining forces is helping group members refrain from using them. Changing the emotional one-upmanship communication pattern requires that the individual enter into a peer relationship, which is often very difficult for such a person to do.

Intellectual One-Upmanship

Contentious communications tend to paint people into a corner, leaving them little choice except to comply or fight. This is another communication pattern that is relatively easy to change, provided the individual

TABLE 5.3. Emotional One-Upmanship: Fighting for One's Place

Driving forces	Restraining forces
Asking open-ended questions; owning mistakes, frustrations and disappointments; asking for another's opinion; paraphrasing another's communication accurately before responding; etc.	Attack–counterattack, sarcastic rebuttals and putdowns, diatribes, relentless questioning, blaming and indirect complaining, sarcastic jokes.
	Asking "helpful" personal questions about the other person's problem instead of joining and exploring the self.
	Making an identified patient.

TABLE 5.4. Intellectual One-Upmanship

Driving forces	Restraining forces
Open disagreements stating an opinion without implying that the other should agree. Decoding the yes–but by clear owning of what is the yes (I agree with this) and separately, what is the but (I disagree with that), etc.	Arguing, yes–buts, leading questions, disagreeing, discounts, interrupting, preemption, etc.

has the will to abandon the restraining forces and substitute the driving forces (see Table 5.4).

Some people practice a less obvious intellectual one-upmanship that uses the language of persuasion and often leaves others not quite sure why they feel dissatisfied with the conversation.

An effective way of changing this communication pattern is to interweave the driving forces and the restraining forces and then gradually reduce the latter (see Table 5.5).

Moral Righteousness

Those who give and withhold approval on the basis of moral righteousness use one of the most influential communication patterns (see Table 5.6) in motivating others to cooperate. They wield influence by playing on others' wishes and fears. The alternative pattern bases cooperative work on information that is consensually validated and related to the goals of the work.

Self-Protection

Communication that enables a person to maintain a safe distance from all kinds of relationships functions like a smoke screen in which the per-

TABLE 5.5. Less Obvious Intellectual One-Upmanship

Driving forces	Restraining forces
Keeping conversational balance, giving opinions with facts and conclusions, questioning for someone else's response, being descriptive, etc.	Establishing a question–answer pattern, giving opinions without a reference, using "uh-huh" and "hmm" as reinforcement, interpreting, giving advice, using persuasion, being prescriptive, diverting through jokes, etc.

TABLE 5.6. Moral Righteousness

Driving forces	Restraining forces
Consensually validating data and descriptive information, making clear connections between the act and the consequences, etc.	Giving advice couched in terms of oughts and shoulds, using words like "always" and "never," making threats, using gentle persuasion, making compliments and approval contingent upon compliance, etc.

son disappears (see Table 5.7). This is the language of disaffection and disinvolvement. It is unlikely that the restraining forces will be reduced until the person is motivated to emerge from their obscurities and into relationships with significant others. Once the person is motivated, the driving forces are available to disperse the smoke screen.

There is a variation of the self-protective communication pattern (see Table 5.8) that often makes for a lighthearted climate. People who use this pattern display good social skills, but they fail to enter relationships. In spite of the social atmosphere, it is improbable that any real communication takes place.

The Doctor–Patient One-Up–One-Down Role Relationship

Built into any therapeutic situation is the stereotypical one-up–one-down doctor–patient role relationship (see Table 5.9). In many forms of therapy, potentiating a one-up–one-down relationship between the therapist and the patient is not a problem; in fact, in some forms of therapy, particularly those in which transference is a major therapeutic tool, this role relationship is an asset rather than a liability. In SCT, however, where the work is based on a continual exploration of all aspects of the reality of the interdependently created treatment context, the tendency to form one-

TABLE 5.7. Keeping Oneself Safe in Authority and Intimacy Relationships

Driving forces	Restraining forces
Exploring the differences and similarities in one's opinions and experience, defining the goal, sharing resources, etc.	Giving double messages, maintaining incongruities, saying one thing but doing another, being ambiguous, presenting an expressionless face (or a good-child gaze with "nobody home" behind the eyes), avoiding contact, etc.

TABLE 5.8. Behaviors in a Variation of the Self-Protective Communication Pattern

Driving forces	Restraining forces
Connecting in the here-and-now, resonating and maintaining a balance of contribution and response, etc.	Gossip, telling funny stories, crossing from present to the past, crossing from present to future, parallel talk, etc.

up–one-down relationships is a clear liability and is addressed as a defense. The tendency to form such a relationship interferes with the recognition that each role in this dyad has a different goal and a different blueprint for work: Therapists are responsible for transferring problem-solving techniques to patients, who are learning how to discover their reality and free themselves from the symptoms and anguish that their defenses against discovery cause; patients are responsible for learning how to use the techniques.

THE INITIAL INTERVIEW

The initial interview in SCT follows the traditional course of any diagnostic interview. Every therapist's initial interview style is unique, and every therapist will have his or her own specific goals for the interview. SCT techniques are compatible with all therapeutic styles where the goals include clarifying the issues that brought the person into therapy, making a differential diagnosis, and getting a good enough overall clini-

TABLE 5.9. Communication Behaviors Indicating the Driving and Restraining Forces

Driving forces	Restraining forces
Being specific, reducing ambiguity, decoding contradictions; asking "what," "how," "when," "where" questions; answering questions for relevant information; encouraging experiencing, discouraging explaining; being behind one's eyes; being interpersonally responsive (but not initiating); reframing by normalizing, humanizing, legitimizing, universalizing, and depathologizing experience.	Being vague, general, ambiguous, contradictory, or redundant; asking "why" questions or answering "why" questions; interpreting; giving opinions without the facts; directing; pathologizing; not being behind one's eyes; keeping an unresponsive face; not owning mistakes; not apologizing; taking silent, unilateral responsibility for interdependent work.

cal impression to be able to take the first steps toward a treatment plan and an appropriate disposition. An SCT initial interview is, therefore, also a therapy session.

While the goals of the SCT initial interview are different from the goals of later therapy sessions, the structure and process of that session are no different from those of any other SCT session. Each session in SCT is a minitherapy in itself. Each session, including the initial interview, follows a therapeutic sequence in that the patient brings as much of the authentic self into the treatment situation as possible, learns to identify and use phase-appropriate SCT techniques to modify defenses, and consolidates the work of the session before leaving.

The initial interview can be used to illustrate how SCT modifies social defenses in as much as the major defense modification techniques—which are the hallmark of SCT—are introduced to the patient as part of the diagnostic process. As the social defenses are modified in the initial interview, SCT patients learn to tell the difference between (1) the interpersonal defenses that come between them and an authentic relationship with the therapist and (2) the intrapersonal defenses being used against frustration, as different from the conflicts and mixed feelings that are frustrating. This is the work of Module 1 of defense modification and the major work of the first half of therapy. In the initial interview patients discover that the *experience* of their feelings is often quite different from the way they *think* their feelings feel. As they explore their experience, they are introduced to the idea that everyone has defenses that characteristically build a defensive reality no one would consciously choose to live in. They learn that explaining and exploring lead in different directions: Explanations, albeit disturbing, introduce certainty (or, at least, probability) into an uncertain world whereas exploration requires one to endure uncertainty while discovering the world. By exploring instead of explaining, patients learn how to live in the present instead of the past or the future. It is in the world of existential reality that transformations through therapeutic change take place.

One of the advantages of using SCT techniques for modifying social defenses in the initial interview is that the therapist has an opportunity to detect the presence of any distress signals. Any such signal indicates that all defense modification with the prospective patient (including the relatively simple modification of social defenses) must be put on hold. (Distress signals, of course, can occur within any of the modules of defense modification.) Although defenses are addressed one at a time in therapy, they do not occur one at a time, and in the beginning of therapy the social defenses against communication are often impossible to address without also addressing some of the defenses in the triad of symptomatic defenses (see Chapter 4). The initial (diagnostic) interview often yields a particularly good example of the relationship between social defenses against communication and cognitive defenses against anxiety. It also illustrates why modifying social defenses is sometimes suspended in favor of either containing or deconditioning symptoms.

For each stage of defense modification, defenses are first recognized and named; then their costs and benefits are identified. Identifying the costs and benefits of the different defenses allows the full impact of the defenses on the individual's life to be understood and experienced. Never is this more important than in the initial interview.

The Status Defense

The first social defense that can be expected in an initial interview is the status defense. The status defense that patients use most often in therapy is one that places the therapist in the position of an authority who is responsible for their welfare. This is a good example of how social defenses typically reflect the social norms that reinforce the status hierarchy in society, in this case, the traditional doctor–patient relationship. The status defense is technically a role-lock (discussed in detail in Chapter 10), and SCT prefers to avoid working directly with role-locks until the patient has become equipped with some of the preliminary defense modification methods. Otherwise, the role-lock could become a barrier experience where both the patient and therapist maintain a disconnection between their thoughts, sensations, and feelings with respect to their interpersonal relationship or, worse, a mutual role-lock or mutual barrier experience between patient and therapist. Modifying the social aspects of the status defense requires a different technique from modifying the more serious one-up–one-down role-locks with authority. The modification of the fundamental dynamics of role-locks (which involve transference and the repetition compulsion) will come only through an exploration of the underlying conflicts that the patient is acting out by going one-down or one-up in a relationship. The initial interview is not the context for this complex work. Therefore, in the initial interview the doctor–patient role-lock is modified through common sense, as is illustrated in the following dialogue:

THERAPIST: I am noticing something that I want to bring to your attention. I have the impression, when you look to me, that somehow I should know more about you than you do. Do you have that feeling? [Notice that the cue that is cited is nonverbal, which vectors the patient's attention to both the intrapersonal and the interpersonal aspects of the current relationship.]

PATIENT: Well, you're the doctor!

T: That is true. And it is true that I do know things that you don't know yet—like how to tell the difference between feelings that come from your thoughts and the feelings you have that come from your experience—and we will work with that. However, let's first explore the idea that I know more about you than you do.

P: Well, you have more experience with people like me.

T: That is also true. I have experience working with people who come to therapy. How I get to know them, however, is by working with them, the way we have been working together in this session. Do you believe that I can know you without us working together?

P: I suppose not.

T: What will happen if we work together as if I can know you without learning about you?

P: Well, I suppose it wouldn't make sense.

T: I agree; it doesn't make common sense. I think we will find that you have to work just as hard as I do if we are to reach the goals we have today, which is to understand enough about why you are here for us to decide what next steps we can take. Your work will be to discover what you don't yet know you know about what is best for you. My work will be to show you some methods that will help you to do the discovering. How does that sound to you?

In the initial interview it is often difficult for the patient to give up being the helpless victim whose solution is to become an identified patient. In a group this same work is typically done during boundarying at the threshold of subgrouping, as well as during active subgrouping. It is usually easy to find subgroup resonance around the wish that the therapist do the doctoring without any help from the patient. There is a true goodness of fit between the appearance of the wish to "be doctored," as well as other flight issues, and what SCT theory predicts will occur in the early phases of group development. With subgrouping, a method that encourages members to explore their experience as it is occurring in the moment (rather than speculating, or talking about their memories of their experience in the past), it is much easier for the group therapist than for the individual therapist to shift the patient's attention away from the transference aspects of the wish to be doctored (which are deep and painful) and toward the functional effects of living out that wish.

In individual therapy the work of managing the therapeutic relationship is a constant focus for the therapist. In the early phases of therapy, one-up–one-down relationships are pointed out each time the therapist (or patient) recognizes that the role relationship is interfering with the work. To reiterate, it is not appropriate for the therapist to focus on the role relationship defense itself until preliminary defense modification is done and the patient is equipped to address the role locks he or she gets into with others, with authorities, and with the self. A fundamental SCT principle in defense modification is that aspects of the therapy that cannot be worked without involving transference modification are not addressed *as work* until the patient has mastered the methods for recognizing and modifying cognitive distortions, somatic and psychosomatic symptoms, depressions, and abusive acting out. It is only then, and not before, that the patient is equipped to work with more complex projections.

The "I Don't Know" Response

When patients respond, "I don't know," they have removed themselves from the work of therapy. This response has many functions: It can defend against involvement in the work of therapy, it can defend against the experience of mixed feelings, it can serve to avoid knowing about a conflict, or it can be a distress signal. Most important of all, the "I don't know" response always signals a lack of choice: Either the patient has no choice or the therapist is being given no choice. It is important to know which. Therefore, unless it is a distress signal, this response is always met head on in SCT.

Before the therapist confronts the "I don't know" response head on, he or she must be able to tell the difference between this response as a social defense that enables the patient to take refuge in obscurity and its use as a distress signal. "I don't know" is essentially an *ambiguity response*, and ambiguity signals either a cognitive disruption or noncompliance. Cognitive disruptions are a signal of potential fragility. When there is a cognitive disruption, there is a *barrier alert* (i.e., a cognitive disruption or a sudden, intense somatic response that signals that there exists a threat of breaching the barrier, or disconnection, being maintained between a person's thoughts, sensations, and feelings). When any barrier alert exists, the patient is not able to work in therapy until the defensive constellations that created the barrier are undone. The SCT method of confronting and differentiating between "I don't know" as a social defense, as a cognitive disruption, and as noncompliance is illustrated in the following material.

Confronting the Response

The following dialogue illustrates one way the SCT therapist might manage a patient who responds to questions with "I don't know." Note that the therapist ends this dialogue by bluntly asking the patient what is going on. The therapist is confronting the patient with his or her reliance on the "I don't know" defense.

T: You say you are feeling something. What are you feeling?

P: I don't know.

T: What I am asking is, How do you know you are having a feeling?

P: I don't know.

T: You know you have a feeling? *(Silence ensues.)* [The therapist now confronts the patient.] Is saying "I don't know" keeping you distant from your feelings and whatever experience goes with them?

P: I don't know.

T: Saying "I don't know" is a way many people have of remaining uninvolved with the work that they are here to do in therapy. Is that what is going on with you?

Differentiating between Noncompliance and a Cognitive Disruption

Instead of confronting the patient with his or her "I don't know" response, the therapist may attempt to differentiate between cognitive disruption and noncompliance as the source of the response. This is particularly important in the initial interview, when each step of the way must be taken cautiously

T: You say you are feeling something. What are you feeling?

P: I don't know.

T: What I am asking is, How do you know you are having a feeling?

P: I don't know.

T: You know you have a feeling? [This is a diagnostic question.]

P: Yes.

T: But you don't know how you know?

P: No.

T: Is that usual or unusual for you? [This is the diagnostic question.]

P: It's unusual.

T: Have you ever asked yourself that question before?

P: I don't think I have.

T: Do you want to ask yourself that question?

P: Yes.

[The responses to the diagnostic question and the questions that follow it suggest that the "I don't know" response was being used defensively.]

T: Ask yourself the question and see what you can learn.

If the preceding dialogue unfolds as follows after the diagnostic question is asked, the therapist must consider this variation a barrier alert and must differentiate between cognitive disruption and noncompliance. These phenomena are addressed in detail in the following sections.

T: Is that usual or unusual for you?

P: I don't know.

T: Is there something happening right now that makes it difficult for you to remember things about yourself? [The therapist is now vectoring the patient into testing his or her reality in the here-and-now.]

P: I don't know.

Cognitive Disruption

In both group and individual therapy, it is always important for the therapist to be alert for a cognitive disruption, that is, behavior indicating that the patient is having difficulty processing information and can no longer participate fully in the therapeutic process. The signals are usually consistent and easy to identify once one has learned to look for them. The person goes white, tends to look up to the ceiling, speaks more slowly, and becomes vague, pausing in midsentence. Restlessness and tension (which typically signal resistance or earlier stages of anxiety) are rarely manifested in a cognitive disruption. Whereas anxiety may be manifested by a twisting of the hands or hand wringing (or by general agitation), cognitive disruption may involve quite flaccid hands, almost as if they were disconnected from the person. Many of those in whom these symptoms frequently appear have learned some good social cover-ups. It is for this reason that it is a good idea when the communication pattern has either fragmented or become vague and slow for the therapist to check for a cognitive disruption by questioning whether or not the person is having difficulty thinking:

T: Are your finding it difficult to think right now?

P: Yes, I am.

T: Are you anxious?

P: I don't know.

T: Is your mouth dry?

P: Yes.

T: Hands cold?

P: Yes.

T: Butterflies in your stomach?

P: Yes.

T: Those are symptoms of anxiety. Are you spacey?

P: Less now. For a moment or two I thought I was going to faint!

Drawing the patient's attention to the physical self connects him or her to a reality that can be checked. Directing attention toward the physical self also encourages "centering," a technique that opens the person to a heightened awareness of the here-and-now and his or her participation in it. Technically, attention is vectored across the boundary from irreality to reality. This is the technique called "discovering reality," which differentiates the reality of the experience from the defenses against it (which are, in fact, often the source of the anxiety).

Cognitive Restructuring. In SCT it is never enough for the therapist to undo a defensive experience, patients must also recognize that there is an authentic experience that triggered the defensive response. As soon as there is good enough evidence to reassure the therapist that the patient is in no danger of fainting, the patient is encouraged to discover what it was in the communication that triggered the cognitive disruption:

T: Do you remember what happened just before you first started to feel spacey? [This technique is called "backing up the fork-in-the-road." The therapist carefully watches the color in the person's face. If the person goes white, and particularly if there is a green tinge to the complexion, the therapist returns to the technique of asking the patient to report the facts of his or her physical self.]

P: Yes, when you asked me how I was feeling.

T: Something about that question was difficult for you and you became anxious and then you were not able to think as well as you usually do. How are you now?

P: Better.

If the person seems to be in good shape again, the therapist can test to see if the patient has enough curiosity to want to start exploring what it was about the experience of being questioned that triggered the discomfort. The patient may discover that he or she had a forbidden reaction to some external stimulus (e.g., annoyance at the therapist's question) or a response to an unwanted internal stimulus (e.g., threatening feelings). In group work this would be a good place to call for a subgroup of people who also experience difficulties in thinking when they are anxious; members of this subgroup can explore the contexts and find the path in the fork-in-the-road they turned away from when they took the path into anxiety.

Deconditioning Fainting. There are cases, however, when a cognitive disruption is serious enough that the person not only feels faint but is likely to do so. In this case, the person is suffering from both anxiety and a psychosomatic symptom. The deconditioning of psychosomatic symptoms will be addressed in the chapter devoted to psychosomatic defenses (Chapter 7). Here, it is sufficient to note that deconditioning fainting is done in the same way that cognitive restructuring is done. The difference is that both therapist and patient agree to be alert for the first symptoms of fainting, so that they can interrupt the cognitive restructuring process and undo the anxiety. Whenever a disruptive (or dangerous) symptom serves as a major defensive response in therapy, it is important for the therapist to encourage the person to divulge information about other times when that symptom appeared; those contexts are described until enough of a picture emerges to identify the connection between the symptom and certain stimuli. This is best done in the initial interview, so that the reaction can be taken into account in the treatment plan. In any case, the cognitive restructuring process is halted whenever a patient needs to restore his or her ability to work. This happens more frequently when treating fragile patients, that is, those for whom self-observation is a tenuous and sporadic experience.

Because fragile patients have difficulty tolerating frustration and containing uncertainty, the therapist must be alert to a whole sequence of behaviors indicating defenses against anxiety and the experience of irritability. These must be brought to the patient's attention and sequenced over and over again until the patient recognizes them. For example, the therapist might instruct such a patient as follows:

"You notice, it has happened again. You felt impatient when I spoke and then you withdrew and looked away. I pointed that out and asked you to turn your head and look at me. This was difficult for you to do. Then when you looked at me, your inner experience

changed somewhat. I asked you to talk to me, and you became restless. I said that was frustration, suggested that you were experiencing the irritability in frustration, and asked you not to withdraw
from it but to stay in contact with me. You notice that when you did,
you became almost agitated, you felt very impatient, banged the
arms of your chair with your fists, and kicked your foot. I said that
was turbulence at the boundary, the irritation that is aroused when
you come out of your withdrawn place, and I asked you to try and
talk to me. You sounded cross when you said, "What do you want me
to do?" and then we were talking."

Of course, this sequence is far too long for fragile patients, who have
difficulty remembering. The challenge with fragile patients is to make
the connections between the stimulus, the response, and the experience
in such a way that they cannot only see the sequence but also begin to
make these kinds of connections for themselves. Many people have withdrawn to such an extent that they in fact notice so little about what goes
on around them that it is almost as if they live in a world of half-formed
shadows with little sense of how one thing follows another. Being able to
see cause and effect, stimulus and response, is a fundamental skill that
must be acquired before they can make sense of their world. Therapists
who use such aids as diagraming the sequence of events or writing code
words for their patients while they talk make this learning process somewhat easier. This approach is easy to introduce into individual therapy
and even in an initial interview.

Surprisingly enough, this approach is often of great interest to the
SCT group, even for those members who have no trouble remembering
or grasping the constellation of behaviors that make up a specific
defense. The ideal is for the fragile member to make a representation of
the stimulus–response sequence while the therapist describes the stages.
The therapist thus serves as the fragile member's memory and will continue to do so until the person can connect (1) the inner experience to
his or her response, (2) that response to the sequence of events, (3) the
sequence to the process, and (4) the process to the context of the frustration. This exercise is most effective when the frustration can be clearly
linked to some aspect of the therapy, since therapy is, in truth, often frustrating and is therefore a reality arena in which patients can practice
increasing their frustration tolerance. Art therapists have known for a
long time that capitalizing on eye, hand, and brain coordination is a
great help in therapy; thus, asking SCT group members to draw their
understanding of how their defenses work can be a great help to them in
the early stages of defense modification. Moreover, watching while a
member's sequence of stages is drawn is usually of interest to all group
members.

In SCT groups, members serve as each other's and the group's memory. Most members seem to have an easy grasp of the sequencing steps that occur in the difficulties encountered by others in the group. This capacity is particularly important when it is used for the benefit of members who split good from bad and then forget the bad when they feel good and forget the good when they feel bad. Particularly when life has once again closed over for such a member, it is remarkably reassuring to that member to be reminded that he or she reported the same experience before and was later able to go on and experience a good mood. (It is also of great benefit to people who suffer from bipolar disorder to feel the group's empathy about their wish to enjoy ups—and to be reminded by group members of how bad the downs are if they do not take their medication.)

Noncompliance

We have seen that the "I don't know" response may be a defense or an indication of cognitive disruption. It may also be a sign of noncompliance. If there is noncompliance, the therapist attempts to discover the reason for it so that motivational work can be done.

Presented below is a variation of the dialogue presented earlier, beginning with the diagnostic question. This variation may indicate either anxiety or noncompliance.

T: Is that usual or un usual for you?

P: I don't know.

T: Can you ask yourself the question "Is there something happening right now that is making difficulties for me?" and see what you can learn.

P: I'd rather not!

If such a dialogue occurs and if nonverbal clues suggest that the "I'd rather not!" is masking a cognitive disruption, the therapist starts work on lowering the anxiety and cognitive restructuring. If there is no doubt that the patient is exhibiting noncompliance, the therapist confronts the patient and either brings the compliance into the context of reality or reframes and poses consequences and choice to the patient:

T: Is there something about you being here today that makes you avoid talking about what is going on with you?

P: Yes!

T: Will you tell me what that is?

P: No! [This a clear signal of noncompliance!]

T: So you know you have a feeling; you don't know how you know; you haven't asked that question before; you don't want to ask it now; and you don't want to tell me what it is about you being here today that makes you want to avoid talking about what is going on with you? [The therapist is summarizing the patient's communication.]

P: That's right!

T: Given that is true for you, what work do you think we will be able to do? [The therapist begins framing the reality consequences of the patient's communication.]

P: Not very much.

T: Is that the way you want it, or do you have some mixed feelings about the stalemate we are in? [The therapist is presenting the patient with a choice.]

If the patient now replies, "Yes. I have some mixed feelings," the therapist can respond, "Then shall we see what we can do about the stalemate we are in?" If the patient's answer is again "yes," work can continue with reality checking, reality education, and reality testing. If the patient is still noncompliant and says, or signals "no," the therapist continues questioning and framing the stalemate situation (e.g., "Are you here of your own free will?") until either work begins or the stalemate becomes a loop. If the latter occurs, the therapist then frames the consequences:

"If we continue to be stalemated in this way, we will not be able to do anything useful with our time today. [The consequences are stated.] You will not get anything out of coming, and I will have failed as a therapist. At the end of the interview I will feel bad that we have not been able to work together, for whatever reasons. But I can afford to fail as a therapist, because I know one cannot always succeed. You will go away not having gotten what you came for. Can you afford that? I wonder if there are not other times in your life when you might have gotten something from a situation but became so resistant that you were unable to take advantage of it? [The therapist is suggesting to the patient that this is a matter of choice.] Do you feel at all that you are locked into a familiar pattern of behavior that you don't know how to change? [The therapist is pointing out the patient's resistance to change.]"

It is extremely unusual for a patient who has come to therapy voluntarily to be this resistant. However, in the rare and sad case in which the patient is this resistant, there is a true fork-in-the-road between entering therapy or leaving it. Presenting this impasse to the resistant patient as a fork-in-the-road, as a junction at which one has the choice of staying or going, and refraining from putting any pressure on the patient to choose one road over the other, is the best that any therapist can do. If the person decides to go, the therapist's final step is to make sure the person knows how to return if there is a later change of heart. This final step, as is true of all other techniques in SCT, is done in detail.

In group work the unmotivated member is a good springboard for subgrouping around ambivalence about being in group therapy. There is seldom any difficulty in forming a subgroup for the resistance, and the exploration almost always ends with the discovery of how hard the work is and how angry it makes everyone that the work is so hard. When a member is adamant about leaving—and however much the subgroup resonates with the desire to leave therapy—the following communication from the therapist (which is taken from an initial interview) is appropriate. The group will learn much, as it always does, when the relationship between action and consequence is brought across the boundary into reality and dealt with by common sense.

> "I support your going if you are certain that you cannot work with me in therapy at this time. We have one last piece of work to do together before we separate, and that is to make sure that you have the other branch of the fork-in-the-road available to you should you change your mind. If you change your mind, would you want to come back and see me or would you prefer a different therapist?"

If the person wants a different therapist (he or she may need help saying so), it is important for the therapist to make sure that the person knows how to find one. It is also appropriate to discuss with the person the different approaches to therapy and how to find therapists who follow these approaches. If the person says that he or she would return for therapy, it is equally important to ensure that he or she has thought through exactly how to do that. The temptation for the therapist in this situation is to take it for granted that if a patient has come for therapy once, he or she can come again. This, however, is not necessarily true. Helping people think through the steps increases their freedom to choose. Once again, it is crossing the boundary into reality. There is no substitute for common sense.

Chapter 6

Cognitive Defenses

T
he triad of symptomatic defenses, which are the next cluster of defenses to be addressed after the social defenses, defend against the experience of frustration and involve the mind, body, feelings, and behavior (see Table 4.4). Frustration occurs whenever something comes between the self and the impulse to act. There is energy in frustration. SCT makes a distinction between potential energy and actual energy. Potential energy, undefended, is a state of arousal and readiness; it is equivalent to the state athletes are in as they wait for the signal to actualize their potential.

The ability to contain potential psychological energy requires frustration tolerance. As long as frustration is tolerable, system energy is available for solving problems and managing conflicts. When frustration becomes too difficult to contain, pressure builds up and the energy is either discharged into the environment or constricted within the system. Constriction generates anxiety, tension, and irritability, against which defenses are mobilized. In other words, system energy is vectored away from the original frustration or conflict and is redirected into defensive experience. Thus, defensive experiences end up taking precedence over addressing the original problem.

A major goal in SCT is to increase the patient's ability to contain frustration (and anxiety, tension, and irritability) so that the potential energy again becomes available for managing the primary conflicts of internal and external reality. Unfortunately, in most cases the secondary conflicts that have been generated by the defenses have preempted the primary conflicts; that is, false (defensive) experiences have replaced the original, spontaneous authentic ones. To restore the original connection to the nondefensive self, energy must first be released from the defenses and symptoms so that anxiety, tension, and irritability can be recontained as potential energy, that is, as energy that is available to be actualized in the direction of the primary conflicts that originally spawned the defenses.

SCT AND THE DEFENSIVE USE OF THE IMAGINATION

As creative and imaginative human beings, we live a large portion of our life in our head. When we do this defensively, we are misusing our intellect to solve our problems. This tendency is easier done than undone. Using imaginary reality as a solution to problems generates additional anxiety, tension, and irritability, as well as other secondary experiences like guilt, dread, and worrying. The human system reacts to emotionally imagined reality in exactly the same way it responds to actual reality. In other words, we are capable of experiencing anxiety, tension, and conflicts of feeling that have no basis in reality! After fleeing from primary experience to defensively constructed reality, a person still has the problems that existed in primary reality and now compounds them with the problems generated by the secondary reality. Recognition of one's defenses introduces the element of choice: Through therapy one can choose between obsessively ruminating and reality testing, between explaining and exploring.

SCT encourages patients to frame their experience only after they have discovered it. This almost always requires people to discover that their expectations of their experience not only do not reflect their actual experience but often distort it. When encouraged to explore the experience of their frustration, they discover that there are differences between the experience of the frustration, the experience of irritability, and the experience of maintaining defenses against irritability and frustration. When these discriminations are made, people discover that what was unpleasant about the experience arose mostly from their defenses against it. Once experienced without tension and anxieties, frustration energy is a not unpleasant mixture of readiness and arousal, together with some apprehension and curiosity.

Intellectual versus Affective Insight

In Chapter 4, emotion and feeling were differentiated and recent findings in neurophysiology (that there is no common sense in intelligence without emotion, a fact for which there is a biological basis) were presented. The fact that people need emotional intelligence to connect their ideas and actions accounts for the findings that intellectual insight alone is not transformative and that it is affective insight that leads to therapeutic change. These findings also support the SCT goal of defense modification, namely, making the boundary permeable between comprehensive and apprehensive knowledge.

The lack of correlation between intelligence (as defined by IQ) and behavioral change also explains why some cognitive therapy patients can make themselves *feel* better when they apply cognitive therapy techniques to undoing their cognitive distortions, and yet still lack the sense that they *are* better. Unfortunately, changing the way one thinks does not change the emotional meaning of life. SCT techniques owe much to the methods of cognitive therapy (Beck, 1976; Burns, 1981). However, in SCT, undoing cognitive distortions is only one step toward the goal, not the goal itself. Undoing cognitive defenses, and reducing the symptoms they generate, solves a secondary problem; it does not address the fact that all secondary problems are a substitute for the primary problem that was defended against. This is why the fork-in-the-road concept is basic to every SCT technique. In choosing one fork-in-the-road the patient learns more about his or her defenses. In choosing the other fork, the patient learns more about the primary conflicts that he or she defended against. Thus, to work with defense modification alone is only half the task. The other half is to enable patients to disconnect from their defensive selves and discover the conflicts they have around experiencing their primary human emotions and impulses. This is the work that restores access to emotional intelligence, and it is emotional intelligence that understands the meaning in life.

In extremes of emotion, most people have little difficulty recognizing the sensations of emotion. However, when emotion is inhibited or denied, considerable focus of attention is needed to regain awareness of the full experience. Regaining the ability to experience full feelings, without defending against them, is one of the major goals in SCT. The work of Module 1, the first module of defense modification, which targets both the social defenses and the triad of symptomatic defenses, which are first modified in Phase One of group development (see Table 4.3), takes a giant step toward that goal.

Primary versus Secondary Reality

For SCT therapists, the subliminal nonverbal signals of thought, feeling, and emotion are a significant source of information about the patient. SCT recognizes three components of emotion: cognitive, affective, and sensory. The affective component is the experience itself of the emotions of joy or grief or anger or sadness or love or hate. When we ask people how they know that they are having a feeling, they often talk not about the experience of emotion but about their thoughts. However the source of thoughts differs from the source of the sensations they experience with the emotion. When our thinking is descriptive, we are describing our feelings in words. We are talking feelings! When we interpret our feelings, we are talking about our thoughts. What is more, the activity of thinking can generate feelings, and often these thought-generated feelings substitute a secondary experience for the primary emotional experience. Thus, there is a difference between what we *think* we feel and what we *sense* we feel. What we sense we feel is the primary emotional experience, and when we describe our inner signals of emotion, we are putting words around primary experience. It is always important to differentiate between the kinds of experience we are verbalizing by indicating whether the experience is primary (experience first, words second) or secondary (thoughts first, experience second). These are primary and secondary sources of knowledge, respectively, which can be congruent (when the boundary between the two systems is appropriately permeable) or incongruent and stressful (when it is not).

Awareness of the signals of feeling is an important source of information in SCT therapy. Here SCT owes much to pioneering work done by ethologists, particularly Tinbergen (1951), as well as those who analyzed nonverbal communication, Shefflen (1973), Birdwhistle (1960), and Davanloo (1987) and his SDTP's method of analyzing videotapes of therapy sessions, as well as those involved in the fine discriminations that go into neurolinguistic programming (Bandler & Grindler, 1979).

SCT therapists are alerted to two sources of nonverbal information: the outward signals of feeling that are manifested in behavior and the inner signals of sensation that reflect psychophysiological states and are manifested in changes in skin color and somatic tension. These are signals about the body's state of arousal. What is particularly important in SCT is the notion that the person manifesting these signals is often unaware of them. It is the therapist, therefore, who has the responsibility to collect this information for therapeutic use.

Primary experience essentially signals experience common to the species, universal on the one hand, unique to each human being on the other. It is important for SCT therapists to keep in mind the universal meaning of the species signals as they work with a person to understand the specific relevance of the signal in the here-and-now context. Thus, from a species perspective, the frozen body signals fear, the white face signals an intention toward flight, the red face or clenched fist signals the impulse to fight. In a therapy group, a species signal from one member to another might be an indication that an impulse is in resonance with the work of a subgroup, or it may be a personal defensive gesture that signals a role-lock; from the perspective of the group-as-a-whole, such a signal may indicate the presence of an as-yet-unheard group voice. How to use the information from a signal requires a judgment by the therapist.

Checking Secondary Reality

The management—or, more precisely, the mismanagement—of the anxiety response to frustration and conflict is the source of much of the psychological pain and suffering for people who come for treatment. Significant relief is experienced when the defenses of negative predictions and other cognitive distortions that generate an ominous imaginary reality are undone. Technically, this is accomplished by requiring the patient to cross the boundary between irreality and reality by checking secondary, constructed, reality against primary reality. This level of relief often occurs in the first or second therapy session and sometimes even in the initial interview.

Cognitive defenses defend us from anything in our experience we are afraid we cannot contain by explaining it away. Cognitive defenses basically defend us from our fears about our fears. When we create a defensive cognition, that is, when we intellectualize as a defense, we translate nonverbal information into words. As a defense, intellectualizing inserts steps in between our direct perceptions and the sensations of our feelings and our body. Intellectualizations "explain" our experience according to a preexisting map, but they may not reflect our experience. Worst of all, defensive explanations focus us away from exploring our experience.

COGNITIVE DISRUPTIONS

Cognitive disruptions, like the loss of the ability to remember, abstract, or concentrate, happen to all human beings under stress. So do physical disruptions, like increased heart rate, dry mouth, cold hands, and sweaty palms. Stress can also generate more self-destructive physical disruptions, like colitis, ulcers, or heart attacks. Whereas defensive communications and constructed realities serve to stabilize the self-system in a way that is still in the service of system survival (even though stabilization is achieved at the expense of system development and environmental mastery), discharge into the inner system environment in the form of a cognitive disruption threatens the very survival of the system. For this reason, therapeutic work at any level cannot be undertaken until the threat to survival is removed. Work with a system that is discharging into itself is counterproductive because it increases the requirement for discrimination and integration and consequently introduces still more dissonance and still more discharge. The importance of this cannot be overemphasized. The proper sequence of goals in all SCT interventions is the rechannelling of the dissonance in such a way as to, first, maintain system survival; second, foster development; and third, achieve system transformation. This sequence holds true at every system level of group therapy.

COMMON COGNITIVE DEFENSES

Explaining

Explaining is an important cognitive defense. Rather than explore our problems, we can explain them away by making them too small, too big, or too far away to address or we can blame them on the past, on others, or on our own helplessness. Defensive explanations relocate problems.

"Interpreting" Reality

"Interpreting" is a particular way of explaining that puts the source of the problem out of reach. Interpreting unconscious motives relegates the problem to the speculative, and the potential for "trying on" motives is infinite. There is no end to guilt when people are accused, or accuse themselves, of unconscious motives.

Externalizing

Interpreting fault, or blaming, is a way of externalizing the problem and moving it as far away as possible. Externalizing relocates intrapersonal problems to the outside world, that is, to the world outside the self and to the world outside the here-and-now. There is no end to disappointment, hurt, and outrage when people project unconscious motives onto others.

Externalizing is like a boomerang. When we attempt to throw away our problems, they return and hit us from outside as well as from inside. Unfortunately, because externalizing is usually done without awareness (unconsciously), it can feel like the outside world is throwing things at us (constructed reality). All too often we throw back yet again, never knowing that we are now building a conflict in reality based on a distorted internal map—the well-known self-fulfilling prophecy.

Externalizing into the Past

Cognitive defenses involve the imagination in telling stories that simplify complex experiences and make them understandable. Unlike fairy tales, however, where the good are good and the bad are bad and everybody lives happily ever after, the stories or myths we tell ourselves about good and bad parents and about the significant relationships in our past do not have happy endings. Moving from the past to the present means coming to terms with mixed experiences and mixed feelings about the real frustrations and satisfactions of past life. Exploring the reality of the past, instead of explaining the past, leads to quite different sorts of insights and understandings.

Negative or Positive Predictions

Worrying about the catastrophes that the future might bring darkens one's experience of the present and fills one up with foreboding and dread. Positive predictions bring a different color and tone to one's experience—but are no less an escape into the future. Both negative and positive predictions are the stuff that obsessions and ruminations are made of. Both lead to experiencing oneself as tossed by the whims of fate. For example, being in love involves negative and positive predictions that catapult us from the heights of joy to the depths of despair on a roller coaster ride that defends us against the reality that one cannot have the relationships one *wants*, one can only have the relationships one can *make*. Making a relationships involves the hard work of tolerating differences. However, making a relationship is likely to be less disappointing in the long run than waiting for one's dreams to come true.

Mind Reading

When we imagine that others are thinking humiliating, denigrating, or critical things about us, we introduce a source of distress and inhibition and create a world of wariness and distrust. Few things color reactions more than attributing to others the kinds of opinions we would least like them to have. This imaginative exercise is the source of much suffering. Mind reading is a loop: The more we think we know what others are thinking about us, the less motivated we are to test reality and the more our responses to others reflect our untested conclusions about their thoughts. Mind reading is basic to the development of both blind trust and mistrust and is an essential ingredient in obsessive relationships and in paranoia.

Using Cognitive Holding Patterns

Obsessions, ruminations, and rationalizations serve as cognitive distortions that focus the person's attention away from the frustrating conflict in reality and onto an alternate reality that functions to bind the original anxiety in a holding pattern. Maintaining and repeating thoughts that begin with "If only I had" or "I wish I could have" or "It never should have happened" creates a world from which it is almost impossible to escape. This defense has the disadvantage of generating a secondary anxiety, which instead of being a signal about the real state of the system merely signals the dissonance of the symptom itself. The same is true of negative predictions and mind reading. These defenses reduce the dissonance between the map and the real territory by *creating* a negative outside world to live in that fits the negative internal map with less dissonance than the real territory does (Festinger, 1957).

The attempted solution of an imaginary reality generates still more anxiety, tension, and irritability, as well as other secondary experiences like guilt, dread, worry, and a tendency to make negative predictions and engage in mind reading. By fleeing to defensively constructed reality, a person not only still has all the problems that existed in the primary reality but adds to them all the problems generated by the secondary reality. Recognition of these defenses through therapy gives the person the opportunity to choose between obsessively ruminating and reality testing.

MANAGING ANXIETY ARISING FROM COGNITIVE DEFENSES

The Barrier Alert and Deconditioning

A barrier experience is characterized by boundaries that are impermeable to problem-solving communications, that is, boundaries that are maintained by selective perceptions, open only to information that is compatible with the existing organization of information (the constructed reality), and closed to all differences. Patients who are not aware of their inner sensations of anxiety have a barrier or disconnection between their thoughts and sensations and feelings. When there is the threat of breaching this barrier, an alert is sounded in the form of a cognitive disruption or a sudden, intense somatic response. A barrier alert may be a signal to the therapist to do reconstruction work with these patients before exerting any more pressure on them to undo defenses.

When anxiety and the somatic symptoms that anxiety can generate are not differentiated, the very process of undoing anxiety may risk precipitating a somatic response. As soon as a somatic response occurs, energy is discharged into the biological system. Somatized anxiety can generate a range of somatic symptoms. Symptoms of cognitive disruptions can appear as confusion, impaired memory, or disorientation. Cognitive disruptions can also generate somatic symptoms. Feeling faint can escalate into actual fainting; feelings of nausea can become dry heaves or vomiting. These symptoms *must* be deconditioned before any further stress is placed on the individual. And if the individual is a member of a group, it is certainly not going to help the group if a member faints! Possible communications by the SCT therapist to a patient who appears to be developing a somatic symptom are as follows:

"You say that you are beginning to get faint [naming the symptom]. That is a response to anxiety [framing the experience as fact]. Did you notice that you started to get faint when you mentioned your husband [connecting the symptom with the probable trigger]? Are you aware of any other symptoms of anxiety besides faintness [continuing to direct attention to physical reality]?"

"You are noticing the beginning of a cramp in your stomach [naming]. Your muscles are reacting to your anxiety with tension [framing]. Did you notice what triggered that response? Do you have other anxiety symptoms right now [directing attention to physical reality]?"

Such interventions lay the foundation for the fork-in-the-road technique, whereby the person is asked to look for what triggered the response. Identifying the trigger also provides a clue as to what experience is being avoided when the focus is on a symptom.

In short, when anxiety is diverted or discharged into a symptom and that symptom distracts the person from seeing the relationship between anxiety and the defense being explored, the symptom has to be undone first. This undoing is accomplished through the process of education, rechanneling, and increasing motivation through confrontation aimed at achieving recognition of the costs and benefits accruing from the use of the symptom.

The Technique of Description: Naming and Framing

One of the most powerful techniques for undoing anxiety is that of describing, which involves identifying a symptom clearly by name; framing it factually rather than focusing on pathology; and making simple connections between the symptom and the trigger, which are not obvious to the patient until they are presented as such.

Describing introduces the process of reporting data and requires people to be aware of their physical self. If anxiety has flooded out the person's observing system, asking for a description of the physical self requires the person to become aware of the facts of his or her experience and is a preliminary step that must be taken before the therapist can ask further questions about anxiety. Experiential grounding in the physical symptoms of anxiety is the preferred SCT technique for lowering anxiety. It is expected that by the time patients have finished identifying their symptoms of anxiety, they will be much less anxious and will be ready to learn where the anxiety is coming from. As in most SCT techniques, there is a logical order to follow: Moving from symptoms in the head down to the symptoms of the abdomen draws a person's attention toward his or her center. There is a connection between focusing on one's internal experiences and the lowering of symptoms, distress, and somatization.

In using the technique of description, the SCT therapist might say to a patient who is experiencing panic, "Those are the thoughts that scare you. What are you experiencing physically at the same time? Are you having sensations in your body?" As the patient begins to identify the fast beating heart or cold hands and tremor—and thus learns to pay attention to the symptoms of anxiety in the body—the focus of interest becomes physical and descriptive, requiring ego functions that move the person away from an orientation to the escalation of panic.

Differentiating between Anxiety and Feeling

If the patient does not know how to recognize anxiety, education is appropriate. As in all SCT methods of education, a reality basis for the learning is developed first. Recognizing anxiety, therefore, requires that patients pay attention to their sensations and identify those sensations that accompany different experiences.

Anxiety releases adrenaline, as do other strong feelings. Some of the symptoms of anxiety are adrenaline symptoms: the fast-beating heart and the feeling of arousal and readiness. Other symptoms of anxiety are dry mouth, cold hands, sweaty palms, and the sensation of butterflies in the stomach. Thus, the symptoms of anxiety are signs of adrenaline production; such symptoms accompany any strong feeling. Anxiety, however, has some differentiating characteristics.

Differentiating between Anxiety and Tension

The first step in deconditioning the symptoms of anxiety (a great deal of pioneering work on deconditioning was done by Wolpe, 1958) is to teach patients that many of the symptoms that have brought them to therapy are actually symptoms of anxiety. Discriminating between the defenses that generate anxiety and the anxiety itself is rarely obvious to a person at the beginning of therapy. Until the differentiation is made, the person will not be able to understand the implications of the difference between the experience of the conflict that generates the anxiety and the symptoms and tension that attempt to bind the anxiety. It is often a surprise to people to recognize that worrying, ruminating, obsessing, expecting the worst, and being scared are all experiences generated from a secondary reality that is constructed as a cognitive defense against anxiety. This defense is designed to bind the primary anxiety that is a natural systemic action to facing an unfamiliar situation. SCT labels the natural reaction to the unknown "apprehension" to differentiate it from the symptoms of anxiety generated by defenses. (Apprehension has two meanings: to understand intuitively, and, as here, to be fearful.)

The first step in the ongoing, painstaking educational work of the first phase of systems-centered group therapy is learning how to discriminate between the psychophysiological experience of anxiety (the tension that binds both the anxiety and the conflict in the muscle system) and the hostility aroused by the frustrating internal conflict. This work in a group is often done with an individual member before it is done in subgroups. Selecting the member with the least difficulty is the ideal choice in that there will be initial success and symptom relief. This initial work at the individual level educates the group to continue the work through subgrouping. The group learns, through resonance and observation, the fundamentals of undoing the defenses against the frustration arising from conflict. Ultimately, as subgroups explore the consequences of defenses—and the secondary gains that often accompany them—and learn to undo their defenses, cognitive distortions like mind reading and negative predictions become ego-alien.

The factual reporting itself of the symptoms of anxiety can be expected to lower anxiety; this is often followed by a perception of tension. It is then possible to move through the tension to the conflicted feelings that were bound by the tension. Before patients can pay full attention to the signals of emotional arousal, their defensive cognitive misconstructions must first be tested against reality. This is as true for emotions of joy and sexuality as it is for emotions of fear or grief or pain. It is important at this point to go slowly and carefully, because the closer the work moves toward the experience of conflict, the more easily the next defensive threshold is aroused. It is not unusual for the previously nondefensive person to suddenly replace a cooperative and rewarding exploration with a stubborn character defense or an even more difficult transference defense in which a victim-bully scenario or a stalemate gets played out. Such stubbornness requires immediate attention from the therapist. Emerging stubbornness always signals that it is time to alert patients to its cost: While stubbornness usually wins the battle, it also always loses the war. The SCT group therapist may expand on this by saying, "Stubbornness is like locking oneself up in jail. Stubbornness makes it impossible to relate either to oneself or to anyone else. It is important for us in the group to get a subgroup to explore what it will cost us to support stubbornness as a defense in this group."

Stabilizing the Fragile Patient Flooded with Anxiety

The following dialogue illustrates one of the first techniques used by the SCT therapist for stabilizing the fragile patient who is becoming swamped with anxiety:

T: Signals of anxiety are a dry mouth, cold hands, sweaty palms, some jitteriness or shivering. Do you have any of those symptoms?

P: Well, yes. My mouth is dry, and my hands are cold. My heart is beating fast, and I'm also tense.

T: So are you aware that you are anxious?

P: Yes, I am anxious.

Requiring patients to focus on their physical symptoms and report them descriptively does in fact orient them to reality in time and space and requires them to become aware of themselves as a source of data. When patients are unable to access physical experience about themselves, there is a significant disruption.

Locating the Source of the Anxiety

If the patient with anxiety has already learned to recognize and report anxiety signals, the therapist can proceed to teaching him or her how to recognize the sources of anxiety—thoughts, sensations, feelings, or the unknown. The therapist starts by asking the patient three questions. The patient is asked whether he or she is:

1. Thinking anything that arouses anxiety, for example, negative predictions or mind readings
2. Aware of any frightening feelings or sensations, for example, the irritability that goes with frustration or feeling turned on
3. Sitting at the edge of the unknown: the fork-in-the-road between certainty and uncertainty

If the patient is still in the early work of therapy, he or she cannot yet answer these three questions as to the source of the anxiety. Nevertheless, the questions are still asked inasmuch as they serve a didactic purpose at this point. Asking the three questions also educates patients in differentiating between feelings that are generated by their imagination and those that come from their experience of reality. Being able to locate the source of anxiety quickly when questioned about it only happens when people become used to making these connections for themselves.

The context for this work is introduced at the beginning of each group therapy session, at the boundary crossing and by means of the distraction exercise (see Chapter 3)—or whenever a member is having difficulty clearing his or her own distraction in the group. And, of course, it is used in individual therapy.

Negative Predictions and Mind Reading

When it is determined that negative predictions or mind reading is the source of a patient's anxiety, the SCT therapist follows a specific set of steps to undo the disruption:

1. Connects the anxiety with the thought: "Are you telling yourself something that is making you anxious?"
2. States the thought: "What are you telling yourself?"
3. Labels the thought as a negative prediction or a mind-read: "That is called a negative prediction" or "That is called mind reading."
4. Asks about the feeling generated by the thought: "How do you feel when you think that?"
5. Makes the connection between the feeling and the thought: "Do you see then that it is your thoughts that are giving you your feelings?"
6. Asks whether the person believes the thought: "Do you believe you can predict the future?" or "Do you believe that you can read people's minds?"

If the patient indicates that he or she can predict the future or read another's mind, the therapist sets up a dialogue that results in checking the belief against reality. When the patient's belief is challenged and undone by reality, the therapist then repeats and reframes the experience:

"So you see, you felt anxious and found that you were making a negative prediction [or an assumption about another person's thoughts] that was making you anxious. You also found out that you felt awful when you were making that negative prediction [or assumption]. Then when you were asked whether you believed the thought, you found that you didn't. So do you see that you were feeling anxious about a thought that you didn't believe when you brought it into the light of reality? Do you think that the next time you get anxious, you can notice if you are having a thought that is making you anxious and see if bringing it into the light of reality makes you feel better?"

Illustration of Anxiety Management: Sample Therapy Session

Dialogue from a therapy session is presented in the following pages to illustrate how the SCT therapist manages a patient whose anxiety stems from the use of cognitive defenses. Note how the therapist uses the SCT technique to undo a negative prediction and how, later in this session, deconditioning occurs.

T: Are you anxious?

P: Yes.

T: Are you telling yourself something that is making you anxious? [The therapist connects anxiety with a thought.]

P: I'm not sure what you mean.

T: Do you have thoughts—are you thinking things in your mind—that are ideas about what is going to happen next or what I am thinking or how you are going to do in here that make you anxious?

P: Well, yes, I suppose so.

T: What are some of them? [The therapist encourages the patient to state the specific thought.]

P: Well, I'm afraid I won't be able to tell you the things I need to tell you so that you'll be able to help me with my problems.

T: So you're afraid you won't tell me things that you want to tell me, and I won't be able to help you.

P: Yes.

T: You are making a negative prediction. [The therapist labels the thought.] How do you feel when you make a negative prediction about our future? [The therapist asks what feeling goes with the thought.]

P: I feel bad.

T: Do you believe that you won't be able to tell me what is wrong and I won't be able to help you?

P: Well, sort of —

T: So you have mixed feelings? You both do and you don't?

P: Yes.

T: When you think that I won't be able to help you, how do you feel?

P: Terrible.

T: And when you believe that I *will* be able to help you, how do you feel? [The therapist is making the connection between feelings and thoughts.]

P: I feel better.

T: So your feelings change as your thoughts change!

P: Yes, they do.

T: When you make a negative prediction you feel bad, and when you make a positive prediction you feel good!

P: Yes, I suppose that's right.

T: So far, it seems as if your anxiety is coming from your thoughts, and we don't know whether there is anything in reality to make you anxious. Would you like to check it out?

P: All right.

T: When we talked about what brought you here in the beginning, do you remember what happened?

P: Yes, I found it difficult to be clear about it at first. And then I stopped being vague, and it seemed clearer.

T: I understood that you often feel very anxious; that you are afraid to go out and meet people or go into new situations; and that you're very disappointed in your husband, who doesn't seem to help you or take you seriously. Is that what you wanted me to know?

P: Yes, it was.

T: So did your fears come true? Are you still afraid you won't be able to tell me the things that you need to tell me so that I'll be able to help you with your problems?

P: (*Laughs.*) No!

T: In fact, do you see that anxiety is one of your problems and we are already working on it?

P: Yes, I do.

T: So do you see how making negative predictions about what is going to happen makes you anxious and miserable?

P: Yes, I do—and I do that all the time.

T: And do you see that when you checked your negative predictions against the real world, you were scaring yourself with your thoughts and not with the reality?

P: Yes, I do.

T: So now how do you feel about your crystal ball? Do you still feel you are that good at predicting the future? [The therapist asks whether the person believes the thought.]

P: (*Laughs.*) No, I don't.

T: So do you think that the next time you look into your crystal ball and make negative predictions about the future, you can remind yourself that doing that makes you feel awful?

P: I can try.

T: And do you think that if we keep working with this, you might become less anxious?

P: Yes, I do.

T: So now how do you feel about your being able to get help in this therapy?

P: I feel quite confident that I can.

T: You look as if you are getting anxious again. Are you? [The therapist will continue to focus on anxiety and to make the connection between anxiety and defenses against experiencing frustration as well as making the connection between frustration and the three responses to frustration: anxiety, tension, and irritability.]

P: Yes, I'm afraid I am.

T: Are you telling yourself something that is making you anxious?

P: Well, if I think about it . . . er . . . yes, I suppose I'm afraid I'm not doing so well in here after all. I'm disappointed in myself.

T: You are afraid you are not doing well in here? I suggest that we check that out against reality, like we did last time. What would doing well be like?

P: Well, I'd not be making all these mistakes.

T: How do you know you keep making mistakes?

P: (*Nervous laugh*) Well, you keep pointing them out to me.

T: Would you please tell me what I say when I do that?

P: Well, last time I said I was feeling scared, you said it was because I was making a negative prediction.

T: Yes, I did say that, I remember. I am teaching you that one of the sources of your anxiety is the way you think. Is it frustrating when I interrupt you in the middle of talking about something important to you?

P: Yes, it is a bit.

T: How do you feel toward me when I frustrate you like that?

P: Oh, I don't feel anything. It's for my own good, and you are just doing your job.

T: Yes, it is my job, and perhaps you will indeed learn something that will be good for you. But it is also frustrating to have me interrupting you all the time. Would you check out your experience and see if you *do* have some feelings about how frustrating this work is?

P: Well, I wish it was easier.

T: And what feelings do you have that it is not so easy?

P: I'm frustrated.

T: Whenever people are frustrated—you, me, or anyone else—we often feel some sort of mixture of anxiety and tension and some irritation. Are you aware of any anxiety or tension or irritation?

P: Well, we know I am anxious.

T: Yes, we know that anxiety is one of your major problems, and we are trying to find out what makes you so anxious. We know that one of the things that makes you anxious is a tendency you have to make negative predictions. Are you anxious because you are making negative predictions right now?

P: No.

T: Well, thoughts aren't the only way we scare ourselves. Having feelings or experiences that we don't want to have can also make us anxious. Are you having any feelings you wish you didn't have?

P: Well, I wish this was easier.

T: You're frustrated.

P: Yes.

T: Are you also tense?

P: Yes.

T: Where?

P: My shoulders.

T: Does having tension make you anxious? [The work here is mainly to connect anxiety to thoughts; more intensive work on connecting tension to the feeling that it is containing comes later.]

P: No, I'm used to it.

T: Are you also irritated?

P: Well, I was.

T: Does being irritated in here make you anxious?

P: Well, it did a bit.

T: So we are discovering another source of your anxiety. Thinking anxious thoughts made you anxious, and when you checked them with reality you felt better and the anxiety went away. And now we are discovering that irritation at being frustrated also makes you anxious. Now, we can't do anything about what is frustrating you. Everyone finds this work frustrating at the beginning. So we can't change the frustrating situation. But we may be able to do something about your becoming anxious if you get irritated. Do you want to do some work on that?

P: Yes, I would. I have a lot of trouble when I get irritated or cross or angry about anything.

T: All right, let's see if we can go back a few moments ago, when you were aware that you were irritated. Do you remember? [The therapist is trying to help the patient differentiate between anxiety and irritation.]

P: (*Pause*) No!

It's not at all unusual for patients who are anxious to be unable to remember an incident, even one that occurred only a few moments before, if the feelings about the incident are what is making them anxious. When there is a good treatment alliance, as in this case, it is usually easy to undo this cognitive disruption. There are two main ways of approaching this task. Which one is chosen will be influenced by the current goal of the therapeutic work at the time: If the therapist is using the recall as a frame for the next step of work, as in this case, it is useful to get into the work as quickly as possible. (Doing the remembering for the patient is also useful for fragile patients who cannot use their own memory for themselves.) If, however, the current goal of the work is to help the patient learn how to use his or her memory, then the technique to choose would be to contain the patient while he or she does the work of recalling.

T: I asked you how you feel toward me when I interrupt you in the middle of talking about something. Remember?

P: (*Pause*) Sort of.

T: And then you said that it was frustrating but that you didn't feel bad because it was for your own good and you knew I was just doing my job.

P: (*Pause*) Yes.

T: And that was when I wondered if being frustrated was making you anxious. (*Pause*) And you said you wished this was easier. Do you wish it was easier right now?

P: Yes, I do.

T: Do you know what feelings go with that wish?

P: I know this is silly, but I feel a bit like crying.

T: So we were trying to remember what it was like for you to feel frustrated and irritable, and now you feel like crying instead?

P: Yes. I often cry when I'm frustrated.

T: So we are at a fork-in-the-road. Which experience would you like to explore first—your impulse to cry when you are frustrated or your irritation?

The patient has diverted into tearfulness and away from exploring and experiencing her irritability. This is a choice point for the therapist. Two different therapeutic scenarios are possible here. The first is to pursue the branch of the fork-in-the-road in which the tearfulness diverts the patient away from the anxiety aroused by exploring irritability. Much later in therapy, a different scenario is possible, one that involves a deeper stage of work in which exploring the tearfulness is now the road to the pain and grief of hurt feelings. In the early stage of therapy, the major focus of the work is deconditioning the defenses that reroute experience away from primary feeling.

P: I'm not irritated anymore.

T: You are teary instead?

P: Yes.

T: If you had a completely free choice, which would you like to explore first—your irritation or your tears? [This is a "containing situation," which keeps the patient related to the goal and at the same time leaves her free to choose her own path. It is very important for the therapist not to have a preference for which route the patient will take. As long as one or the other side of a conflict is explored, work in therapy is being done.]

P: I don't know.

T: "I don't know" is a position that makes it impossible for you to choose and leaves you helpless. Do you want to be in a helpless position?

P: No.

T: Then which experience do you want to explore in yourself first? Your irritation or your tearfulness?

P: I feel absolutely stuck. [Notice that several other roads to different levels of defense analysis have appeared. Feeling stuck, for example, is a sign that the patient needs to work on resistance to change. However, the therapist must remain focused on the work of the moment, which is the patient's defense against experiencing irritation in a frustrating situation. Unless some other defense now serves as a barrier to further work, it is ignored by the therapist; the time to modify it will come later in the sequence of defense modification.]

T: Is being stuck also a frustrating experience?

P: Yes, it certainly is!

T: How would you describe your reactions to your frustration at being stuck right now—anxious, tense, or irritable?

P: Is this multiple choice?

T: Yes.

P: And what if I don't want to choose?

T: Then we would both be stuck and our work would be stuck. We would not learn any more about the difficulties that brought you here today.

P: (*Pause*) Well, I seem to be getting irritated.

T: Will you choose to explore your irritation, or would you rather recall your tearfulness? [This question is important in that it brings the idea of choice itself into the patient's awareness. It also gives the patient the freedom to actively choose which part of the work she will do first.]

P: I'll choose irritation.

T: How do you know you are getting irritated?

P: I feel it.

T: And what is the experience that you're feeling?

P: I'm feeling impatient.

T: Frustrated, irritated, and impatient with this process?

P: Yes.

T: And anxious?

P: No, not right now.

T: So what is like for you to be here and know you are irritated and not be anxious about being irritated?

P: Well, it feels all right, actually! [The deconditioning process is working. The patient is now able to experience irritation without being swamped by anxiety.]

T: Good. Before, you said you had a lot of trouble when you got irritated. Are you in any trouble right now?

P: No . . . I seem fine. And, as you said, it's all right to be irritated when it's so hard.

T: And how do you feel about me for being part of what makes it so hard?

P: All right. As I said, you're doing your job, and I think you're doing it well!

T: It's true that I'm doing my job. But that sounds like a thought rather than a feeling. What is the feeling that goes with your thought that I'm doing my job well?

P: It's a good feeling.

T: And what about the feeling when you are irritated with me? Am I correct that you also get irritated with me for doing the things that make it hard for you, even if you do appreciate me doing my job?

P: Well, yes.

T: So how are you when you are irritated with me?

P: Well, that's not so good. I feel out of sorts with you and out of sorts with myself.

T: Which "out of sorts" do you want to explore first—with you or with me?

P: Well, I know the ones with me very well. I feel like you're thinking that I'm stupid and slow and that I'm boring and—

T: But those aren't thoughts about you. They are thoughts about me. You're at your crystal ball again, and this time you're not reading the future, you're reading my mind. How do you feel when you think I'm thinking critical things about you?

P: Well, I don't like it. (*Pause*) I feel bad about myself.

T: I think we have the boomerang here! Do you know what a boomerang is?

P: Yes, it's a curved piece of wood that you throw and it circles round and comes back again.

T: Well, is it possible that you are "boomeranging" your thoughts into my head and then having them come back and hit you and make you feel bad?

P: Well, I haven't ever thought of it like that.

T: Are you mind reading critical thoughts? And do they make you feel bad?

P: Yes.

T: Whose thoughts are they?

P: Well, the right answer is that they are mine! (*Pause*) It's funny: It makes sense, but somehow it doesn't feel like that.

T: How does it feel?

P: It really feels like you're being critical.

T: You believe in the critical thoughts even though you are no longer quite so sure that I'm the one that's thinking them?

P: Yes, I both believe it and I don't.

T: Nobody in boomeranging recognizes that they threw the boomerang; if they did, boomeranging wouldn't work. You understand that the whole purpose of the boomerang is to get rid of the thoughts that you cannot bear to have and give them away to someone else. You gave your critical thoughts to me. But the trouble with boomeranging is not only that the thoughts come back at you but that they hurt just as much, if not more, than the ones you threw away. Which is worse for you—for you to feel critical of me or to believe I'm feeling critical of you?

The Reprise Technique

It is in the process of modifying the cognitive defenses against anxiety in Module 1 of defense modification that SCT patients discover that thought-generated experience not only defends them against reality experience but also preempts reality. Being introduced to the fork-in-the-road, the concept of choices, is the first and major step in SCT therapy for people learning to actively and deliberately shift their attention away from defenses and symptoms and search instead for whatever authentic aspect of direct experience they were unwittingly defending against. There are many small steps to master before patients can do the work of modifying cognitive defenses against anxiety on their own.

At the end of each significant section of work, particularly when there is a large component of education, as there is in the earlier defense modifications modules, SCT therapists use the technique of reprise. This technique encourages patients to review the steps they have just taken that led them to discovering alternatives to living defensively. The reprise, an essential technique in SCT, serves to increase the probability that patients will make the techniques they have been using with the therapist their own, that is, that they will use them by themselves, without the aid of a therapist. The reprise technique also gives the therapist an opportunity to see how much of the work that has just been completed "belongs" to the patient, how much still "belongs" to the system of therapy, and how much is still simply potential. The following dialogue illustrates the reprise technique:

T: Let's go through it again so you can do it by yourself. What do you do when you don't know what you are feeling?

P: I start by getting some energy.

T: How do you do that?

P: Well, one thing I do is change my posture—sit up so that I can feel myself and give myself room to breathe.

T: And what does that do for you?

P: Well, first of all it shifts me from my social role to my working role. Also, it takes me out of whatever defensive role I may be in—and my body knows it even if I don't. If I change my posture, I won't be acting out my role anymore.

T: OK. And what is the role you tend to go into when you are in conflict?

P: I got into the one-up–one-down: You become the teacher or parent, and I become the beaten child. Trouble is, I go stupid in that role and can't think for myself. I rely on you to tell me what to do—and then comply and do it right—but I don't learn and I can't remember what to do when I come to do it for myself.

T: How about now? I'm asking all the questions, and questioning is a leading behavior. Are you feeling one-up–one-down right now?

P: No!

T: How do you know?

P: (*Laughs.*) Because I know the answers, and the answers are coming from my own experience—not just the ones I think you want to hear.

T: That fits with what I see: You aren't ducking your head and looking out at me from under your eyebrows, and you're not nodding all the time as I talk; I also don't get the feeling of you as compliant. And we know we can both be fooled so it's important for us to keep watching out for that shift in role.

P: OK, so I get the energy and I focus it on what I'm feeling—sort of look inward and see. As I do that now, I feel sort of fluttery in my stomach. I recognize that feeling: It's anxiety.

T: OK, now there are several ways you can work with that anxiety. Do you remember what they are?

P: Yes, I think so. The easy one is to make sure I've diagnosed it right. So I check to see if I have other symptoms of anxiety, like dry mouth or cold hands or heart beating fast or whether I'm sweaty.

T: Do you remember how it used to be when it was worse than that?

P: Yes. That hasn't happened for quite a while now. I used to get confused and light-headed: Sometimes things didn't look or feel real, and you'd get far away.

T: I'm glad that isn't happening to you. OK, so as you check, do you have other symptoms?

P: Now, just the butterflies.

T: OK. And what are the three questions you ask next?

P: It's so funny. It's so easy to remember now, but that whole thing took me so long to learn: thoughts, feelings, or the unknown! The first two are the things I can do something about—if I'm scaring myself with my thoughts or getting afraid of feeling or already having a feeling that scares me. The third is being scared of the unknown—and I remember how surprised I was and what a difference it made when we talked about everyone being apprehensive when they don't know what's going to happen next and how much it helped when you helped me notice my curiosity as well as my fear.

T: I know. That helps me, too, every time I have to sit on the edge of the unknown.

P: I still don't like feeling apprehensive, and sometimes I go back to thinking there's something wrong with me instead of accepting that it's just part of being human.

T: Curiosity is part of being human, too! It's the fork-in-the-road: Are you going to put your energy into the apprehension, or are you going to put your energy into the curiosity? Which are you going to do right now?

P: I know the right answer to that! (*Laughs.*) I'm going to find out whether I'm curious, and if I am, I'm going to find out whether being curious changes how I feel! And then I'm going to follow my curiosity wherever it leads!

COGNITION AND PERSONALITY STYLE

Certainly, one of the most popular human defenses is the tendency to explain reality instead of exploring it. Negative predictions, obsessions, and ruminations are used as defenses in every stage of therapy. Cognitive defenses are accompanied not only by anxiety but also by suspiciousness, paranoid thinking, and depression. Their presence or absence characterizes the predominant personality style of the patient. For example, patients whose style is histrionic flood their system with feelings. When they first try to explain their experience, they are so overwhelmed by feelings that they are only vaguely aware of what they are thinking. Under stress, people with a histrionic style collect information from reality but neither discriminate between what is collected nor organize it well enough to use it. When the therapist helps them contain their anxiety and guides them into reality testing, they are usually able to follow quite easily and to get almost immediate relief.

People whose thinking style is predominantly obsessive jam their system with ruminative, redundant, circular thinking. Information about reality is so "overdiscriminated" that it makes no sense. Helping these people take the intervening step into common sense is difficult, as they will have to abandon the security of their defense and allow themselves to be uncertain before they can collect the information about what in the real world is troubling them.

For the patient in the following dialogue, whose thinking style is obsessive, there is also a passive dependency role-lock to bypass.

P: I woke up anxious again this morning.

T: What did you do about it?

P: I reminded myself that my anxiety was generated by my thoughts and that thoughts were not reality, just like you and I worked last session.

T: So you recognized that anxiety-provoking thoughts are a defense that generates your discomfort and distracts you from reality.

P: Yes.

T: Did you discover what the reality was that you were defending against when you woke up this morning?

P: No!

T: So you did half the work. Do you remember what the other half is?

P: No!

T: Last time, when we went through the three questions, what did you discover?

P: I saw that I hate uncertainty and that however anxiety-provoking it is, obsessing creates a familiar world. That when I have thoughts that I am going to be fired and that my boss doesn't like me, I am no longer in uncertainty and have constructed a world that is familiar, even though it makes me miserable.

T: Yes, that is one fork-in-the-road. You seem to have a good fix on that. Do you remember what you discovered when you explored what you were avoiding in reality?

P: Something about ambiguity.

T: Anything else?

P: Something about ambiguity scares me.

T: Do you remember about your own ambiguity?

P: I don't seem to.

T: Well, you have just more or less told us that you are frightened by ambiguity and that when you are in an ambiguous situation you take flight into your obsessions and that makes you miserable. There was another side to this that I thought was very important. Do you remember us working with the amount of ambiguity in the way you talk and think?

P: Vaguely.

T: We were talking about preparing to do the performance appraisal for your secretary.

P: Oh, I remember! I was afraid that I wouldn't be able to do it properly.

T: Yes, and do you remember when I asked you what kind of appraisal you would give her, how vague you were and how ambiguously you replied?

P: I kind of think I sort of remember something like that.

T: We spent a lot of time on the way you use language.

P: Yeah, you sort of said that I hide out in something like a smoke screen, kind of like so that nobody can find me, and you thought maybe that this might be a way that nobody gets to pin me down.

T: Yes, ambiguous communications are like a smoke screen, and people can hide out in them. Did you notice that you became much vaguer just now when you weren't quite sure what you remember? (*Pause*) What you and I were noticing last time is how vague your thinking can be, how general and global your thoughts are about your work and how difficult it is for you to shift from the general to the specific.

P: I remember. Ambiguity—that's what you said it was.

T: Yes. You hate ambiguity in the world. You retreat from it up into your head and suffer from your anxiety-provoking explanations about why you are anxious. When you try to think about what it is in reality that you are avoiding, you think about it so ambiguously that you get frightened all over again and defend yourself with more anxiety-provoking explanations.

[Generating anxiety-provoking explanations is a common problem for patients. Until this patient has learned to tolerate the normal apprehension that comes from real-life uncertainties (SCT calls this "learning to sit at the edge of the unknown"), he will defend against it by attempting to explain the world. His explanations, however, will be generated by his anxiety rather than his curiosity. Hence the anxiety-provoking negative predictions and mind readings that characterize his obsessions.]

T: Do you remember what you discovered about your real world when you explored it?

P: No, what did I discover?

T: We seem to be using my memory more than yours at the moment. If you pause and think back right now, can you recollect what we found?

P: Not much more than the word "ambiguity."

T: OK, so let's use my memory. What I remember is that you had not thought about the criteria for the performance appraisal, that it would be easier to think about whether your secretary was doing well or not if you were clear about what she had to do on her job.

P: Oh, I remember. And we noticed that when I stayed ambiguous, I couldn't even begin to think about it. But when we changed my generalizations into descriptions, it became quite easy to list the tasks she had to do and then to see whether she was doing them well or not.

T: Yes.

P: And then you asked me if the firm already had a performance appraisal form. Do you know—I forgot this—they did! And I had no trouble filling it out. Then I started to obsess about whether she would get angry with me all over again.

T: It takes a while to change a pattern. We are just beginning this work. We all have to learn how to change our anxiety-provoking generalizations into specifics. No one is born knowing how to do that. Everyone has to learn. And everyone has some turbulence at the boundary when they don't know what they are looking for and have to go and collect their data. And it helps everyone to be curious about the task rather than be afraid of the unknown. What we are learning about you is that you defend yourself against normal turbulence at the boundary by retreating into obsessional explanations instead of getting curious so that you can collect data about the real world to solve the problem.

Chapter 7

Psychosomatic Defenses

S uccessful socialization contains the spontaneous expression of energy so that it can be harnessed in the service of both the individual and society. However, learning how to contain spontaneity is inevitably frustrating. Requiring children to manage their energy before they are developmentally ready results not in containment but in inhibition and constriction of their energy through tension. Tension is like constricting spontaneity inside a muscular straightjacket. In the course of SCT therapy, it nearly always follows that the energy released when cognitive distortions are undone will be constricted once more in a straightjacket of tension. Until there is enough containment for spontaneity, reducing one defense will call into play the next one in line. Thus, when the defenses against tension are modified, there will first be a shift in the person's experience toward tension and irritability and then toward greater irritability until, ultimately, he or she feels more irritable than either anxious or tense.

People often do not make the discrimination between anxiety and tension. However, it is precisely difficulties in the process of discrimination that SCT identifies as responsible for generating defenses and symptoms. Developing the ability to differentiate between anxiety and tension is understood as essential to the integration of emotion, feeling, and cognition. Not only is a patient's ability to discriminate between anxiety and tension important to the therapeutic process, but it is also an important diagnostic measure used by the SCT therapist in judging when to shift from one defense modification to the next. For example, as soon as the SCT patient becomes more tense than anxious, tension, rather than anxiety, then becomes the focus of defense modification.

Tension is a somatic, not a cognitive, defense. The anxiety-provoking map of the world that is created by the cognitive defenses is subject to the influence of rationality and can therefore be modified by appealing to common sense. Thus, the work of undoing the cognitive defenses establishes a method for reality testing in which ideas about reality are tested against reality. In contrast, the somatic world created by defensive tension is not subject to rationality. Speculating about what tension is defending against is a cognitive process and will not lead to discovering the physical experience of emotion that the tension masks. Although people readily become aware that they are tense and can recognize that tension is in fact a different physical experience from anxiety, they are seldom aware that tension functions as a straightjacket for spontaneous experience.

The work that patients do in the beginning phase of group development and at the beginning of each group session connects cognitive fears of their feelings to their actual experience of their feelings. In the initial stages of group therapy, as in the initial stages of individual therapy, tension is used as a signal of how much pressure can be maintained on a patient's defenses. The signal alerts the therapist to do the work of deconditioning psychosomatic symptoms if they occur. Although rechanneling work is perhaps more easily done in individual therapy, it can be done in a group—provided the group-as-a-whole is paced to the steps needed to undo the somatic defenses.

DIAGNOSING THE SIGNALS OF TENSION

Monitoring tension in the patient is the single most useful method for diagnosing the readiness of the person for work. The way tension is manifested in a patient is a signal to the therapist as to when it is therapeutic to continue the work of defense modification and when it is not. If the tension is serving as a straightjacket for feelings, there is no clinical reason not to undo it. Tension-induced muscular aches and pains are uncomfortable but not dangerous. These can be worked with in the group, just like any other defense. For example, it is safe to work as fast and as hard as possible when tension is located superficially in the hands or jaw or neck and shoulders. Even tension pains experienced in the stomach, chest, or back, as long as they involve only the striated muscle system, constitute a signal that the patient is still able to do good work in therapy. This conclusion also applies to conversion symptoms like glove anesthesia, where the probable diagnosis is hysteria, because the insensitive area ends sharply at the wrist, which is a physiological impossibility!

Absence of Tension

The absence of tension is not necessarily a sign that all is well: It may signal a serious disconnection between the patient's reason and emotion. Such patients cannot say how they feel because they have no access to their emotional experience to put into words. Feelings are the translators that make the apprehensive world of emotion comprehensible (Damasio, 1994). Indeed, comprehension requires both cognitive and emotional information. These patients will have a hard time benefiting from anything but cognitive therapy until they gain access to their apprehensive, nonverbal experience. SCT can be a shortcut in this process.

Clinical judgment about how freely to modify the defense of tension rests on determining whether there are signs that a patient's tension is being rerouted into the body (autonomic system involvement) instead of being more safely maintained in the striated muscles (central nervous system involvement). Whenever the therapist is uncertain, the possibility of a need for restructuring conversion symptoms should be kept in mind.

Conversion Symptoms

Some conversion symptoms can be dangerous and need to be "reconverted" before further defense modification is done. It is important for all therapists to be able to tell the difference between tension as a straight-jacket and tension that involves more serious psychosomatic symptoms. Benign conversion symptoms involve central nervous system responses. Conversion symptoms which are not benign involve the autonomic nervous system and produce a more serious form of constriction, one that signals physical problems (much gratitude to Habib Davanloo for this clinical clarification). It has already been emphasized (Chapter 6) that it is not therapeutic to put pressure on a patient's defenses if it will lead to a cognitive disruption—confusion, loss of memory, extreme detachment, or fainting. Worse still is to put pressure on a patient's defenses and precipitate an attack of ulcerative colitis or a migraine. For this reason, it is important to diagnose conversion symptoms before a person enters either group or individual therapist. Nonverbal signals are an excellent diagnostic clue. When in doubt, the therapist must take the initiative and ask a patient directly for any physical diagnosis that may affect the therapy, particularly if the therapist does not have this information from the diagnostic interview. No work that increases frustration (and therefore increases anxiety, tension, irritability, and the psychosomatic defenses against them) should be done until the tendency to channel defenses into the body has been deconditioned.

It is also important to discriminate between somatic symptoms that can be reconverted (both benign and non benign), and somatic symptoms that reflect an underlying disease process that can only be ameliorated. Reducing the defenses against the realities of an illness like multiple sclerosis, for example, will not change the overall course of the disease but will certainly make more energy available to the person for managing it.

UNDOING TENSION

When twitches, muscle aches, and tension pains in the chest or gut are recognized as superficial signals of stress, that is, as indicators of constricted emotion, pressure to work can be put on the patient. Undoing symptoms requires choice. Choice requires that the conflicts and forbidden impulses be contained as they arise, *before* the patient becomes defensive. Standing at the fork-in-the-road, the patient has the opportunity to address the previously unnoticed stressor and to explore either the emotion or the defense. Once the patient becomes defensive, he or she no longer has a choice. Choice must be regained by undoing the straightjacket of tension so that the internal experience is freed.

It is important in SCT to work with all symptoms in such a way that they are neither minimized nor magnified but, rather, normalized, legitimized, and depathologized. In SCT, all restraining forces to crossing boundaries are weakened as consistently as possible. This includes discussing defenses and symptoms in such a way that the descriptors themselves aid the process of weakening the restraining forces. SCT therapists follow a specific sequence in guiding a patient through the process of undoing what they call "the straightjacket of tension."

1. *Have patient describe the experience.* This step requires patients to pay attention to the information they can gather from their senses and to notice the discrepancies between what they think they are experiencing and the actual experience.

2. *Help patient differentiate between tension and feeling.* This step continues the ongoing work of helping patients discriminate between the different components of an experience rather than assume that there is a single component.

3. *Have patient locate areas of tension in the body.* Gathering experiential information makes it possible for the patient to differentiate the physical experience of tension from other experiences.

4. *Guide relaxation.* The therapist introduces the idea that the straightjacket can be relaxed. This is particularly important with patients who tend to be tense. Immediately asking them to undo the straightjacket would be like pressuring them to achieve, which would introduce other problems. For some patients, this step is an introduction to relaxation methods. It is important to guide such patients through the different regions of relaxation, from head to face to neck to shoulders to

diaphragm. Bringing the patient's attention systematically downward to the center of the self automatically reestablishes the center of gravity in the pelvis. This simultaneously reduces anxiety. Intentional relaxation encourages people to take an active stand with their symptoms by introducing the notion of a voluntary modification of the physical state.

5. *Pause at the first sign of tension person cannot undo.* As with all SCT work, the goal is to reduce tension in small, practical increments—an approach that provides an experience of consistent achievement.

6. *Frame tension as a straightjacket for feeling.* Objectifying tension as an active constriction introduces the idea that it can be undone as well as done. Normalizing symptoms and weakening restraining forces involves using language to describe defenses and symptoms in such a way that the descriptors themselves contribute to the process. Therefore, tension is labeled as a straightjacket for feelings.

7. *Frame fork-in-the-road.* SCT therapists help their patients identify the choice between explaining the experience of tension or exploring for the feeling inside the tension.

8. *Contain the person while he or she is exploring.* Being "contained" by the therapeutic process is what encourages a person to face the unknown. Acquiring the ability to contain while exploring for new experience, instead of turning toward old familiar defenses, is done more easily with the therapist's support and encouragement. The SCT therapist reminds the patient that apprehension at the threshold of the unknown is less frightening if their curiosity is actively involved.

9. *Undo defenses against anxiety, if any.* At this stage of work, it is seldom necessary to do more than guide the person through the already learned technique for undoing anxiety: (1) checking anxiety-provoking thoughts about experience against actual experience and (2) reframing fear of the unknown into curiosity and normal sensations of arousal.

10. *Contain while the person takes time to discover the experience inside the straightjacket of tension.* The cooperative work of containing—by the group, the therapist, and the person who is actively working—builds the norm that people come to their experience in their own time. This is an important step in SCT, as each person's internal rhythm is different. The adapted self (or "false self") is afraid of taking too much time. This fear makes it difficult, or impossible, to discover spontaneous experience. Legitimizing the process of learning to take one's own time is an important step in reestablishing the natural rhythm of work in a person and in a group.

By encouraging people to undo tension and focus on the feeling that is contained within it, the SCT therapist is asking them to pay attention to their sensations of arousal. This entails continuing to ask patients to check if their expectations or explanations of experience match their actual experience. In the following dialogue, the person is exploring the experience of frustration and the therapist is drawing the person's attention to the difference between anxiety, tension, and irritability:

T: What is your physical experience at the moment?

P: Well, my heart is beating fast and I'm tense.

T: Tension is different from either your feeling of irritation or your anxiety. Where are you tense?

P: My face is tight, my shoulders—and I have knots in my stomach. [If the patient had mentioned butterflies in the stomach, the therapist's response would have been to label the butterflies as anxiety and undo the anxiety.]

T: We say that your tension is a straightjacket for your feelings. How tight is the knot in your stomach? [This question begins the diagnostic questioning for benign or nonbenign psychosomatic symptoms.]

P: Pretty tight.

T: Where exactly?

P: Here! (*Puts hand on stomach.*)

T: How big is it?

P: About the size of a large fist.

T: You say it is tight?

P: Yes, it's so tight it hurts.

T: Does your stomach often get painfully tight?

P: Only now and then.

T: And then what happens? Does it get worse or go away again?

P: It usually goes away.

T: It seems as if the knot is tied so tight that it is giving you pain. Focus on the feeling that is straightjacketed inside the knot and see what happens. [A clear instruction is useful to patients and makes it more likely that they will focus and follow the instruction than the vaguer "See if you can kind of . . . " or the concealed command "Why don't you . . . ?" Notice also that the suggestion is to explore and discover.]

P: It gets tighter and hurts more.

T: Do you want to knot up your feelings painfully like this? [The therapist is suggesting that the patient has a choice.]

P: No, I don't.

T: You are at a fork-in-the-road. Which do you want to explore first—the way you knot up your feelings and hurt yourself or the feelings inside the knot? [Once again the therapist is emphasizing choice, as a means of keeping the patient in the driver's seat and bypassing the power struggle.]

P: I want to explore for the feelings.

T: Go for it! Relax through the knot and into the feeling inside. Are you aware of anything inside the knot?

The work that follows is a good illustration of why tension is framed as a straightjacket in SCT.

P: Well, there is some sensation in my abdomen.

T: A sensation in your abdomen! I see. And what is the sensation?

P: I feel warm.

T: You notice you are warm?

P: Yes.

T: And what else?

P: I feel kind of excited . . . energized.

T: You notice that there is energy? What else? What other sensations in your body?

P: A sort of fizz.

T: You say a sort of a fizz? And how is that fizz—pleasant, unpleasant, or neutral?

Almost always, the experience for patients, once they have undone the tension, is one of excitement and arousal, which involves—when they are not afraid of it or misinterpreting it—a pleasant state of alertness and readiness. That is, patients can experience the potential energy in frustration when frustration (1) does not arouse tension, anxiety, or irritability and (2) does not mobilize the defenses against anger, with which it is often confused.

DECONDITIONING PSYCHOSOMATIC SYMPTOMS

Undoing tension is not always simply a matter of focus and choice. Sometimes tension and a psychosomatic symptom are so linked that one cannot undo the tension without exacerbating the symptom. It is even more serious when the symptom is sufficiently distressing to preempt any awareness of the tension itself. In either case, the symptom has to be deconditioned before the emotional experience that is being locked up in tension can be accessed. When tension is linked to a psychosomatic symptom, the original stress that initiated tension has been rerouted into the body, with the result of the person no longer having a tense abdomen but a psychosomatic symptom—like diarrhea or worse. Deconditioning psychosomatic symptoms is different from deconditioning a headache, which can be relieved simply by undoing the straightjacket of tension. Undoing a psychosomatic symptom must be done in steps. The patient must understand that he or she defended against an emotional response to some stressor with tension. Then, when muscular tension failed as a defense, the response was rerouted into the body and became a psychosomatic symptom. The connection between the emotion and the response must be brought to the patient's attention without triggering the somatic response. This is done by the bracketing technique.

The Bracketing Technique

Deconditioning psychosomatic symptoms involves bracketing, which gets its name because it requires people to put brackets around the symptom to identify the time just before and after the symptom started.

Bracketing is an early step in a deconditioning technique. First, the therapist asks the patient to describe the symptom and his or her relationship to it. This provides a frame of reference for the defensive experience that can be contrasted to a prior nondefensive experience. Then the therapist asks the patient to remember when he or she first became aware of the symptom—whether the patient went to bed feeling like this, woke up feeling like this, felt like this at breakfast, and so on. The therapist does as much as possible to encourage in the patient an attitude of exploration and to engage the patient's curiosity in identifying the transition moment when the defensive experience began. Curiosity is the best antidote to anxiety about the uncertain or the unknown, and it is curiosity about the unknown that sooner or later enables it to be explored. Once patients become curious, they are on their way to discovering what stimulated the underlying conflict or impulse they defended against.

Bracketing Benign Psychosomatic Symptoms

When symptoms are benign, like muscle cramps, simple headaches, or fatigue, the first step for the SCT therapist is to help patients recognize that they are not suffering from an illness but from a defense that has involved the physical self. Patients are taught that these conversion symptoms mean that they have converted stress into a physical experience by discharging energy into the body instead of directing it to manage whatever it was that was stressful.

Helping patients understand this notion is a great deal easier in group therapy, where members can witness other members experiencing their own somatic defenses and undoing them. New members are often surprised at how easily their headache or stomachache disappears when the emotion it was substituting for appears. A version of the following dialogue occurs often in SCT groups with new members:

P: I have a headache.

T: Did you have it at the beginning of group? [The therapist starts the process of bracketing.]

P: No, it started just a little while ago.

T: Do you remember what was happening at the time?

P: I think you had asked me if I would see whether I would feel any different if I didn't sit with my arms folded and my legs crossed.

T: What was your reaction to that?

P: Fine. I tried it, but it didn't work. And I noticed I had a headache.

T: How did you feel about me suggesting that you try something that didn't work?

P: I thought it wasn't working because I wasn't doing it properly.

T: That's the way you related to yourself. How did you feel toward *me* for suggesting something that wasn't working? [Here is another example of staying goal focused, which is to identify the fork-in-the-road between symptom and defense. The patient's substitution of a thought for a feeling is ignored at this point.]

P: I wasn't annoyed. These things take time.

T: Yes, they do take time. However, right here it's possible that you missed a fork-in-the-road. What you know is that I suggested something, you tried it, it didn't work, you blamed yourself, and you exonerated me—all this at about the same time you got a headache. Is it possible you took the fork-in-the-road into a headache and away from your reaction to me? You notice we still don't know what it was!

P: I remember—it's amazing! I *did* feel annoyed. I thought you were going too fast with me. It's amazing! I don't believe it. My headache's gone!

In this example the situation that stimulated the defensive headache was in the patient's recent memory and was therefore easy to access. What is important about the bracketing technique is the requirement to backtrack to the time just before the symptom started. This reinforces the concept of a fork-in-the-road, the junction between the onset of the symptom and the alternative, the feeling that is ignored in favor of symptom formation. Notice that this approach specifically avoids any attention to the symptom other than describing it (any preoccupation with the symptom itself almost always exacerbates it).

Obviously it is not always as easy for patients to identify the event triggering a psychosomatic symptom as in the example above. What if the patient in our example had not been able to recall the moment of anger? There is a good chance that he might have been able to accept that there *is* an alternative path from the fork-in-the-road even without being yet aware of what the alternative is. Even without an awareness of a specific alternative path, the very idea of its existence makes a significant difference to new patients and prevents them from taking an automatic plunge into the symptom. This is particularly true for potentially more serious symptoms, like a cramping colon. Even if the alternate path is not discovered, the fork-in-the-road model introduces patients to the concept of choice, to the idea that they can choose to contain and explore the experience rather than acting it out somatically. When patients can contain the stress, they are also able to make the connection between the missing experience (the trigger) and the substitute defensive symptom. Sitting at the fork-in-the-road with a choice, that is, containing the experience until both paths are explored, is the technique for rechanneling psychosomatic symptoms from abnormal to normal channels.

Bracketing Nonbenign Psychosomatic Symptoms

What if a patient's psychosomatic symptom is not benign? The following dialogue, which takes place during individual therapy, demonstrates the difference in response when the patient's symptom is not benign:

T: How tight is the knot in your stomach?

P: It's so tight it hurts.

T: Does your stomach often get painfully tight?

P: Yes, it can get tighter and hurt even more.

T: Do you want to knot up your feelings painfully like this?

P: No, I don't.

T: Are you aware of anything inside the knot?

P: Yes, it's beginning to cramp again.

T: Beginning to cramp again. Has it been cramping before?

P: I always get cramps when I'm anxious.

This remark is a cue for the therapist to ask for a history of the patient's symptom. If the patient reports a connection between anxiety and, say, an upset stomach that sometimes moves on to cramps and diarrhea, it is important to find out whether this is the first step in a more serious disorder that can get triggered in the process of defense modification. If it is not, then defense modification can be continued, with the expectation that the cramps will be modified.

For the purpose of illustration, let us say that this patient has diverticulitis, which flairs up when he is stressed and for which he takes medication. The issue here is not simply deconditioning; what is also required is a process that decreases the patient's sensitivity to what triggers the symptom. In this sense, the therapeutic process requires helping the patient identify early warning signals, thus affording the patient time to respond to stress at lower levels before the symptom is activated. Benign somatic symptoms clear up easily in a group that is used to dealing with such symptoms during defense modification. Deconditioning, and desensitization (to be discussed shortly) of nonbenign symptoms can be done in a group, but the first steps are typically easier in individual therapy, where every small nuance of response can be monitored.

T: We are going to go very slowly. It won't help us for you to get an increase in pain in your stomach. So, we'll continue to work, and your job is to let us both know as soon as you notice a twinge. (*The patient puts his hand to his side and rubs it.*) Is it starting now?

P: Only very mildly.

T: That's what we want. We want a mild early warning signal to give us a chance to see what it was that your stomach reacted to.

P: (*With hand still on his side*) It hasn't happened yet.

T: Do you know what cued you to put your hand to your side?

P: A slight tension.

T: Do you remember what we were doing when you first noticed the tension?

Constant monitoring of the earliest signs of the symptom will help make a connection between any triggering event in the therapy session

and a somatic reaction in the patient. This event can be something as
seemingly neutral as a car alarm in the street or the ringing of a tele-
phone. Or it can be something related to the therapy itself, such as the
pace of the therapy (too fast or too slow). It can be quite subtle, like the
therapist's breaking eye contact with the patient for a moment or not
appearing to respond in the way the patient would like; it may be quite
specific, like the patient's feeling of annoyance at a particular therapeutic intervention or his or her reluctance to do the work of modifying a
defense. Whatever the triggers, the important thing is for the patient to
use the slightest pain as a signal to identify it, and to then immediately
look for the experience that the symptom distracted him or her from.
The work with a patient who has a nonbenign psychosomatic symptom is
exactly the same bracketing technique that succeeded for the patient
with the headache; what is different is the therapist's and patient's careful monitoring of the involved body part and the readiness to back up
and investigate all aspects of the therapeutic situation at the slightest signal that the somatic symptom is occurring.

Once stress has involved organs of the body, all defensive modifications are applied slowly and cautiously. In these cases, the conversion
symptoms have converted the physical self. The first goal is to ameliorate
symptoms by reducing the frequency or intensity of the attacks experienced by the patient. Some symptoms, like migraines, may never completely disappear, but they can become significantly less frequent and
less severe.

TENSION AND ORGANIC ILLNESS

Some somatic symptoms indicate a progressive disease process. The
goal of the therapeutic work for patients with organic illness is to
reduce the defenses against the symptoms so that patients have more
energy to manage their illness. This is true of illnesses like emphysema
or multiple sclerosis (MS). Tension and depressive responses to the illness itself reduce the person's ability to manage the illness. I am thinking of one patient in particular: an agile, active, artistic, and energetic
person whose MS has progressed over the years to the point where a
wheelchair is increasingly becoming a part of her life. We work with all
her defenses. We regularly undo anxiety and tension, work on depression and blame, differentiate between depression and despair, grieve
the loss of her physical self, and struggle to accept reality as it is and to
sit at the edge of the unknown. She says, as I draw her attention over
and over again to the fork-in-the-road between reality and her defenses
against it:

"Oh, I know. I'm ricocheting off the wall of reality again. You'll say I've got to go through the turbulence. I do know that reality is very hard. It hurts a lot, it makes me sad and angry, and I hate my help-lessness. And I do know that when I stay this side of reality I'm in 'victim' and feeling sorry for myself and furious at everyone else. And when I cross into reality, it's awful. There's frustration and pain, and I'm sad. But I also have joy and delight and happiness, I love my family and friends, I have energy, and I'm creative. You say you can't have one without the other. I don't want to believe that but it seems to be true."

My work with this patient has taught me many things. Most impor-tant, for this chapter, is the lesson that it is not kind to soften defense modification in the face of debilitating illness. People who struggle with organic illness need their full, undefended self if they are to make the best they can of what they have available to them. When I work with this woman, I always have immediate feedback as to whether we have had a successful session. When we have worked well, she walks out of the ses-sion with a little more energy and balance than when she walked in.

DESENSITIZATION

A better word for the process of desensitization is perhaps *sensitization!* The process entails a systematic increase in vectoring patients' energy and attention into their experience and encouraging them to have it and contain it.

Sample Therapy Session (Restructuring Sexuality)

The most frequent barrier experience in difficulties with sexuality is the tendency to move to a world of negative predictions and anxiety at some point during the sexual experience, and sometimes at the first signal of sexual arousal. This permits the person to have, at best, a mixed experi-ence of pleasure and anxiety; at worst, it transforms the sexual experi-ence into one of frustration, inhibition, humiliation, shame, and perhaps impotence.

The defensive world of sexual dysfunction seems to require an auto-matic shift into the role of identified patient or bully, depending on whom the person blames for his or her difficulty. The dialogue below illustrates successful desensitization in undoing a psychosomatic symp-tom in sexual dysfunction.

The restructuring process is similar to all other restructuring where an internal boundary has become closed to information and a deconditioning and reconditioning process is needed. First, the fork-in-the-road between sexual responsiveness and the imaginary reality must be identified. Then the conflict has to be contained. Once it is, the patient can take the path to sexual responsiveness.

T: You say that when you know that you and Sara are likely to make love, you immediately imagine that the same old thing is going to happen all over again and get anxious?

P: Yes.

T: That, as you know, is a negative prediction, which takes you away from the present experience. Do you remember how you felt with Sara when you were turned on? [The therapist begins the restructuring process.]

P: Yes.

T: Will you recall a specific experience and describe it please?

P: (*Pause*) Well, last week when I came back from a business trip, she met me at the airport and we hugged. And it felt wonderful. [This is a low-threat memory and therefore an ideal context in which to start sensitizing the patient to his spontaneous feelings.]

T: What was wonderful in your experience?

P: Well, I felt welcomed and wanted and happy.

T: And what were the sensations in your body that accompanied those good feelings? [The therapist encourages the patient to describe the physical sensations he was experiencing as well as the exact way the couple were standing, particularly which parts of their bodies were touching and which were not. The therapist then repeats the patient's description in a natural tone of voice.]

T: So you had your arms around each other, and you could feel her breasts against your chest, your thighs against her thighs, and her buttocks under your hands. The contact felt warm and had a sensation of a spreading warmth inside you. It sounds very nice.

P: Yes, it was lovely.

T: Are you recalling the sensations now?

P: (*Colors.*) Yes! [The color of the patient's complexion is an important signal that his recall and his physiology are in harmony. The barrier is not yet interfering with the natural internal communication between the mind and body.]

T: So you are feeling good now!

P: (*Smiles.*) Yes!

T: You feel warm in your chest?

P: Yes.

T: Where? (*Patient indicates with his hand an area across his chest and down to his diaphragm.*) And you can feel the warmth in your thighs?

P: Yes, here. (*Rubs his upper thighs.*)

T: So, you have a warmth in your chest that reaches to here and in your thighs reaching to here. (*Gestures, using his own body.*)

P: Yes.

T: What about this part? (*Again gestures with his hand on his own body, showing how the genital area has been missed.*)

P: I don't feel anything.

T: Back up to the warmth you were feeling. You could feel her breasts against your chest, your thighs against her thighs, and her buttocks under you hands. The contact felt warm, and you had a sensation of a spreading warmth inside you. Can you still feel it?

P: I'm getting it back again.

T: Do you have any tension?

P: No, I'm pretty relaxed.

T: Can you remember anything else about the pleasure you had greeting Sara?

P: Yes, her hair smelled wonderful . . . and it was soft against my face.

T: Pleasure?

P: (*Smiles.*) Yes.

T: Make plenty of room for it. Fill up with it.

P: I am.

T: Is your diaphragm relaxed also?

P: Well, that's a little tight.

The diaphragm is often a source of unnoticed tension. When the tension in the diaphragm is relaxed, there is an increased flow of energy and warmth. When anxious thoughts intrude, these effects are undone and the patient continues to focus on the sensations of physical pleasure.

As always in SCT, but particularly in this process, it is important for the therapist to maintain the structure so that the patient is free to explore his experience in it. This helps the therapist to stay ready to be surprised.

In this case, as the sensation of warmth gradually began to suffuse the lower part of his body, the patient became anxious, sensations were starting in his anus although he had expected them to be in his penis. It is important for the therapist to normalize, and not pathologize, physical sensations. For example, references to homosexuality at this point would be unlikely to increase the patient's ability to continue to explore his unfolding experience. If the patient himself associates his sensations with homosexuality; there is once again the fork-in-the-road technique. In the present case, the patient reported thoughts of homosexuality.

T: So the thought of homosexuality comes into your mind. Does that word increase or decrease the sensations of pleasure that you are having in your anus?

P: I stopped noticing them when I got anxious.

T: Is that what you want?

P: Not really.

It is not unusual to find that erotic feelings are accompanied by shame. Shame is typically accompanied by a sinking feeling, which some people call dread. By following the sinking feeling the person discovers the source of shame and dread. This technique is used frequently in the more advanced stages of SCT therapy. In this case, it is important for the patient to have a sense that his sexuality is imprisoned by a barrier of shame. This is one of the moments in therapy when it is useful for the therapist to give the patient a preview of the work he will be able to do when he is ready.

T: You are ashamed, you say, of your feeling. If you follow that shame feeling, where does it take you?

P: I can't. It's as if the shame I feel is like a thick and awful feeling that blots out everything.

T: Yes, that does sound like shame. See if you are free to back away from it now, and go back to the pleasure you were having in your anus before it got drowned out by shame. As we work, we will gradually find a way through that thick and awful feeling of shame to whatever part of you is being shamed. It is probable that you will find that there is a free and spontaneous sexual part of yourself behind the shame barrier, which you can have again when you are ready to find it. You say you are afraid you will always be impotent. You remember having erections in your teens, so you know that you were certainly not born impotent. The good thing about our physical selves is that given half a chance, we regain our natural functions when we no longer inhibit them. What happened to the pleasure that you were experiencing in your genitals when you thought about being impotent? Did it increase, decrease, or stay the same?

The therapeutic work continued with this patient, enabling him to regain the experience of sexual pleasure. He was able to follow the spread of sensation from his anus to his scrotum and then to a tingling in his penis, which he experienced with pleasure.

Modifying defenses as a person gradually becomes sensitized to his or her body is a journey with many forks-in-the-road. Both deep and superficial fears emerge. In SCT these are acknowledged, normalized, and framed as a fork-in-the-road with branches that lead toward or away from the discovery of the sensations of the self. The taboos against sexual experience often have their source in early experience, when learning tends to be "all or nothing." Therefore, in gradually encouraging the patient to regain the experience of pleasure, a range of defenses must be undone.

C h a p t e r   8

Masochistic Defenses

FRUSTRATION AND AGGRESSION

Throughout Module 1 defense modification, the focus is on the patient being able to discover that frustration, when defended against, creates anxiety, tension, and irritability. Once anxiety defenses and defensive tension have been rerouted and the anxiety and somatic symptoms have been deconditioned, the last of the defenses in Module 1—the masochistic and sadistic defenses—are addressed.

As anxiety decreases in the course of therapy, tension increases; as tension decreases, awareness of frustration increases—and so does the impulse to retaliate against whatever is frustrating. For some people, the masochistic depressive defenses are now aroused that constrict the retaliatory impulse. Others discharge this impulse in hostile acting out. Undoing the defenses against the retaliatory impulse is the first major step toward regaining the energy of primary aggression, which is essential to survival.

Animals "educate" their primary aggression by acting it out in play, but no human being has grown up unpunished for the same attempt to educate aggressive impulses. Just as the baby kicks randomly to express the mixed distresses of frustrated impulses, the small child kicks a parent or a door, the older child mentally kicks a human object, and adults scapegoat others, the world, or themselves. "Getting even" is as old as the human race. The impulse, when frustration hurts, is to hurt back. When there is a considerable store of unassuaged frustration and emotional pain, people tend to have conscious or unconscious fantasies of revenge.

In SCT, the connection between frustration and aggression is not seen as a direct connection. Rather, it is the defensive constriction in frustration that makes frustration uncomfortable. It is the discomfort, added to the frustrating delay in gratifying an impulse, that arouses aggression. When SCT members learn to make space for the experience of frustration they discover an experience of arousal energy that is not unpleasant. Being open to the experience of the energy in frustration enables them to center themselves in the frustrating situation, and by being centered, they are able to see the frustrating situation in its systems-centered as well as its self-centered context.

Until the actual experience of aggression is explored, and its many manifestations are recognized, it is typically misinterpreted as danger-ous. When the retaliatory impulse is misinterpreted, not only that impulse but all forms of aggression become feared. The aim of this chap-ter and the next is to differentiate between the various manifestations of aggression: irritability, anger, outrage, hostility, and impulses to retali-ate. These manifestations range from spiteful or sadistic fantasies to the acting out of murderous rage.

In SCT, depression and tantrums are treated as two different ways of defending against the retaliatory impulse. Depression turns the retalia-tory impulse in on the self. Tantrums turn it out. SCT work promotes the alternative of containing, exploring, and experiencing the retaliatory impulse in order to discover the information it contains for the manage-ment of the situation that is arousing it. As in all SCT work, exploration involves a sequence of steps. The depressive boomerang, if it is present, is the first to be addressed. Next, the experience of having a retaliatory impulse is explored. Once the impulse is acknowledged, the defenses against it are recognized as defenses rather than as helpless responses. Finally, there is the work of making the defenses ego-alien by recogniz-ing their costs.

In the initial phase of group, frustrated members are easily irritated, and experience their own irritability as threatening. Their defensive responses to threat only increase the problem: Members either further defend themselves by producing cognitive distortions about what being irritated means, put themselves into a straightjacket of tension, or dis-charge their irritation in hostile thoughts or actions toward themselves, others, the leader, or the group. At this stage of group development (the transitional subphase between the flight and fight subphases of Phase One; see Table 4.3) the probability is that members will defend against acting out their hostility against others by turning it back on themselves and becoming depressed.

FRUSTRATION, IRRITABILITY, AND THE RETALIATORY IMPULSE

In preparation for the work of modifying depression, some preliminary discriminations must first be made between frustration and irritability and between irritability and hostility. When the experience of frustration is not well tolerated, it is often reacted to with impatience and irritability. The first step in preparing to modify a patient's depression is therefore to help him or her discriminate between the experience of frustration and the experience of impatience or irritability. Making this discrimination paves the way for the next step, which is to differentiate between the experience of irritability itself and the impulse to retaliate against what is frustrating. It is only when the retaliatory impulse is recognized as separate and discrete from frustration and whatever stimulus has aroused it that the work of undoing depression can proceed.

The less differentiated feelings are, the more they are likely to flood the system and be experienced as overwhelming, chaotic, and dangerous. In SCT, all undifferentiated experience signals the need for discriminatory work. Flooding is immediately addressed by separating facts from the feeling; then work proceeds on differentiating the feeling into its components. SCT patients learn (1) to differentiate between being irritable and being enraged, which dispenses with the belief that being irritable is the same as being enraged, and (2) to recognize how frustration, irritability, the retaliatory impulse, and defensive rage differ.

DEFENDED VERSUS UNDEFENDED EXPERIENCES OF FRUSTRATION

Confusing frustration and irritability has serious consequences. When frustration is thought to be intrinsically explosive, it is the explosion, not the frustration, that people think they must defend against. All stimuli arouse sensations, and in the process of becoming afraid of the stimulus people also become afraid of the arousal of sensations. Thus, the *experience* of frustration, with or without irritability, becomes misinterpreted as an omen or signal that the system is about to go out of control. Often, the association between arousal and loss of control becomes so frightening that people learn not only to defend against the specific experience of frustration but to anesthetize themselves to all other feeling experiences as well. This creates a split between thinking and feeling, which also separates comprehensive knowledge from apprehensive knowledge. Common sense is then no longer available to counteract cognitive misinterpretations of reality. The goal of SCT is to make the boundary between comprehension and apprehension (intuition) appropriately permeable so that the patient has access to both cognitive and emotional experience. The work of SCT continually requires discrimination and exploration of differences and similarities in experiences until these are, through the technique of containment, understood and integrated. Learning to tolerate frustration requires discriminating between the following:

1. The sensation of energy in frustration and the experience of defensively constricting or discharging it
2. The irritability people often feel when frustrated
3. The impulse to retaliate against the frustrating person, object, or thing
4. Depression and acting out in hostility, sadism, or rage, which are the two major defenses against the retaliatory impulse

In the work of SCT, the first three discriminations are fundamental preparation for the work of undoing the depressive defense. In turn, learning how to undo the depressive defense is essential before one can explore the sadistic and masochistic aspects of the retaliatory impulse. Without these basic discriminations it is difficult for the patient to "contain" the complex responses to frustration. When irritability is not contained, it is turned out or in, that is, discharged in rage and histrionics or constricted in depression. Rage and histrionics draw heavily on the constructed reality of righteous indignation, entitlement, and externalized complaints and blame. Depression draws heavily on tension, negative predictions, obsessions, worrying, and alternately externalizing and internalizing complaints and blame. Irritability that is turned in leads to the role of victim and identified patient. Irritability that is turned out leads to the role of scapegoat and bully. Thus, it is a defense against the retaliatory impulse that is behind irritability routed into both rage and depression (and, as we will see in Chapter 10, into role-locks as well).

DISCOVERING REALITY

Irritability is often mistaken for rage; defended against as if it were rage; and consequently reacted to with all the fears that are linked to rage that is uncontained, explosive, and out of control. Exploring frustration leads to recognizing not only the differences between the experiences of frustration and irritability but also the difference between these experiences and the defenses against them. This discrimination enables the irritability that often accompanies frustration, and the rage that is aroused by whatever conflict is frustrating, to be recognized as two separate and distinct experiences. Frustration is an experience of *potential energy*. Irritability is the experience of the *pressure to discharge* the energy.

   The first step in working with irritability is to teach the patient what it is not. One of the more striking differences between SCT and other psychodynamic therapies is the relative absence of interpretation in SCT; the emphasis in SCT is on what and how, not on the traditional therapeutic "why" questions, which tend to elicit explanations or interpretations. This difference in orientation means that a different kind of material is dealt with in therapy. Nowhere is this difference more striking than in the way SCT approaches irritability, frustration, and aggression. A traditional "Why are you angry?" will predictably be followed by a patient's complaint about a parent, a sibling, a friend, a spouse, a boss, and so on. In contrast, the SCT therapist helps the patient discriminate between frustration, irritability, and anxiety by using "how" and "what" questions.

EXPRESSION VERSUS EXPERIENCE OF FEELING

As was emphasized in the discussion of cognitive defenses (Chapter 6), the way people *think* they feel often makes it difficult or impossible for them to experience their *actual* feelings. For patients who have done previous work on defense modification, who are already familiar with simple methods for undoing negative predictions and testing assumptions, moving cognitive distortions out of the way of the experience of frustration is relatively easy.

A major cognitive distortion is the conviction that expressing a feeling is the same as having the feeling. For example, some patients believe that a diatribe or a tantrum is the experience of primary rage, rather than simply an *expression* of defensive rage. This confusion is not confined to patients. There are forms of therapy that encourage the expression of aggressive discharge and that induce patients to beat a pillow, throw tin cans against a wall, or duel with foam rubber bats. The thinking behind such techniques is the belief that working with the expression of defensive rage changes patients' relationship to their experience of it. In the short run, the patient certainly has a catharsis and temporarily feels better. Rarely, however, is there a permanent change. The same is true when patients are encouraged to rant about events that have hurt and angered them. The problem with both these methods is not that they generate good feelings, which they do, but that they are addictive. The more frequent the discharge, the greater the pleasure and the greater the impulse to find opportunities to discharge. There is thus a risk that there will be an increase, through reinforcement, of both the aggressive feelings that are generated by outrage and the impulses to act out.

SCT makes a clear differentiation, as illustrated in the following dialogue, between the expression of feelings and the experience of it. It is in this area that Davanloo's research has made another significant contribution:

T: I notice that you are looking irritated, you are restless, and sometimes you tap the arm of your chair and sometimes you tap your foot. How do you experience yourself?

P: I'm irritated.

T: Yes, I see that. However, that restlessness is an expression of your irritation, not the irritation itself. Do you know how you experience your irritation?

P: What do you mean?

T: I mean in yourself, in your body. What is the experience you are having inside that you are expressing by tapping your finger or your foot?

When patients recognize that the way they are expressing their irritability is not the same as experiencing irritation, the way is paved for exploring the difference between frustration, irritation, and rage. The first step is to explore the difference between frustration and irritability and the various ways of defending against these experiences. The patient's characteristic defenses will emerge, including those used in role relationships, usually the one-down defenses but sometimes the one-up defenses. Role relationship defenses will be discussed later in terms of role-locks, which are the subject of Chapter 10. Frequently, when asked for their experience of a feeling, patients do not recognize their feeling. This is particularly true with the feelings that are generated by aggression. Experiencing a feeling requires paying attention to the reality of the immediate physical experience of its emotional component, which is often quite different from the experience people think they are having or expect to be having or are afraid they will have if they allow themselves the full experience. What is more, most people do not know the difference between the experiences of frustration, irritability, and rage. Perhaps because there is aggressive energy in all of these experiences, people often mistake their irritability and frustration for rage—and often fear them as if they were murderous rage. For this reason, it is important for the SCT therapist to help the patient to identify what the feeling is *not* before identifying what it *is* when working with any of the aggressive experiences.

Parenthetically, careful attention to the technique of "reprise" (see Chapter 6) is required with patients whose relationship to themselves is more tenuous and who are not able to remember much about their experience or their interactions in a therapy session. The therapist or the group must serve as their memory and provide the context for their changes. Repeatedly, the whole sequence of behaviors, from defenses against anxiety to the experience of irritability, must be noticed and sequenced over and over again until the patient recognizes it and can remember it.

The Seven Discrimination Steps

In the following pages, the SCT technique for recognizing the connection between frustration and irritability and for undoing defenses against the experiencing of them is presented in the form of a dialogue between therapist and patient. Briefly, the technique involves the following seven steps, in which the therapist helps the patient to

1. Recognize irritability
2. Separate the experience of irritability from explanations of why one is irritated
3. Separate the experience of irritability from negative predictions about where it will lead
4. Separate the experience of irritability from tensions that attempt to straightjacket the experience
5. Differentiate between the defenses against irritability and the energy of frustration
6. Experience the fullness of the energy and the feeling of potency it provides
7. Contain the energy and explore the fork-in-the-road between (a) the impulses aroused by frustrating conflicts and (b) defenses such as psychosomatic symptoms or depression

The discriminations in these steps, which are predominantly relevant to preparing for the undoing of depression, are required to differentiate between irritability, hostility, sadism, and primary rage, which are addressed in the next chapter. Note that the intrapersonal aspect of depression and rage involving internalizing and externalizing defenses is still squarely within Module 1 of SCT defense modification but that as the interpersonal components of defiance and compliance emerge, the focus shifts toward the role-lock defenses of Module 2, a subject discussed in depth in Chapter 10.

Step One: Recognize Irritability

Consider the following exchange between therapist and patient:

T: You recognize that you are frustrated; are you also feeling impatient and irritated?

P: Yes.

If such an exchange occurs, the therapist must make sure that the patient's experience is irritation and not anxiety or tension or rage:

T: How do you know you are irritable?

P: Well, my heart is beating fast and I'm tense.

T: What else are you aware of?

P: Well, I have butterflies in my stomach.

T: Butterflies in your stomach are probably not irritability. They sound more like a symptom of your anxiety again. What else are you aware of?

P: My mouth's dry, my heart's beating fast.

T: What you are describing seems to be your anxiety, not the feelings that go with either irritability or anger. Are you aware that you are anxious as well as irritable?

P: Well, I suppose so. Yes, I'm anxious about being irritable.

T: Let's separate out the sensations that you have that belong to your anxiety and the sensations that belong to your irritability or anger so that you can learn to tell the difference.

If, on the other hand, the patient denies feeling impatient or irritated, the therapist then starts the process of drawing the person's attention to the signals that he or she is sending without realizing it:

T: The reason that I ask is I notice that you are looking irritated, you are restless, and sometimes you tap the arm of your chair, and sometimes you tap your foot.

P: Frustration makes me restless.

Step Two: Separate Irritability from Expressions of It

Once patients acknowledge feeling irritated, SCT therapists help them separate the experience of irritability from expressions of it:

T: When you say you are restless because you are frustrated, that certainly seems to explain it. However, that does not tell us how you are experiencing your restlessness and irritation.

P: Just like you say—I'm tapping—

T: Tapping is an expression of your irritation, not your irritation. Do you know how you experience your irritation? Physically, I mean, in your body?

P: I'm just frustrated. I'm not irritated or angry or anything like that. [The therapist is attempting to help the patient discriminate between the experience of irritation and the way that irritation is expressed behaviorally.]

Step Three: Separate Irritability from Negative Predictions

The therapist then helps the patient separate the experience of irritation from any negative predictions of where the irritation will lead.

T: You say you are not angry. I would agree with you; you appear to me to be simply frustrated and irritable. However, you don't seem to be comfortable. Are you thinking that it will be bad in some way if you are irritable? And does that thought make you anxious?

P: Well, getting irritable never did me any good. Certainly, I got yelled at if I talked out of turn as a kid.

T: Yes of course, it is impossible for any of us to grow up without being difficult for adults to tolerate at times, and certainly noisy or fidgety and irritable children can make adults very annoyed.

P: Yeah, and I notice I'm uptight and tense as I think about it.

Step Four: Separate Irritability from Tension

After negative predictions have been exposed and tested against reality, the therapist helps the patient separate the experience of irritation from the tensions that straightjacket that experience:

> "Tense as well as irritable! Two separate experiences now! And yes, I can see it. You look quite stiff, and although your fingers were drumming, your arms and shoulders look tight. Well, we know that tension is a straightjacket for your feelings. Can you undo that straightjacket and find out what you are feeling inside it this time?"

The irritability that follows frustration is frequently mistaken for rage and defended against as if it were rage. When these defenses are undone, irritability is replaced by an experience of arousal energy. It is at the point after patients have filled up with arousal energy and are no longer irritable that there is the potential for them to take the next step and recognize that they are angry with the therapist, who is orchestrating the frustrating situation. This work is parallel to bringing feelings into the relationship in the distraction exercise (see Chapter 3) and reinforces the ideas that the people's feelings belong to them and that it is possible to bring a feeling into a relationship without having the other person take it personally. To help the patient recognize his or her feelings at this point, the therapist might say:

"I notice that not only are you tapping your foot but that you look as if you are irritated with me. I would not be surprised if you were. I would find it irritating if someone kept interrupting my usual ways of making a relationship and required me to pay attention to my own experience instead. How do your experience your irritation with me?"

If the earlier work holds, the person will access the experience inside the tension. If there is a regression, the work of undoing the tension is repeated.

In the early phases of group therapy, the group reality is frustrating and responses to the frustration are aroused and undone at many levels before the differences in experience and response have been explored and differentiated in the group work. Members give lip service to the idea that the thought or wish is not the deed—but without any real conviction at the primary level of experience. The less differentiated the experience, the greater the fear that it will overwhelm one's ability to contain it. The more primitive the fears, the stronger and more primitive the defenses against the fears. This is where the discrimination between the experience of frustration or irritability and its expression is fundamentally important. When there is an explosive feeling inside the straightjacket of tension in the abdomen, the person is too afraid to accept an invitation to have the experience because it is interpreted as an invitation to mayhem. Here the partially conscious fantasies of disaster, rejection, and trauma should be made fully conscious within the security of one-on-one or subgroup work. This is another point where the therapist is wise to choose the member (or members) with the greatest potential for success to do the initial work for the group.

"(*Speaking to an individual*) Look how tense you are: You are putting a straightjacket around yourself and your feelings. You say you are afraid to experience your rage because you will have a tantrum, turn the chairs over, and put your fist through the wall! You are mistaking having a tantrum for being *in* a rage. A tantrum is not your rage! Turning over chairs is not your rage! Putting a fist through the wall is not your rage! All of these things are how you would *express* your rage if you were to act on it. Do you believe that you will act on it, in here, in the group? Come, let's find the subgroup to explore the impulses to act, and let's learn the difference between the impulse to act and actually acting. (*Speaking to the group*) Where do you feel the rage in your body?"

Abusive words, hostile behavior, and other discharges of the energy in frustration are frequently confused with rage. When they are mixed with hostility and sadism and directed toward a target, they have the potential for violence. However, the group must learn that tantrums, abusive words or gestures, or violent acts are all *expressions* of feeling, *not* the feeling itself. Again, the technique of the fork-in-the-road introduces the choice of exploring the experiences of frustration or irritability instead of acting them out. The patient has the opportunity to discover that acting out, particularly violent acting out, is *not* the same experience as arousal. The experience of acting out has a carefree pleasure to it. If guilt follows, it arises not from the experience of acting out itself but from fears of its consequences. It externalizes the conflicted experience into behavior that engages the environment instead of the self. Undefended arousal or aggressive energy is quite different: It is an unconflicted experience of power, potency, and containment. It is the context, not the impulse, that determines whether or how to act on the primary aggressive drive.

Discriminating between irritability and tension can frequently be done in conjunction with work that discriminates between irritability and feeling. However, more than any other primary affect, the energy of irritability is most often defended against somatically. Psychosomatic symptoms are a stalemate between the impulse to discharge and the impulse to bind. This work must be done slowly, carefully, and thoroughly. It often entails crossing a time boundary into the past, with a resurrection of memories of tantrums and depressions; these memories are accompanied by fears that there will be a repetition if the here-and-now impulse is experienced.

Step Five: Differentiate Defenses from Energy

The goal of Step Five of this work is to separate the experience of the natural energy of frustration, an adrenergic fizz of readiness, from the defenses that constrict or discharge the energy. It is not appropriate to go deeply into the experience of anger at this time. The exploration of all forms of aggression, hostility, and rage are best worked on in a containing relationship (usually with the therapist). Therefore, the work with irritability and sadism, primarily an intrapersonal experience, precedes the exploration of the hatred, anger, and murderous rage that is essentially an interpersonal experience.

Typically, a person first notices heat, and then some sort of internal movement, perhaps described as a tingling or a feeling of energy. The therapist may respond to the patient's descriptions as follows:

> "You notice that you have a tingling in your arms and that the tightness in your chest is loosening and you are experiencing some heat? And that feeling of energy—is it pleasant? Unpleasant? Neutral?"

Typically, the person will first say the feeling is unpleasant or neutral. If so, the therapist will ask the person to attend to the feeling more carefully. To the great surprise of many people, the actual experience of frustrated energy is a pleasant fizz of arousal. What is more, when people become able to let themselves have their full energy, they discover that they feel bigger and more powerful, with more space inside themselves to be themselves. Frequently, they are amazed or amused that this is the experience they had expected to be dangerous and terrible.

Step Six: Experience the Fullness of the Energy

The following exchange is typical of Step Six, when the patient begins to experience the fullness of the energy and the feeling of potency it provides:

T: You look surprised when you say that the experience is pleasant. Were you expecting it to be unpleasant? Well then, you have a pleasant surprise at the actual experience and another example of how there is a difference between what you think you will experience—your negative predictions—and your actual experience. How would you describe what you are experiencing?

P: Well, I experience a feeling of warmth . . . a tingling . . . sort of an excitement. I feel alert. [The *experience* of irritable energy is almost always a sensation of warmth deep in the abdomen that gradually suffuses the body; it is accompanied by an increasing experience of arousal and potential energy.]

T: Let yourself fill up fully with your feeling. Make room for yourself. [Almost always, there is not enough "space" to have the full experience at the beginning. It is as if people have learned to constrict themselves to avoid their expansive feelings and they now have to learn to open up again to their full size. This is true not only of irritability but of all the primary feelings: joy, happiness, love, sexuality, grief, pain, rage, curiosity, and arousal.]

P: Well, I find that I am tight here. (*Points to waist.*)

T: Is your belt tight?

P: No, it's not my belt. It's as if there is not quite enough room inside.

T: It sounds as if your diaphragm might be tense. Breathe deeply into yourself and make room.

P: (*Laughs.*) Well, actually that *is* better. I am feeling very full. I feel heat, and it's spreading through my body. I feel tingling in my arms and hands. I feel very big. I seem to have grown in size.

T: How is that experience for you?

P: I feel powerful and strong and clearheaded. I feel great.

T: You look centered: solid in your chair and solid in your body. Is that how you feel?

P: Yes.

T: Well, now that you are in your centered self, go and live there and see what you know about yourself as irritable.

P: It's all right. Of course, I get irritable when you interrupt me and stop me from being the way I usually am, but that's all right, too, because I am learning things I do want to learn even though the way I'm learning them is hard.

T: So when you are centered in yourself, you understand—you have your common sense again. And your irritation, which upset you earlier, has turned into a pleasant sensation of warmth and energy and arousal and excitement—even a feeling of potency and power!

It cannot be overemphasized how important it is to take the step of introducing the arousal and readiness component of frustration. For as long as frustration is experienced as urgency and stress that must be defended against, the energy in frustration will be in danger of either exploding into outrages, constricted in tension and psychosomatic symptoms, or imploding into depression.

The Boomerang Defense against the Retaliatory Impulse

We all have the impulse to blame people, events, or the world when frustration exceeds tolerance. It is then that defenses against impulses to retaliate are brought into play; these in turn require further defenses to manage the resulting symptoms. There is much potential energy in the impulse to retaliate. When it is difficult for us to contain energy, we do one of two things: discharge it or constrict it. Discharges and constrictions manage energy in opposite ways. Defensive discharges of energy fuel diatribes, righteous indignation, hostile confrontations, sadism, and murderous rage. Defensive constrictions fuel depression.

The first stage of depression involves the boomerang defense, which turns the retaliatory impulse toward the self. Then comes the constriction, like a psychomotor straightjacket.

The word *boomerang* is used as a label to describe the experience of things coming at the self without knowing that they are one's own feelings on the rebound. The boomerang defense defends against a fleetingly experienced and then denied or ignored attack impulse toward some frustrating person, thing, or event in the outside world. The impulse then rebounds back to the self, like a psychological boomerang, causing the familiar mixture of self-deprecation, blame, and anguish that accompanies depression—as well as tension, psychosomatic symptoms, psychomotor retardation, cognitive disruptions, and irritability. The first sign of the boomerang defense is the experience of a barrier alert, without any sense of what triggered it. Until people know that depression is a defense, they cannot undo it and they cannot cross the reality boundary into the here-and-now. Thus, there is little energy available to deal with the frustration of real-world conflicts. Once depression has set in, both the mind and body are heavy and sluggish and there is little energy available for everyday tasks, let alone for any kind of active retaliation. Typically, depressed people are unaware of how effectively they are retaliating with a passive depression.

Through an adaptation of the bracketing technique, a person can mentally back up and recall the state prior to the depressed reaction. Through focus and recall, and with the help of reinforcement from the therapist, the person can recover the original impulse that was denied. Undoing depression requires identifying the trigger, that is, the missed impulse to retaliate. When the patient's sadistic impulses are severely inhibited, the therapist can help by working with the patient's comprehensive imagination and fantasy, that is, by joining the patient in developing the fantasies of retaliation. The therapist must be careful not to suggest content to the patient while encouraging him or her to decondition their anxiety by fantasizing about the kinds of retaliation that they have inhibited and put out of their consciousness. This work, however, is only a deconditioning step and must not be confused with the deeper experience of primary aggression, which spontaneously emerges in intuition and imagery.

At this point it is appropriate to state that techniques for undoing depression are an adjunct to, not a substitute for, medication in cases where depression is biological, chronic, or diagnosed as endogenous rather than exogenous. Nevertheless, many people who have been depressed for as long as they can remember, even those who have been diagnosed with manic-depressive illness, report that SCT techniques help them contain the experience, and that depressions do not last as long and occur less often.

Step Seven: Contain the Energy and Explore the Fork-in-the-Road

The instant before the defense takes over is the point for containment. After that there is no turning back; one has missed the opportunity to explore the fork-in-the-road between impulses aroused by frustrating conflicts and defensive depressions and rages. This is a major difference between SCT and many other therapies. In SCT very little attention is paid to the symptoms that are generated by defenses, but a great deal of attention is paid to the primary experience that is defended against. The first step toward creating choice is to identify the triggering event that precipitated the defensive response. Note how this is achieved in the following dialogue:

T: It looks as if you just slid into depression. Did you notice yourself go? What was happening just before? Can you trace it back? What was happening just before you went?

Often, the very fact that there *is* a context for the slide into depression is a revelation for the person who has spent a lifetime dealing with depressive tendencies without being aware of any connection between the depression and a precipitating event. The context of the shift into depression has to be explored over and over again before the person comes to recognize the kinds of triggers that occasion the slide.

T: You felt yourself go that time. Did you have a moment, maybe, when you could have slowed the slide?

Even though the person may not have access to the moment of choice, this intervention provides a frame for future work and encourages the person to remain alert for the fork-in-the-road. It also gives such patients an idea of what they are to look for and encourages them to believe that sooner or later they will find it.

The following exchange between the therapist and patient in the preceding dialogue occurred later:

T: You're sitting on the edge and refusing to slide?

P: Yes. It's like I'm hanging on by my fingernails and refusing to go.

[It is often very moving to notice the first time the person has color in his or her face while actively battling the terrible suction of the depressive defense.]

T: Do you have any sense of where the alternative fork-in-the-road is?

P: No. Intellectually, I can guess it's that I'm mad. But I don't *know*! [When patients are unaware of any alternative branch at the fork-in-the-road, it is important to reinforce centering so that they can make themselves available to knowing.]

T: So you are managing to hang on and contain the impulse. You are sitting at the edge of the unknown and don't even at this point know in which direction to look. Can you hope that if you manage to hang on, sooner or later you will find another way?

P: I don't know.

T: Hope is often almost unbearable. Can you bear to hope?

P: Yes.

T: So for the moment, hope is all you have for the other branch of the fork-in-the-road. Can you put your weight into hope?

P: Yes.

This person was able to gain some hope of containing the energy and therefore had potential energy available for awareness of context, as well as of the self. The therapy had a happy ending.

Despite outward appearances, people who implode their energy, and are therefore frequently or consistently depressed, are in some respects like those whose energy explodes into noise and action. It is very important for both types of people to learn to trace the steps back along the path to the point just before they slide into depression or explode into activity. It is the ability to observe the context of distress that makes the difference.

Depression and Rage as Barrier Experiences

A self-system without an awareness of context is imprisoned in a barrier experience; it is as if there is no other perspective. Indeed, the barrier experience creates an encapsulated system within the self-system. It functions to split the self-centered person from a systems-centered context. The boundaries of this encapsulated system are as impermeable to intrapersonal communication as they are to interpersonal communication. Communications that do cross the boundaries are governed by selective perceptions that are self-reinforcing. In a barrier experience, it is as if this is the way things are, always were, and always will be.

Depression and rage are essentially barrier experiences in that they are relatively impermeable to influence. Therapeutic intervention cannot be effective until the self-observing system can be revived and engaged. Successfully reframing the barrier experience in the context of space and time is like taking a quick look over a wall and suddenly understanding that there is more to life than one has known. The process of working to get free from the barrier experience is no different for people who explode into rage or implode into depression than it is for those who respond with any of the many other defenses to sudden frustration.

UNDOING DEPRESSION

The work of undoing depression is similar to the work of deconditioning any other symptom. Thus, in deconditioning depression the occurrence of the symptom is bracketed between the memory of the last time the person was free of depression and the first time since then that he or she remembers being depressed. Events in the space between these brackets are then subjected to a step-by-step microanalysis until the gap is located. The memory gap is the interval of time within which the retaliatory impulse was elicited but went unnoticed. Recall of the retaliatory impulse makes the alternate branch of the fork-in-the-road available; this is the pathway to exploring the retaliatory impulse, the sadistic component of the impulse, the constellation of the projective identification, and the restitutive component in the projective identification.

Depression (unless it is endogenous) is also treated as a defensive symptom in an SCT group. If group members become depressed during a group therapy session, the connection is first made between the precipitating event in the group and the depressive reaction to that event. The group is encouraged to focus on the context, to look for the moment before they became aware of feeling depressed, and to recall how they were feeling about what was happening. The group will notice that there was a flash of a negative, disappointed, or critical reaction followed almost immediately by a turning of the criticism onto the self. Group members are encouraged to contain the emotion in the original reaction, a not unpleasant full feeling. By learning to "bottom out" on their feelings and resonate with each other at deeper and deeper levels, the group learns to subgroup around even more primal work.

Chapter 9

Sadistic Defenses

THE ENERGY OF FRUSTRATION

In SCT, containing is the necessary transitional state between comprehensive and apprehensive knowledge. When one is poised at the edge of
the unknown, one cannot predict when (or whether!) the transition into
apprehensive experience will come. The more frustration tolerance and
impulse control one develops, the more one can learn to tolerate uncertainty and remain curious while one waits.

The amount of energy available for managing impulses is directly
related to the ability to "contain" the energy of primary aggression
when frustrated. Primary aggression experienced without conflict is
simply an experience of potential energy. In the very young, the
expression of aggression follows frustration so fast that there is little, if
any, discrimination between frustration and aggression. Later in development, it becomes possible to experience frustration and primary
aggression as separate and nonconflictual experiences. For everyone,
young or old, there is a point at which frustration becomes too much
to tolerate and a regressive dedifferentiation of experience takes place.
When that occurs, frustration is experienced with irritability and irritability may activate the impulse to retaliate. The impulse to retaliate
generates the conflict between the impulse and the defenses against
the impulse. Each transition increases the energy the person must
attempt to contain.

When the energy in frustration is too much to contain, it tends to
explode or implode. The major implosive defenses are depression and
somatizing (see Chapters 7 and 8), which turn the hostile impulses back
on the self. The major explosive defenses are tantrums and hostile acting
out. There is an important difference in the SCT methods for modifying
explosive versus implosive defenses. The primary work for people who
discharge into defensive (i.e., sadistic or violent acting out) involves
reducing the permeability of the boundaries to their aggressive energy
whereas increasing permeability is the primary work for people who
implode their energy. Although somatizing and depression (discussed

fully in preceding chapters) are related to the explosive defenses, they will be referred to here only in passing.

Somatizing and Deconditioning

More than any other primary affect, primary aggression is most often defended against somatically. Psychosomatic symptoms serve as a power-lock on the impulse to discharge. Undoing somatic defenses (Chapter 7), by using the technique of bracketing, must be done slowly, carefully, and thoroughly. Deconditioning somatic defenses against aggression is frequently complicated by cognitive distortions. When anxiety-laden memories of tantrums are described in detail and brought into the light of reality, they are almost always normalized and depathologized. When earlier rages have had serious consequences, the process of reality testing during therapy must include an assessment of the patient's present ability to contain before any deconditioning is done.

Differentiating between Experience and Expression of Aggressive Emotion

There is frequent confusion about the difference between the concepts of experiencing and expressing anger (i.e., aggressive emotion). Most often, those who are afraid of their anger fear their negative predictions of what they might do or their misconstrued memories of what they have already done. To help a patient understand the difference between experiencing and expressing anger, the SCT therapist might say something like this:

> "You are recalling having a tantrum. But a tantrum is not your anger, it is just one of many kinds of expressions of anger. You also remember sulking. Sulking is another kind of expression of anger. And you remember calling your brother names? Another expression. Expressing your anger has to do with raging and shouting and hitting things and all the other ways of discharging your anger energy. It is important that you recognize the difference between how you express your anger and the experience you have of the anger itself, so that, however angry you are, you can still decide whether to express it and how to express it."

It is always important in SCT to recognize the difference between exploring an experience and acting it out. Because the consequences of acting out masochism and sadism are so personally and interpersonally destructive, it is particularly important that the aggressive emotion be experienced and contained instead. Sadism and masochism are often experiences that are as difficult for the therapist to explore as they are for the patient in as much as a therapist may have the same defenses the patient has against these impulses, as well as some of the same cognitive distortions.

Differentiating between Thinking, Feeling, and Doing

Swearing, shouting, or having a tantrum are often thought to be the same as being frustrated, irritable, angry. This confusion fails to differentiate between the expression of experience and the experience itself and taps into the early belief that there is no difference between thinking, feeling, and doing.

Confusion between thinking and feeling and doing has nothing to do with intelligence. Even extremely intelligent and well-functioning professionals are surprised to discover that although their common sense knows that thinking, feeling, and doing are separate activities, they do not always behave as if they believe it! Discriminating between thinking, feeling, and doing begins very early and is an ongoing developmental task that results in ever more complex discriminations. This is true throughout life itself, as well as in therapy. Over and over again, at different stages of development, people find themselves as upset over an angry thought as they would be if they had actually behaved aggressively toward the person they are angry with.

T: You are as upset as if you are really hurting someone. But this is a fantasy, and it exists only in your head.

P: I know . . . but I seem to forget that I know!

T: Do you have any fear that you will actually do the things that you are thinking?

P: No.

T: You are quite sure and confident that you would never do this?

P: Yes.

T: Then, you see, your fear is of your thoughts, not of the reality of your experience. That is just like we discovered before, when you felt terrible about your negative predictions and mind reading. When you checked your terrible feelings against your reality experience, you found that they went away. Do you see you are having the same kind of terror now? This time you are confusing thinking and doing, and you are as upset as if they were the same thing—which, in reality, they are not!

Negative predictions about one's expression of irritability or frustration or anger are checked out through testing reality in exactly the same way that negative predictions of social reality are tested. It is through discovering one's own reality that a person learns that irritability is not necessarily a tense and anxious experience charged with restless electric energy that will discharge inappropriately at any moment; nor, one learns, is it necessarily a constricted, tense, or even anesthetized experience of heaviness and weight. SCT patients learn that it is possible to experience a restless, but not necessarily unpleasant, energy that can transform into a "fizz" of alertness and readiness that makes them feel full of themselves. When contained, rather than controlled or restricted, the experience of frustration is one of being "all ready," without, as yet, anywhere to go.

ACTING OUT

Both acting out hostility on the environment and turning it in on the self are behavioral discharge defenses. The major SCT method for managing discharge is directing group members' attention to the fact that a flood of apparently undifferentiated feeling contains many identifiable differences. This is the work of subgrouping. Parenthetically, defense modification applies equally well to individual and group psychotherapy. The work of "containing" the person who has poor impulse control is the same in group and individual therapy. The group, however, has the additional advantage of subgrouping. Subgrouping cannot be duplicated in individual therapy until the patient has moved into the phase of intimacy. What can be emphasized in individual therapy is the universality of the human experience of feeling overwhelmed by strong emotion.

Addressing acting out is one area in which the valuable technique of education goes a long way. The SCT group learns that a tantrum is not anger itself but an expression of anger. Confusion between the experience of anger and an expression of it plays a big part in generating fear in groups when anger is aroused. Group members may give lip service to the idea that the thought or wish is not the deed, but they are without conviction at the primary level of experience.

Particularly in the early phases of group development, group reality is frustrating. Responses to the frustration are aroused at many levels before the differences in members' experience of frustration and response to it have been explored. The less differentiated a person's experience of frustration, the greater his or her fear of being overwhelmed by it and unable to contain it. The more primitive the fear, the stronger and more primitive the defenses against it. Typically, a person's fear of being destructive when frustrated directly relates to his or her internal sadistic fantasies. There is also, unfortunately, the occasional patient whose satisfaction comes from acting out sadistic fantasies on willing or unwilling partners. (The therapeutic work with these people is discussed later in this chapter, when working through the fantasies of sadism results in making the underlying projective identification conscious.) Unless one is working with a special population, fear of loss of control rarely reflects an actual tendency toward loss of control. It is the patient's failure to understand the difference between a hostile thought and a hostile deed that almost always needs attention. This is especially true when sadistic fantasies start to surface.

For some patients, the fear of expressing anger is connected to the physical sensations of emotion swelling inside. It is important for the therapist to differentiate between the patient's fear of sadistic fantasies and the fear of internal sensations of emotion. Fear of sadistic fantasies is a conflict between having a sadistic fantasy and judging oneself for having it; fear of emotional sensation, on the other hand, has to do with a fear of experiencing the emotion of anger, that is, fear of a relatively undifferentiated emotion that poses the danger of flooding the system and discharging into the environment. For some people, the simple sensation of frustrated energy can be experienced as almost unbearable; the therapist must actively help them reduce the intensity of their experience by giving them reassurance and information and by pacing their ability to contain the energy in frustration by presenting them with a series of "just noticeable" experiences before flooding occurs.

Shifts in degree of aggressive arousal are nearly always signaled physically, as with a jutting jaw, a clenched fist, or a kicking foot. These are cues that the therapist can use to slow down experience. Drawing a person's attention to these signals and asking for a description of what is observed almost always lowers the arousal of emotion. Having patients focus on the early warning signals of aggressive emotion encourages them to explore their experience when the energy is still low enough to be contained instead of discharged. When experience is maintained below the threshold of acting out, discriminations between arousal, frustration, and irritability can be made and the different sensations integrated. Whenever experience is not successfully titrated, whenever the irritability from frustration is not contained, precipitation of either discharge or regression is likely. In regression, discrimination is lost. Irritability is experienced as rage; when rage is aroused, so is blame. Then either the world or others or the self becomes the target for the human tendency to scapegoat. Therefore, it is useful for both therapist and patient to look for the early warning signals that irritability is in danger of escalating into rage.

Acting out violently or abusively is characteristic of people who do not notice the signal of rage before it erupts. Increasingly, the ability to

delay and contain impulses makes it possible to do the work of discrimination and integration. As with all acting out defenses, it is important for
the therapist to assess the patient's ability to contain *before* undermining
any defense.

If a patient describes the experience of frustration in terms of an
impending explosion, the SCT therapist attempts to help the patient
separate out a fear of exploding from the act itself. The therapist tries to
determine if the patient reaches a identifiable point after which he or
she explodes.

> "You say you are so frustrated you could explode. Let us separate out
> the fear of exploding from the act of exploding. Does that happen
> to you? Do you reach the point you are at right now and then
> explode?"

If the patient merely fears exploding but never actually does so, the
therapeutic work continues. If the patient admits to explosive acting out,
the therapist takes a history and assesses the probability of the patient
acting out in the therapy situation: "Tell me about the last time you
exploded. What was frustrating you? Who were you with?"

It is important to note that the very work of describing the episode
serves a deconditioning function. While the patient describes the
episode, it becomes possible for the therapist to draw the patient's attention to how hostility rises and falls. Basing self-knowledge on self-observation lays the foundation for the self-validating experience of
containing. For example, in response to a patient who had just described
a traumatic encounter with his boss, the therapist replied:

> "Did you notice when you were telling me about how your boss
> called you names, you became quite aroused? And yet, do you see,
> as you went on talking you didn't boil over at all? In fact, you were
> able to tell me about other times when he lost his temper. You told
> me how sometimes you felt he was ridiculous as well as infuriating.
> Looking back now and remembering the experience of telling me
> about your frustration with your boss, can you describe the fluctua-
> tions of feeling that you had?"

This is the SCT work of encouraging discriminations in feeling. The
more feelings are differentiated, the less overwhelming they are. This
work paves the way to making discriminations in the here-and-now:

> "You say you are frustrated again? How difficult is it for you this
> time? Are your feelings as difficult to contain now as they were in the
> story you told me about your boss? Not so bad? How much less?"

The work of developing discriminations of feeling operationalizes the SCT hypothesis that developmental maturation is a function of discrimination and integration. In the following dialogue, the therapist is helping the patient learn to discriminate between feelings:

T: And how do you experience yourself right now with me—being frustrated and able to contain it? Do you think you are finding it a little easier to contain than when we started? Do you have any energy to spare for exploring?

P: Yes, finally!

T: You're frustrated and irritated with me right now?

P: Yes!

T: Well, we've done this before. See if you can center yourself through your irritation.

P: OK.

T: How do you feel now?

P: I feel grounded, balanced, energetic.

T: Now, when you think about my putting pressure on you just now, what do you experience?

P: Well, it seems different. I both like it and I don't like it.

This short dialogue illustrates what a person feels when centered. When they are centered, people do not have trouble knowing what situation is frustrating them or what they must do to have things make more sense for them. Understanding that one cannot, in reality, do as one likes does not arouse the same frustration that is aroused when things are taken "just personally." Containing leads from self-centered understanding to understanding the self in context. Contained and centered, the person is back in touch with common sense.

DENYING ANGRY IMPULSES

So far, we have focused on issues of undoing defenses against irritability, that is, undoing the tendency for irritability to escalate into rage with a discharge of hostile aggressive energy. Defensive withdrawal or denial of the experience of irritability may not seem as important, but it is, in fact, costly to both the person and the environment. Many patients are totally unaware that they are angry—even when it is quite obvious to those around them. They do not see their own tense jaw, tight mouth, clenched fist. Others do. The first step is to bring to the attention of such patients the signals that there may be more feeling inside them than they know.

T: Would you look down at your hands. Do you see how they are clenched on your knees as you talk about this work being difficult in here? Are you also aware of your jaw being tight and that you are frowning?

P: No . . . I don't know.

T: You say you don't know! Then your body knows something we don't know! Don't think! Would you focus instead and see where the source of the energy is in your body that fueled your arms and your hands?

Drawing patients' attention to the fact that much more is going on than they are aware of is the first step. Emotions are rooted in physiology and are allied with an impulse to act, which can be signaled clearly by the body without the person being aware of it. Drawing attention to this introduces an additional source of information to the patient. It also provides an independent way of telling the difference between feelings that are related to thoughts and feelings that are related to an emotional experience. Feelings that are the translation of the experience of emotion into words are always related to physical sensations, and often to intention movements that the emotion triggers. Feelings that are generated by thoughts use a different part of the brain and are not accompanied by instinctual intention movements. In the following dialogue the therapist is trying to help the patient differentiate between these two kinds of feelings:

T: Would you focus and see where the source of your energy is that fueled your arms and your hands?

P: In my abdomen.

T: In your abdomen! I see. And what was the sensation?

P: Heat . . . energy.

T: You say heat and energy? Yes, and what else?

P: Well, I feel like hitting something.

T: Ah, you have an impulse to hit out! Do you see that you are now experiencing the impulse to hit out quite comfortably?

P: Yes.

T: Are you now more likely or less likely to act on the impulse?

Once a person recognizes that there is a direct connection between emotions and physical impulses, it becomes possible to discriminate between the impulse to act, the intention movements that signal action, and the inner experience of the feeling that is fueling the impulse. When there is congruence between what people say, how they are saying it, and the gestures that accompany their words, they have the full feeling, the impulse, and the expression. This, however, does not mean that they are fully aware of this congruence. Before they can use themselves as a guide to their own experience, they must first learn to be open to the information that is contained in the spontaneous signals of experience. This is different from the characteristic ways that people express themselves while they are communicating (i.e., the kinds of grimaces and gestures that are copied when someone else tries to imitate them). Mannerisms have more to do with communicating social role expectations than with the spontaneous self. In the following dialogue, the SCT work of discrimination continues:

T: You notice you fling your arms up and your hands are fists? Can you also remember how that felt in your body? How do you feel the energy in you as you wave your fists? How did it feel?

P: I don't know.

T: You say you don't know! Are you forgetting to focus your attention? Where is the source of your energy that fueled your arms and your hands?

P: In my fists. And in my abdomen.

T: In your fists and in your abdomen! I see. And what was the sensation in your abdomen?

P: Heat.

T: You say heat. Yes, and what else?

P: Energy.

T: You notice that there is energy. What else? What other sensations in your body?

P: Sort of a fizz.

T: You say sort of a fizz. And how was that fizz—pleasant, unpleasant, or neutral?

We know that the actual experience of arousal is one of a good feeling of energy, even when the emotion is painful—if one has not made oneself afraid of it by making negative predictions; *if* one has not framed it in terms of past bad experience; and *if* one has not made it into a painful experience by a straightjacket of tension or, worse, a psychosomatic pain in the gut or the head or the heart. It is important in SCT to insist that patients use their own physical sensations, rather than the thoughts in their head, as the basis for their experience. (This is the ongoing work of revising the cognitive map to fit reality, as opposed to the human tendency to revise reality to fit the map.) It is in the service of this task that there is so much repetition of the fundamentals in SCT. Thus, when a patient acknowledges that the sensation of aggressive emotion is actually a pleasant one, the therapist may respond:

> "You look surprised when you say pleasant. Were you expecting it to be unpleasant? Well, then you have a pleasant surprise at the actual experience and another example of how there is a difference between what you think you will experience—your negative prediction—and your actual experience, which is a pleasant sensation of warmth and energy and arousal and excitement."

RAGES AND TANTRUMS

It was discussed in the last chapter how it often comes as a great shock to people who are depressed to discover that depression is their own hostility turned in. It comes as just as much of a shock to people to discover that their tantrums, diatribes, and expressions of outrage have less to do with expressions of aggressive emotion and more to do with defending against sadistic and frustrated impulses. There is a large cognitive component in outrage, as there is in depression. Outrage and diatribes are just as well rationalized as depressions, and each contains both pleasure and pain. The recreational quality of outrage is easily recognized, and the component of secondary gain is as strong in outrage as it is in an indulged and carefully tended depression.

A good example of how seductive an enraged diatribe can be—and how easily it overpowers common sense—is given in the following clinical episode: The husband of a new and seriously suicidal patient was asked to come in with her to discuss her treatment plan. As soon as they arrived, the husband launched into a diatribe about how angry he was that many therapists and many years in therapy had not cured his wife. After several attempts to reorient the interview, I asked him if he had some pleasure in expressing his outrage at therapists. He said that he did. I said that I knew that it did indeed often feel good to get things off one's chest and that we had a choice: I could continue to listen to his pain and fury at the frustration of not getting satisfactory treatment for his wife or the three of us could work on what we could do to keep her safe, considering the fact that she had told me that she had a habit of putting a loaded gun in her mouth when she wanted to "feel better." To my surprise, he chose to continue his diatribe.

Learning to contain enables the person to explore the two paths at the fork-in-the-road: the path of acting out on the path toward exploration of the inner experience that is being avoided during the acting out. Typically, when outrage and tantrums are explored, there is the discovery that they mask an impulse to discharge irritation in blameful and sadistic thoughts and wishes, targeted either out or in (depression, after all is self-torture). Taking the path toward exploration of the hostility makes all sorts of fantasies available—some quite violent and bloody, others bloodless, cold, and sadistic. One thing they have in common is that they are all ways of getting even.

Everyone knows what it is like to have in imagination the fight we did not have in reality; we try this way and that way to a satisfactory win. Sometimes after a few repetitions and a few revisions of the fantasy, the battle is won and forgotten. Other times, no matter how the mind twists and turns the event, nothing seems to work and angry fantasies become a constant companion to everyday life. The original cause may be quite forgotten, but the fantasies are triggered by even small frustrations; stopping at a traffic light or having to wait to cross a road can set off the impulse to kill.

SADISTIC FANTASIES

So far, the SCT work we have discussed involves matching fantasy against reality so that the feelings that are generated by the imagination can be compared and contrasted with the feelings that are generated from reality. In contrast, the exploration of sadism is done through experiencing and exploring the feelings that are generated by imagination! It is through the use of imagination that the unconscious sadistic fantasies are accessed and brought into consciousness. Thus, the imagination is harnessed in the service of learning to make conscious and tolerate the sadistic impulses rather than act them out. The patients' work is to generate the retaliatory fantasies; the therapist's work is to help them contain their conflicted response and explore their mixed feelings one at a time, separating out thought from thought, thought from feeling, and feeling from feeling. At every step along the way the therapist reinforces the difference between thinking and doing. In each of the following therapist comments, the therapist is attempting to do just that:

"There is a difference between thinking about retaliating and thinking that you should not be thinking about retaliating. You are at a fork-in-the-road. Which would do you want to explore first?"

"There is a difference between thinking about giving her a dirty look, which you hope will make her ashamed, and actually shaming her in the real world. Will you explore what you know about the difference?"

"There is a difference between thinking of drawing blood and actually making somebody bleed. Which do you want to explore first—your impulse to hurt or your fear that thinking is the same as doing?"

The conflicts experienced around exploring sadistic fantasies are both numerous and diverse. People vary in their reluctance to put into words the images that come to mind. Some are frightened by the feelings that are aroused by the scenes they imagine whereas others are filled with a bragging delight and feelings of entitlement and potency. While some people are able to act out the fantasies with satisfaction and pleasure and others cannot even tolerate the idea of sadism, the most common reaction is a mixture of feelings: guilt, triumph, pleasure, and horror.

For those whose sadistic fantasies are never far away, the fantasies unfold freely. There are potential advantages and also potential disadvantages to this. In some cases the sadistic fantasies carry people through various retaliatory imaginings of torture until they access their source—a projective identification. Once the projective identification has been discovered, there is a clear path out of the sadistic layer and into the apprehensive experience of primary aggression as a life force.

It is not always this simple, however. There are also those who not only have ready access to their sadistic fantasies but also act them out. In these cases there is a split: The triumph and pleasure are conscious, but the guilt, horror, and compassionate identification with the victim is unconscious. Before the work of accessing the primary aggression can be attempted, there must first be a recognition that the victims of the sadistic acting out are people who experience pain and not fantasy figures happy to cooperate in a sadomasochistic game. In subgrouping, all the stages of undoing sadism and accessing primary aggression are made conscious in the group. Recognizing the connection between sadism and humanity is a powerful force in recognizing that in acting out sadism there is no real relationship with a living person. Sadomasochistic acting out is the surface communication of a projective identification. There is likely to be much resistance to the masochistic component in sadism and the sadistic component in masochism. Few are aware that the abuser is just as much a victim of the role-lock as the abused. For all people it is probable that getting the sadistic fantasies to surface is the most direct way to insight into sadomasochistic conflicts. This is another context where work is more easily done in subgroups than in individual therapy. In group therapy, much preliminary work is done by the resistant members as they listen to members of the active subgroup discovering their experiences.

The goals of exploring sadomasochism in subgroups are (1) to differentiate between sadistic fantasies and irritability and between sadistic fantasies and instinctual rage; (2) to explore the sadistic fantasies (when fantasies are explored and understood, they are unlikely to be acted out); (3) to understand that the sadistic (and masochistic) fantasies are the surface communication of a projective identification (projective identification is understood as communication of experience with the purpose of being understood through experience); (4) to understand that the pleasure in sadism comes from the feeling of power and control and safety from the feelings of helplessness; and (5) to understand that guilt is a secondary feeling, generated by a mixture of mind reading and negative predictions, triumph, and compassion. SCT works the fork-in-the-road: first discriminating between the feeling of power and control and fears of being punished, and then exploring the conflict between pleasure and pain and between the triumph (related to self) and the compassion (related to other).

There is another response that it is important for therapists to be on the alert for: that of the patient who has learned how to access sadistic fantasies, feels better for it, and has been therapeutically reinforced for this response. Such patients then use sadistic fantasies as an obsessive defense against the experience of their conflict, rather than as a means of understanding what they had been defending against. If the case rests at this stage, the "cure" will have become the disease.

In contrast, there are those whose sadistic thoughts are so inhibited that they are out of any awareness. This is particularly true for people who have long turned all hostility toward themselves without any recognition that they even have an impulse to retaliate. Once such patients can recognize that there was a triggering event to which there was a strange absence of response and once they accept that there is an alternative to depression, their therapist has the opportunity to encourage them to deliberately imagine alternative ways of responding. When fantasies do not emerge spontaneously, it is helpful for the therapist to encourage their creation. It is sometimes extremely difficult for patients to create such fantasies, particularly if their characteristic experience in life is that of dedicated victim. To such a patient the therapist might say the following:

"Yes, I understand. You say you are beaten down, abused, and victimized and you feel helpless and frightened and sad and depressed and hopeless. Do you understand that you are telling me about your relationship with yourself as you are being victimized and that you are not yet addressing your relationship with your abuser?"

"Again, you tell me about how awful you feel when she calls you names, criticizes the way you look and talk, and ridicules you as a lover. Will you now notice what feelings you have toward *her* when she does this?"

"Let us take one of the incidents that have hurt you so badly and go over it slowly to see if you notice any point in which you have a feeling toward her for treating you like this."

It sometimes takes a great deal of reframing before patients can switch their focus from their intrapersonal to their interpersonal experience. Once the focus has switched, they can be encouraged to become aware that they have an active as well as a passive response to the abuse:

T: You cringed when you thought of giving him an angry look. What are you cringing from?

P: I am afraid he will come at me again if he sees—

T: Do you see that you are having a fantasy about how he will retaliate and that it has gotten in the way of exploring how you would retaliate? So you have just turned something back on yourself?

P: Yes . . . I see.

T: So we are at a fork-in-the-road again between your relationship with yourself and your relationship with him. Which would you like to explore first—the impulse you just had that you are cringing from or the impulse you have to give him a dirty look?

The goal of exploring hostility is to work through to the bottom of the masochistic or sadistic fantasies, that is, to the point where the person comes to understand the context of the experience and is thus able to separate from it. Patients who have become free to experience their retaliatory sadistic fantasies will have little or no trouble knowing the words that go with them, although they may have trouble expressing them.

SADISM AND GUILT

Guilt can easily lead to a barrier experience. The barrier experience against the fear of being caught and punished for sadistic thoughts defends against a deeper fear of knowing that sadistic impulses are active and present in the self, whether one approves of them or not, and that one has already acted out sadistically and will probably do so again.

In SCT, guilt is understood as a complex of mixed feelings rather than as a feeling in itself. The feelings in relationship to sadism are usually a mixture of horror, hatred, triumph, and pleasure. Pleasure and triumph are usually the first of the mixed feelings to surface when guilt has been resolved. The source of the pleasure and triumph is not understood until later, when the fantasies of torture are understood to mirror the tortured experience the patient has felt.

SADISM AND REVENGE

When the sadistic fantasy is followed through, there is a predictable message: The person wants to get even, to do unto others what they have done to him or her. What is available in the sadistic fantasies is only the hatred; these fantasies express the primitive talion law (retaliation in kind).

> "I'm taking a long needle and stabbing you through the heart. Your heart is full of little holes, and the blood is trickling down your chest. It's like Jesus on the cross with the spear mark. I don't feel guilty. It's what you deserve for stabbing me with your words. I feel good that you know how it feels."

There is a double message in these words. They contain a condensation of love and hate.

When the sadistic fantasies are completed apprehensive insight follows, the projective identification is resolved, and the split is integrated. In the course of this process it is as if the patient is saying to the abuser, "I hate you for what you did to me and will get even by doing it to you. I love you as I do this to you because, by experiencing what I experienced you will understand how you hurt me and you will love me as I love you."

Sadism in SCT is understood to relate to both comprehension and apprehension. Sadism involves comprehensive knowledge in that the imagination is heavily involved in the details of the torture the patient invents. It involves apprehensive insight in that the scenes of torture are linked to condensations of information that code the splits in the intrapersonal and interpersonal relationships that cause the kind of anguish that only torturing can communicate. Exploring the experience of sadism, rather than defending against it, makes it possible to hear the message that is coded in the sadistic impulse. Experiencing the active energy in sadism without evaluating it negatively makes it possible to decode the message.

THE DIFFERENCE BETWEEN SADISM
AND PRIMARY AGGRESSION

Accessing primal aggression comes from work on centering and learning how to contain frustration and sit at the edge of the unknown experience. It is not at all unusual, particularly through the work of functional subgrouping in SCT groups, for the experience of primary aggression to occur within the first module of defense modification, when centering work is being done. Just as comprehension is the link to the human animal called *Homo sapiens*, so apprehension is the phylogenetic link to the prehuman animal in the hierarchy of living systems. When primary aggression is experienced apprehensively it is nondefensive and there is an apprehensive understanding of universal experience. When it is contained, there is no fear of acting out the instinctive knowledge. The lion is neither sadistic nor guilty as it tears at its prey; neither is the lioness masochistic as she allows herself and her cubs to be warded off until he is sated.

The pathways to and the characteristics of the experience of primary aggression are quite different from those of the experiences of sadism and masochism. The preliminary exploration of sadism is primarily cognitive; it is a function of the imagination and is under the aegis of socialized comprehension. The exploration stage involves a mixture of comprehension and apprehensive insight. Guilt is the product of the collision between comprehensive and apprehensive understanding. It is a mixture of socialized disapproval; horror of the impulse to retaliate, which is disguised in perverted imaginations (the compound defense of sadism); and the impulse to teach others to respect one's goals of survival, development, and competitive mastery, which are threatening to emerge in their most primal form. It is not until apprehensive insight occurs that the understanding of sadism approaches the depth that is reached in accessing the experience of primary aggression. There is an experience of the fullness of instinctive knowledge that comes with primal rage, a transformational experience of apprehension of one's place in phylogeny. In the apprehensive experience of the breakthrough, defenses against sadism are bypassed and the power of the primary aggression in the life force is experienced apprehensively.

However, there is a difference between accessing the experience of primary aggression, apprehending the murderous rage, and having apprehensive access as a method of managing hostility. There are no shortcuts in SCT therapy. Centering and containing the life force without defending against it or acting it out requires different tolerances in the context of Module 2 work with role-locks, of Module 3 work with the defenses against change, and of Module 4 work in the separation and individuation work of intimacy.

There is an important difference in the way SCT defines the source and function of sadistic fantasies and the fantasies that erupt around murderous rage. The fantasies of murderous rage lead directly to primary aggression and require a very different management from the sadistic fantasies that we have just discussed. Like the work on sadism, learning how to open up to the experience of murderous rage is built on all the earlier work in Module 1: connecting the irritability in frustration with the experience of irritable energy; deconditioning the negative predictions and mind reading; understanding depression and withdrawal as boomerang defenses; and recognizing impulsive rages and violent or histrionic acting as discharges.

Before primary aggression is accessed in the group, there is an intervening step in defense modification: the exploration into role-locks. We have already discussed how the first half of Module 1 defense modification is done predominantly in the boundarying work at the beginning phase of every group's development with subgrouping spontaneously occurring around the issues that the different modifications raise (e.g., subgrouping can occur around learning how to make eye contact, discovering reality, exploring cognitive distortions, or undoing somatic symptoms). When defenses against irritability come into focus, they are increasingly worked in the context of subgrouping around defiance and compliance. As compliance and defiance are explored, so are the role-locks between the group and its identified patient and scapegoat. In addition, the issues around authority begin to crystallize, and the fundamental role-locks in relationship to authority coalesce. Modifying role-locks takes the group smoothly into the authority issue, which in turn opens up the potential for experiencing primal rage, which then becomes the fuel for the exploration into resistance to change. Thus, the first three modules of defense analysis pace the unfolding of the authority phase in group development.

C h a p t e r   1 0

Role Relationship Defenses

T he norms of behavior for the individual, the group member, the subgroup, or the group are what give systems their character, for good and for bad. Role behaviors generate transactional potentialities and also limit them. Defensive role responses reflect the compromises in system development and determine the parameters of system survival, future development, and environmental mastery. When defenses in role behavior are modified toward greater adaptations to reality, the system ability to survive, develop, and master is also adapted to reality. "All the world's a stage, and all the men and women merely players. They have their entrances and exits, and one man in his time plays many parts." Shakespeare was a master at portraying the roles we play, not only in the various phases of our development but also in the many contexts of our everyday life.

Typically, group members helplessly, unwittingly, and persistently repeat the major role behaviors they learned in childhood. We are all victims of the repetition compulsion, and nowhere is this more obvious than in our group behavior. As members interact with each other, they subliminally cue each other to treat them in ways that repeat the old familiar role relationships they have entered group therapy to change! In this sense, members "volunteer" for certain roles, like identified patient or scapegoat. However, the power of the group therapy is twofold: First, it is by no means likely that members will be the perfect reciprocal match for each other's scripts. Second, it is only when the group requires certain roles that it will use its volunteers. Even when a member who is usually the scapegoat (or identified patient) volunteers for the role, he or she may still not get the part if there is another member (or subgroup) who is a better fit!

When roles are viewed from the group context, it is easy to see how role behavior represents a solution to conflicts in the group. Conversely, when roles are viewed solely in terms of individual dynamics, it is no longer so easy to identify their group function. Leaders in some forms of group therapy sometimes give members catchy names based on their group role (Mrs. Helper or Mr. Talker or Miss Complainer). The problem with caricaturing members in this way is twofold: First, it is simplistic, belittling, and condescending and encourages stereotyping. Second, it ignores the major dynamic purpose of roles in a group, which is to provide a stabilizing function for the systems of both the individual and the group-as-a-whole.

Defining role relationships by function, which changes as context and goal change, is an important feature of SCT work. A role is understood as simultaneously representing, for both the individual and the group, a solution for managing conflict in a certain context. Thus, roles play an important part in stabilizing the individual and group systems. Indeed, in the early stages of developing a theory of living human systems, roles were the bridge construct that connected the system of the individual with the system of the group (Agazarian & Peters, 1981). Roles can be functional or nonfunctional, according to the context. For example, groups tend to create the role of the compliant "identified patient" to contain their helpless dependency and to serve as a symbolic offering to the "good leader" to nurture and cherish. This can be a transitional role, in which case it is functional for both the member and the group, or it can be permanent, in which case fixation ensues. The same is true of the scapegoat role: The chosen member serves as a container for the group's murderous rage so that the "bad leader" is not destroyed. When scapegoating is transitional, both the scapegoated member and the scapegoating group nearly always make significant progress; when it is not, group sadism and member masochism are reinforced.

Members who volunteer for group roles like the identified patient and the scapegoat are driven by their own impulse to repeat old role solutions from their nuclear family system; their motivation to volunteer is a function of their individual dynamics. However, which volunteer will be chosen by the group to occupy a given role is a function of the group's dynamics. Many volunteer, but few are chosen!

Much work has been done by Ariadne Beck (1981) on exploring the relationship between member roles and the phases of group development. She has identified four key roles: socioemotional leader, task leader, scapegoat leader, and defiant leader. Although Beck associates these roles with individual dynamics, SCT views them as role functions generated by the group. When the task or socioemotional leaders are absent and a "work initiating act" or an empathic resonance is required in the group, some other member will produce the behavior, thus supporting the idea that the creation of the group role is a function of group dynamics and is independent of the person who fills it (even though the individual who fills the role will do so in a way that reflects his or her individual dynamics).

One of the major differences in the way systems-centered and group-as-a-whole approaches address the issue of group roles is in the way role relationships are managed. In interpersonal therapy, for example, the scapegoating of a member's role is deliberately encouraged to make it ego-alien. In contrast, in SCT, interventions that would target the member in the role are avoided. All SCT interventions around roles are directed at the function of the role for the group and not at the person playing the role. The group is encouraged to explore, in subgroups, what is fueling the impulse to set up the role. This subgroup work makes it possible for members who are being volunteered, by themselves as well as by the group, to explore their underlying impulses. SCT interventions aim to bring into group-as-a-whole consciousness not only the function of roles but also the mechanisms the group uses to create the roles and elect qualified members to fill them. When members take their group role personally, they are reminded of the function their role plays for the group—and of the fact that when the group no longer needs the role, it will not be reinforced. This important technique legitimizes exploring the impulse to take on a role. It also highlights the fact that group members cannot change their role unless the group supports the change. For example, it is a fact of group life that a group will discourage the very changes in a member it has been encouraging if there is still a need for that member's old role! In other words, a group will reinforce, encourage, and reward only those changes that are adaptive to the group. This is particularly true in the role-locks that occur around issues with authority in the subphase of fight.

ROLE-LOCKS

Role-locks are barrier experiences that occur when someone becomes trapped inside a role. People in a role-lock with themselves are often in a role-lock with the outside world as well. Those inside a barrier experience have no awareness of the impact on others of their acting out the role or of how acting it out leads to reciprocal role-locks with others. Awareness that one is in a role-lock with the self comes through the work of developing the observing self-system. The self-system has the potential to see over the barriers and perceive the context in which the role is being played out; the role-lock with the self; and the role-lock with others, the immediate environment, or the world. Psychodynamically, this is easily translated into simple transference based on projection, transference based on projective identification, and the as-yet-unboundaried pervasive transference. Until the observing self-system can learn enough about internal and external role-locks to sound the alarm, people are relatively helpless within the barrier experience; they remain convinced that God and might and right are on their side and that others will someday see the light. It is the role relationship with oneself inside the barrier experience that is the major source of human suffering. When people experience themselves within a systems-centered context, real pain, however intense, can be integrated over time.

Interpersonal role-locks occur when two people relate to each other from their own barrier experience and each barrier experience mirrors and reinforces the other. Being essentially an interdependence of opposites, role-locks appear reciprocal in nature. Communication between the participants in a role-lock is unconscious in that it crosses the boundaries between two split-off and encapsulated (unconscious) parts of two individuals (subsystems in the self-centered systems). It is this phenomenon that is experienced as role suction. The roots of role-locks are in projective identification, and involve both secondary and primary transference. What is conscious is the barrier experience, in which each participant experiences the other as an opposite "other"; a compatible one in the case of the identified patient and an oppositional one in the case of the scapegoat. It is at that level that role-locks are addressed in the subgroups. When the projective identification underlying the role-lock emerges, it becomes clear that the experience of each person is a reflection of the other, although the participants each formerly perceived the experience only in the other and not in themselves. How each is the reciprocal of the other is demonstrated when the barrier experience is undone and the split-off part of the self is reintegrated. It is then discovered that parts of both participants of the role-lock couple were in the same subgroup all along: the subgroup of the victims' victim!

Role-locks are not exclusive to patients. Therapists, too, are vulnerable to the compulsion to repeat certain patterns of behavior and to the suction of a reciprocal role. When therapists follow their impulse to take care of the group's identified patient or rescue its scapegoat; when they get into a power struggle or deadlock with the group or a member; when they allow themselves to be seduced into membership; or, worse, when they act out with an individual patient inside or outside the group, they have responded to the suction of the role-lock that can serve no good purpose for themselves, group members, or the group-as-a-whole. For therapists, the technique of subgrouping is sometimes a lifesaving therapeutic intervention. When therapists are concerned that they might be acting out their own impulses instead of containing them or when the pressure of an individual member or the group-as-a-whole is so strong that they begin to take group dynamics personally, they can call for sub-group work around the issue that is provoking or seducing or confusing or frightening them.

Role-locks mark the transition from intrapersonal work in therapy to interpersonal work and are the bridge between the self-centered defenses and systems-centered defenses. Work with characteristic role repetition defenses cannot be done in any depth if the person has not first modified his or her self-centered defenses. It is the necessity to first modify defensive communication, cognitive distortions, tension, and hostile responses that makes it important for SCT therapists to pay more than cursory attention to the signals of role-lock in the flight and early fight subphases (see Table 4.3). It goes without saying that the identified patient role-lock has great salience in the flight subphase, just as scapegoating is salient in the transition into the fight subphase. The SCT therapist, however, will do little more than name the impulses behind these role-locks when they first appear and alert the group to the consequences on the work of the group if the impulses are acted out. Subgrouping around the interpersonal defenses rarely reaches much depth until after the intrapersonal defenses have been modified. When therapeutic regression occurs after intrapersonal defense modification has been accomplished, the characteristic role defenses are elicited at the conscious instead of the unconscious level and within a strong, reality-oriented system structure, one that supports approaching and solving the problems that inevitably exist along the path to the goals of therapy. To try to work with role-lock defenses before members can both recognize and undo their intrapersonal defenses is to increase the probability that they will retreat into a barrier experience and act them out.

CHANGING ROLES

Different roles relate to different goals, different goals require different behaviors, and different behaviors generate different experiences. In SCT, the patient role is strictly prescribed: There are specific behaviors that define the role, and the role has goals that are related to a specific context. At the beginning of the group or individual therapy session, entering the role is facilitated by specific techniques, such as the distraction exercise. Abandoning the role at the end of each therapy session is also facilitated by specific techniques, which serve to reduce the potential for introducing a new role-lock, one acquired in therapy, that might emerge as a new defense. For example, a transference neurosis that is not contained within the confines of therapy may well serve as a role-lock that increases, rather than decreases, defensiveness—and not only in therapy but in everyday life as well.

In the review period before the end of a therapy session, group members are asked to review their current therapeutic experience for "surprises, learnings, satisfactions, dissatisfactions, and discoveries." The feeling of surprise is a powerful emotion. Almost all human beings, whatever their particular defenses against feeling, can recognize the feeling of surprise in themselves. Since this feeling is a common experience, it is possible for all members to join in and contribute information to the review period.

The SCT review period is one of the techniques that encourages patients to differentiate between their patient roles and their personal roles. "Surprises and learnings" enables them to practice changing from roles that are appropriate for therapy to roles that are appropriate for everyday life. Explicitly involving their self-observing capability makes it less likely that members will leave in a barrier experience. This is particularly useful for those patients for whom splitting is a major defense.

UNDOING ROLE-LOCKS

The technique used in modifying role-locks builds on the bracketing technique introduced to identify the trigger for somatic symptoms and depression. The refinement of the bracketing technique for modifying role-locks involves identifying the trigger for the role response so that the people in the role-lock can discover exactly what they are repeating. The act of identifying and describing the facial expression, voice tone, gesture, or posture that triggered the role-lock paves the way for recognizing both the projection and its source from the past. Once the trigger for the role repetition is successfully bracketed, the defensive projection can be isolated, identified, and moved aside so that the underlying conflict that fueled the role-lock can be addressed.

Modifying defensive role-locks lays the foundation for undoing the externalization defense of projective identification, a defense that fuels the crisis of hatred. This work in turn opens the door to the life-and-death struggle with one's own stubborn resistance to change. Modification of this defense occurs after Phase One of group development (authority)—in the transitional phase that precedes the work around intimacy in Phase Two, which is where therapy of the *person* begins! (See Table 4.3.)

With few exceptions, SCT techniques are presented to group members through the teaching of individuals (often in the distraction exercise, when the relationship between the member and the therapist is one-on-one). When the techniques are sufficiently mastered, they become part of the skills of subgrouping, and members can help each other with the methods. The technique for undoing role-locks builds on earlier techniques such as the fork-in-the-road and bracketing. Common to all SCT techniques is the sequential modification of a defense; in the case of projection, defense modification deals first with simple projection, then with more complex forms, and finally with projective identification (Horwitz, 1997a, 1997b).

Undoing projection in role-locks is the first step to undoing a projective identification. The SCT technique for undoing projection is a multistep process, which is the same for both group and individual therapy. The first step is to identify that there is a projection by using a technique learned in the flight subphase of Phase One. Let us say, for example, that a member of a group in the fight subphase of group development says the following: "Janet just raised her hand. She's trying to get the group to notice her and make room for her to speak. I'd like us to do that." If this group had been in the flight subphase, or in the transition subphase between the flight and fight subphases, the major goal for training would be to teach members to check out projections so that the reality-testing climate can be established and consolidated in the group. With this goal in mind, the therapist would encourage the member to check out a mind-read by saying something like "You are interpreting Janet's hand raise as an intention movement that you think you recognize. Would you check out with Janet whether or not you are accurate, as far as Janet is concerned, by asking a yes/no question so that you can validate your reality." However, in the present case, the context is the fight subphase, the major goal of which is to help members work toward understanding the projections and projective identifications in the group. Reaching these goals enables members to undo the two major projections that are acted out in role-locks: taking care of others at the expense of oneself and scapegoating others instead of oneself. This is more complex learning, and the therapist starts the process of surfacing an incipient role-lock by asking the member to identify the observable facts of the trigger:

T: So you interpreted the raised hand as an intention movement asking to be recognized. Was there anything else that caught your attention and fueled your criticism? Voice tone? Posture? Another intention movement?

P: Yes, I think so . . . maybe something in the voice—no, I know, it was the posture! Janet looked submissive. She had her head tilted down, and she was looking out from under her eyebrows. [This identification of the trigger is basic information that will be useful later to this member in recognizing his transference reaction to Janet. However, this is not addressed at this stage of the work.]

T: So you saw Janet in a submissive posture with her hand raised? What did you think when you saw that? [The foundation for answering a question like this has already been laid in the distraction exercise, when the facts of distractions are identified separately from the feelings. Thus, members have already practiced determining whether their feelings are generated by thoughts about the distraction or whether they are generated by the reality of the distracting event itself.]

P: I thought Janet was playing victim.

T: You thought Janet was "in victim." And how did you feel when you thought that?

P: I felt sorry for Janet. I don't think she gets a fair deal when she doesn't stand up for herself. [In this case, the member's feelings are clearly generated from his thoughts about Janet. It cannot yet be determined whether these feelings are similar to or different from the feelings he has in his relationship to the real Janet.]

T: So you thought Janet was not getting a fair deal in the group because she was not sticking up for herself? Did you then try to stick up for her by telling the group to make space?

P: Yes, that's right, I did.

T: What role did you put yourself in, in relationship to Janet, when you did that?

P: Rescuer! [The member recognizes the identified patient–rescuer role-lock.]

T: And do you think by rescuing Janet she will learn to stick up for herself and get herself a fair deal?

P: Now that you frame it that way, no!

T: So do you see that you were moving into the role of helping the identified patient? I wonder if there is a subgroup for that?

As soon as the techniques for undoing the simpler projections are the property of the group, the way is paved for undoing both the projection and the projective identification that is involved in scapegoating. Undoing the role-lock in scapegoating also rests on systematically causing projections to surface: first by recognizing the signs and then by experiencing the symptoms. In the context of the flight subphase, members infer projection by noticing that what they are attributing to the scapegoat is something specifically missing in themselves. After the retaliatory impulse has been recognized by the group, there is a growing awareness of the physical impulse to scapegoat when frustrated. Awareness of the impulse also brings awareness of its strength, and the more terrifying facts of projective identification begin to surface.

Exploring both the impulse to scapegoat and the scapegoating projections are more easily done in a subgroup than in one-on-one interaction between group members and therapist after the transitional subphase between the flight and fight subphases, a phase in which the experience of retaliatory rage is first explored, contained, and depathologized (often in relationship with the leader). In the subphase of fight, the scapegoating impulse can grow so strong that dyadic work between the therapist and a member may precipitate a role-lock instead of insight. The major experience of the scapegoating impulse is therefore better explored in subgrouping. When members' scapegoating impulses are contained in a subgroup, the therapist is more likely to successfully introduce the bracketing technique for encapsulating the projection, and the group is more likely to cooperate with the process of working through to the underlying projective identifications (see Table 10.1). Overall, it is unlikely, that the work of learning how to undo projection and how to bring to the surface the more terrifying facts of projective identification will be completed until after the group has reached Phase Three of group development.

TABLE 10.1. Technique: Undoing Role-Locks

Explore experience in subgroups instead of acting it out.
- *Subgroup* around defiance and compliance and explore the experience.
- *Explore impulse* to make or become an identified patient, victim, martyr, or scapegoat.
- *Discover fork-in-the-road* between turning the retaliatory impulse back on the self in depression and turning it outward against others in hostility.
- *Access sadistic and masochistic fantasies* of retaliatory torturing of leader or other members; explore impulses to volunteer for, and act out, reciprocal roles in masochistic and sadistic role-locks with leader or each other.
- *Gain insight into projective identifications* and the interdependent role suction into reciprocally paired role-locks. Recognize the repetition compulsion in the rationalization "This is my fate and the story of my life!" Understand the communication in the sadomasochistic projective identification "I'll do to you what you did to me, and then you will understand" or "I'll show you! I'll do to me what you did to me, and then you will understand."

UNDOING SCAPEGOATING: SAMPLE THERAPY SESSION

The episode chosen to illustrate the undoing of scapegoating at the individual level is taken from a mature group that has already acquired SCT techniques and considerable acceptance of their underlying impulses. It illustrates the technique of moving aside the simpler projection so that the projective identification emerges and shows how context is the determiner of the therapist's decision about what level of intervention to use. Unless the group regresses under trauma, regression to earlier phases of group development is part of a natural process of deepening and strengthening the ability to work. The sample therapy session includes my own thinking process as I was deciding whether to consolidate current work in the group or to follow the regressive potential. It serves as an example of how SCT manages the dynamics that are undoubtedly familiar to most group psychotherapists. SCT methods for promoting insight into projections may differ from those of other therapies, but the therapist's dilemma and the goals of the interventions are probably very much the same.

The episode in the sample therapy session is a good example of an event that can occur in the context of any phase of group development. How I, the therapist, responded to it, however, was determined by my assessment of several independent criteria: (1) what skills of defense modification had already been acquired by the group; (2) whether the intervention was best targeted to the individual, the subgroup, or the group-as-a-whole; (3) whether the episode was occurring in the context of the current phase or whether there had been a regression to an earlier one. Ideally, defense modification uses the resources available to the system to increase the likelihood of a success experience. This makes it important to determine whether the event is occurring as a regression to an earlier phase, in which case there has been a loss of available resources, or whether the defense is still within the leading edge of the defense modifications that are appropriate to the phase of development the group has reached.

The event occurred in a group that had already revisited issues around authority several different times at differing depths. Approaching this event within the group context of the authority issue would have been salient for the individual involved. However, revisiting the authority issue would not have been as useful for the group-as-a-whole. I therefore made the decision to attempt to undo the projection with the individual member and then to encourage the group to recognize the different levels of experience involved from the perspectives of individual members and the group-as-a-whole. There is a common boundary between the individual system and the group system, just as there is a common boundary between the subgroup system and the member and group-as-a-whole systems. Thus, intervening at the boundary between the individual and the group is an alternative to subgrouping. In this instance the judgment call was supported by the outcome, and both the individual member and the group-as-a-whole had a good experience. It is in thinking diagnostically in this way that the SCT therapist becomes clear about the relationship between the context of the intervention and its goals.

In the distraction exercise at the beginning of this particular group session, I did a considerable amount of work identifying certain members' unconscious intention movements in an effort to increase their awareness of certain defenses. I was probing a deep level of the unconscious dimensions of role-lock, and I was doing so with the belief that the leading edge that was current for the group-as-a-whole was experimenting with how to give and take individual feedback (in addition to the work of subgrouping). Giving and receiving feedback is important work in a mature SCT group in that it consolidates members' taking responsibility not only for modifying their own defenses in and outside the group (the intrapersonal work) but also for modifying the working environment of the group (the systems-centered work). SCT group members often practice steps on the leader before doing so with other members, and at any given time some members are further ahead than others in their work. For some members at this point in the sample group, the restraining forces still outweighed the driving forces to this relatively new group goal of giving and receiving feedback.

The subgrouping and group-member work of the session had gone well, and the group was feeling autonomous and powerful. Two members (I will call them Anne and Bob) had initiated an exploration of the effect of some of my nonverbal intention movements and had questioned whether the effect of these gestures on the group had been neutral or whether they had aroused compliance or defiance. My dilemma was in deciding whether to respond to Anne and Bob's initiative as a regression to the authority issue or whether to cooperate with it as leading-edge work in the service of reality testing and member autonomy. I opted to cooperate, believing that Anne and Bob were trying out new behavior on their leader before experimenting with it on each other.

This transition from working with the leader to working with each other occurred two-thirds of the way through the session, when Anne told Bob that the gesture he made (a dismissive hand movement) when giving me feedback mirrored the very intention movement he was giving me feedback about. In communicating this observation, Anne was crossing another new boundary. This was the first time in this group that one member had given feedback to another member. Not surprisingly, there was some tension in Anne's voice. As soon as she had finished, there was a loud "That's not fair" from Nigel. This was a fight statement, with scapegoating potential. As the leader, I was faced with the need to make another clinical decision: Should I wait to see whether subgrouping would develop around the two sides of the issue of scapegoating author- ity, with member-leaders as the target of scapegoating, or should I work individually with Nigel on the projection? I opted for the second. I wanted to reinforce the skills of undoing projections and also wanted to support the first steps of member-leader behavior. I therefore responded to Nigel with the bracketing technique for undoing role-locks. (In the dialogue below, *N* stands for Nigel, *YA* for me, *A* for Anne, *B* for Bob, and *C* for Claude.)

YA: Nigel, what was the behavior you observed that gave you the idea that Anne was not being fair. [Here I am eliciting a description of the trigger for the projection.]

N: She attacked Bob.

YA: I understand that you experienced Anne attacking Bob. Do you know exactly what the trigger was, what it was that you saw or heard that gave you that idea?

N: The trigger was the way she attacked.

YA: The way she attacked. OK. If you were able to replay the event on a videotape, what would you point out to us as evidence that Anne attacked Bob? [Here I am suggesting a frame for descriptive lan- guage.]

N: What she said and the way she said it.

YA: Do you remember her words?

N: Yes. She said, "You just did the same thing with your hand that you are telling Yvonne about."

YA: And what about the way she said it?

N: Her voice tone was hostile.

YA: OK. And do you remember what you thought when you experi- enced that?

N: Yes, that it wasn't fair that she was trying to get him like that.

YA: And do you remember what you felt when you thought that? [So far, the method I am using mirrors the first steps in undoing a con- structed reality.]

N: That she was scapegoating.

YA: That is another *thought.* Do you remember how you *felt?*

N: I suppose the right answer is that I felt angry.

YA: That isn't the right answer if you did not feel angry. *Did* you feel angry?

N: Yes, I did. I felt angry with Anne. I thought she was not being fair.

YA: OK. Now you know what the trigger was [Anne's communications] and, what you thought about it [unfair], and what feelings were generated by your thoughts about it [anger]. Now, will you move all that aside and find out what relationship you were in, with yourself? [This is a significant departure from earlier techniques with this group. Rather than undoing the constructed reality and pointing out that Nigel's feelings are being generated by his thoughts, which probably do not check out in reality, I am attempting to move the whole projection aside so that Nigel can get direct access to whatever internal conflict triggered his projection.]

N: I don't know what you mean.

YA: I have framed your thoughts and feelings in response to Anne as a projection. It is a projection, whether or not it is an accurate representation of reality. But rather than treating it as a mind-read and asking you to check reality with Anne, I am asking you to pay attention to what your internal experience was. If you move your projection out of your way, do you recall what else was going on in you? [I am suggesting that Nigel himself is the context.]

N: Well, yes. I liked what Bob was doing. I thought it took courage, and I was angry with Anne for scapegoating him.

YA: You liked what Bob was doing. Did you wish you could do what Bob was doing?

N: No. If I try to do what Bob does, I get myself scapegoated. (*Long pause*) But now that you mention it, I would like to do like Bob. But I wouldn't want to be scapegoated for it. It's too easy for me to set myself up as a scapegoat.

YA: So you are at a fork-in-the-road. You can work with Bob in his subgroup, or you can start a subgroup exploring the impulse to scapegoat Anne. Do you know which way you want to go?

N: I'd rather join Bob and ignore Anne.

YA: (*To the group*) Anyone else confronted with the same kind of choice?

C: Well, as a matter of fact, now that Nigel is exploring this, I realize that I was in a different subgroup. I want to be able to do what Anne did, and I had an impulse to scapegoat Nigel.

YA: Nigel mentioned voice tone. Did anyone else react to Anne's voice tone?

C: Yes, I did, but I just thought she was nervous because she was trying to do something new.

A: As a matter of fact, I could hear tension in my voice, too. I was nervous. I had to push myself across the boundary and do it anyway, and I'm pleased that I did.

B: I'm pleased that you did. Nigel, do you believe that I didn't feel scapegoated?

C: Now I do!

For Nigel, with the projection onto Anne moved aside and the incipient authority issue role-lock avoided, it was possible to undo the projection of his conflict with his own authority onto the group and to regain the part of himself that wanted to identify with Bob and to be an authority. It was also clear that Nigel carried the potential for a rerun of the authority issue for the group; with a tendency toward projecting the part of himself that fears being scapegoated into a target that he then scapegoats, just as he initiated scapegoating Anne. By undoing the projection, he saw clearly that his underlying fear was that if he took the personal authority that he wanted to take, he would be scapegoated—much as he scapegoated himself whenever he so much as thought of taking a leadership role in the group. Later, in "surprises and learnings," Nigel reported a flash of insight that linked his response to Bob with his childhood attempts to speak up like his father and say "brave things" in the family, attempts that were aborted by his mother, who would tell him, "You're being too big for your britches." When Nigel first entered the group, he was afraid of being scapegoated; he was very surprised to learn, when he checked it out, that the group was determined not to scapegoat him. Since joining the group, he had made significant changes in his relationships on the job, and he was continuing to work with his tendency to be caught in a passive–compliant role-lock. If the group sequence presented above had been acted out instead of understood, Nigel would have been in a role-lock with Anne, with a potential for a group regression into a fight. As the group discussed the event, other members identified with different aspects of the issues that had been voiced for them by Bob, by Anne, by Nigel, and by Claude. The strong response suggests that this was a fulcrum event for the group-as-a-whole.

INDIVIDUAL ROLE-LOCK DEFENSES AND SUBGROUPING

Role-lock defenses characterize the person's relationships to work, intimacy, and authority. They can be separated into those that deal largely with relationships with authority and those that deal largely with relationships in intimacy. Role-locks are characteristic roles that we play over and over again, as we seek out others who will cooperate with us: identified patient and caretaker, victim and exploiter, martyr and hero, scapegoat and scapegoater, leader and follower. These reciprocal role relationships always serve a function both for the individual and for the social group in which they are repeated. The most important role-locks for Module 2 of defense modification in the fight subphase are the defiant and compliant role-locks with authority. These are the relationships that lock us into a power struggle with an outside authority and blind us to the stubborn conflicts with the authority in ourselves. Recognizing one's own particular tendency to repeat with others reciprocal role relationships is the first step in undoing all the role-lock defenses.

Identified Patient and Caretaker

Undoing the identified patient–caretaker role-lock requires recognizing how one is volunteering for one of these roles and how a split-off part of the self is projected onto one's role partner. Thus, the caretaker of the identified patient reexperiences the part of the self that wants care, a desire that is manifested repeatedly by the tendency to volunteer for the same old role. Undoing the identified patient–caretaker defense requires recognizing defensive denial. When a denied event is brought to our attention, we recognize it as something we have always known. Thus, abandoning the identified patient–caretaker role-lock is not as difficult as it first seems.

Scapegoat and Scapegoater

Undoing the scapegoat–scapegoater role-lock requires working with the mutual projective identification. This work is not as simple as taking back a projection of a split-off part of the self that can be both recognized and reexperienced. The first step in undoing scapegoating entails recognizing one's social collusion. Undoing scapegoating requires education about how to recognize the communication patterns and behaviors in society that set up the scapegoat, including one's own delegation of self or other for the role. Since scapegoating involves both projection and projective identification, unconscious repression must be made conscious before the scapegoating defense is mastered.

Defiant and Compliant Relationships with Authorities

Authority role relationship defenses manage the one-up–one-down relationship between the self and the other in perceived unequal authority relationships. That relationship is manifested in defensive compliance or defiance and is in the service of protecting the self from disappointments in functional dependency. Defiant and compliant role relationships are the most important role-lock defenses to modify in the fight subphase of Phase One, as they would otherwise result in a premature power struggle with the therapist. As role-locks with authority closely mirror difficulties with past and present authorities, it is important to build a solid foundation before they surface in the virulence of the crisis of hatred in Module 3. Like scapegoating, role-locks with authority involve projective identifications. The goal of this work is to have patients recognize the signals in themselves that trigger their defiant and compliant responses, so that they can better manage their impulses to act on those responses. Work with role-locks is preparation for work on the underlying issues, which cannot be addressed without first dealing with the underlying projections. Becoming conscious of the communication and behavioral patterns that set up scapegoating and defiant/compliant relationships with one's self and with others is a significant step in understanding the defenses, an achievement that in turn significantly reduces self-sabotaging role-locks.

Subgrouping around Defiance and Compliance

The techniques derived from the systems-centered view provide alternatives to acting out group tensions in scapegoating. From the beginning of the first subphase of group development, SCT members are introduced to the idea that they project onto others that which they are not able to address in themselves, and they work on "taking back" their projections. They learn that it is the hurt self that is split off and projected into the identified patient and that it is the unacceptable self that is split off, projected onto the scapegoat, and treated as unacceptable. Recognizing the projections that underlie the impulse to scapegoat gives group members the opportunity to become more sophisticated about the process of attempting to take back whatever parts of themselves they can identify. This identification is accomplished either through recognizing a disowned similarity or by recognizing a suspicious absence of any similarities. Functional subgrouping again provides the context for the work, and group members are encouraged to join the subgroup that would be most useful for them in their work. Again, ambivalence is treated as a defense against experiencing the conflict, and subgrouping is presented as a way of choosing to work one side of the conflict. In this way, all members work first with their chosen half of the conflict; they do so, in the context of subgroup support, until the natural development of subgrouping raises the other side of the conflict.

When the authority issue is not acted out but is explored instead, the voices of the compliant and defiant subgroups can be heard clearly. The major role-locks that are relevant to the work of Module 2 of defense modification are the one-up–one-down power struggles that are acted out in conflicts with authority. Through subgroup work, the consequences of the compliant and defiant roles are experienced as giving power to others while keeping powerlessness for the self. This insight is but a step away from revisiting the masochism (and underlying sadism) in compliance and the sadism (with the underlying masochism) in defiance. Subgrouping around defiance and compliance permits the exploration, rather than the acting out, of the behavior that is predominantly stereotypically dependent or counterdependent (or conforming or rebellious), behavior that is rarely relevant to the goals of the group but highly relevant to the politics of survival. By subgrouping, the actively compliant subgroup learns about their identification with the aggressor and their tendency to try to bully other members into compliance with authority. Meanwhile, members of the actively compliant and the passively defiant subgroups explore the many manifestations of their overt and covert sabotage of authority.

The Passively Compliant Subgroup

Exploration of role-locks with authority comes more easily to the subgroup working around passive compliance, since masochism is a more socially acceptable defense than sadism and suspicion, which are part of defiance. The following doggerel caricatures the stereotypical responses to authority that are typically seen in groups in which the early phases of group dynamics are acted out rather than explored and members are trapped in a role-lock with the leader, with the group, and with themselves:

> Tell us to jump and we'll ask, "How high?"
> We promise never to ask you why!

Patients who are caught in the passively compliant role-lock appear to be obedient, conforming, pleasing, adaptive, and lovingly and trustingly merging; they are given to flight and avoidance and expressing love. As such members explore the passive and compliant aspect of their role-lock with authority, it comes as useful insight to them to see how easy it is for them to volunteer as the identified patient in the group and how often the group volunteers them. In exploring this, members of the passively compliant subgroup will typically recognize a consistent and debilitating underlying depression that has defended them against the full experience of both their disappointment and their aggression when they, as identified patients, are not cured in the flight subphase. It is more difficult for this subgroup to experience the aggression they defend against; they tend to act it out in sabotaging their subgroup, the therapist, and themselves by following the letter but not the spirit of the law. It is in successful subgroup exploration in the context of the fight subphase that members in the passive–compliant role-lock deepen their insight into their mutual projections and their tendency to deny their retaliatory impulse and turn it back on themselves.

The Actively Compliant Subgroup

> We'll stand on your shoulders and speak with your voice;
> Enforcing your rules without question or choice.

The discoveries for members in an actively compliant role-lock are hard-won. In exploring their role-lock with authority, individual members of an actively compliant subgroup discover that they are torn between a tendency to be obedient, conforming, and adaptive to the leader (whom they overestimate) and a tendency to bully subordinates (whom they denigrate). Fiercely protective of the identified patients, righteous about obeying orders without question, sadistic and sarcastic to differences, these individuals often live inside a barrier experience from which it is difficult to recognize their similarities to others—even to those in their own subgroup. It is important to ensure that such patients develop their self-observation work in the supportive context of a subgroup. The deeper the exploration, the clearer it becomes that their well-being depends on their being accepted as the right hand of the leader. It is crucial for these members to discover that when they are not rewarded for acting out this role, they are in danger of turning their retaliatory impulse toward the leader back on themselves in a painful, and potentially serious, depressive reaction.

The Defiant Subgroup

> Whatever you say we will do the reverse,
> We dare you to say that we are perverse.

Subgrouping around the defiant role-lock leads members to recognize, with wry humor, that while following the SCT rules makes both intuitive sense and common sense, they would nevertheless rather die than comply. It is in subgroup work that members get a glimpse of how their power struggle is with a role-lock in relation to the stubbornness in themselves and is not just a role-lock with any outer authority. Subgrouping around explorations into defiant role-locks leads members to own tendencies that are rebellious, nonconforming, resistant to influence, stubborn, individualistic, contentious, and authoritarian. The defiant subgroup battles constantly against the impulse to take a stand against any group issue. Paradoxically, it is the work of the defiant subgroup that creates the safety that ultimately enables group members to face their issues with authority and make the transition into the intimacy phase of group development, Phase Two.

ROLE-LOCKS WITH THE PAST: TRANSFERENCE

One of the great tragedies of traditional psychotherapy is the attention to childhood memories without considering the context in which they are being remembered. If the context is the set of defenses addressed in Module 2, memories are filtered through those defenses and are recalled in terms of one-up–one-down (dominant–submissive) relationships. When issues with authority are externalized, the experience of relationships with authority is inevitably framed and fixated in terms of victims and scapegoats. Thus, these one-up–one-down relationships from the past are repeated in the here-and-now of group work in the fight subphase. In contrast, when childhood memories are explored in the context of defenses against intimacy (in Modules 4 and 5 of SCT defense modification), memories from the past are understood in terms of the basic conflict of intimacy, that is, between the relationships one wants versus the relationships one can make.

We see the manifestations of transferential and countertransferential phenomena at every level of the hierarchy of human systems when we focus on reciprocal role relationships. For example, we can see the scapegoating role relationship at all levels of the human hierarchical systems, whether we are hating a part of ourselves, hating the bad apple in the small groups or neighborhoods of our community, or hating some ethnic or religious group in our country. Transferential phenomena are behind recognizable role relationships at all system levels, whether we identify the "other" as the identified patient in a therapy group, the homeless in the community, another group's religion, or another nation's leader.

Transference and countertransference transactions, as well as projective identifications, are familiar to the psychoanalytic experience. It can well be argued that it is in the dynamics of these phenomena, however accessed, that cultural as well as personal transformation takes place. We can see it clearly when we look at dimensions of development in different cultures: Changes in the role of women, for example, or in childrearing practices are not just a change in norms but a change in relationship possibilities; they are a function of a change at the unconscious (transferential) level. It was Jung who focused on the *social* need to work through social projective identifications to preclude a repetition of a worldwide acting out of hate, such as in the role-lock between Nazis and Jews.

The concept of transference can be applied to the psychobiological level as well. There is an isomorphy of structure and function between transferential transactions between the known and the unknown. Biological systems develop from the biological ooze, the undifferentiated matter-energy pool we name chaos, to the living cell and, finally, to hierarchical societies. Psychobiologically, however, it is human beings who have developed a social system that can transfer sign, signal, and symbol over space and time. And I would say that the difference that distinguishes the human from the animal social system is a transferential unconscious communication process (a phenomenon that is more advanced than imprinting) between the unconscious selves of people (in addition to the conscious communication between people) that involves discrimination, integration, and transformation. (Transference will be addressed again when we discuss the defenses against intimacy, the fork-in-the-road between hope and despair, and the role of transferences in the interdependent phase of work.)

Chapter 11

Resistance-to-Change Defenses

*M*oving into the "crisis of hatred" is a fulcrum experience in both group and individual therapy. This experience marks the transition from Phase One, in which issues around power and control are salient, to Phase Two, in which issues around intimacy arise. How this transitional phase plays out will depend to a great extent on how deeply defensive sadism has been experienced and on how thoroughly role-locks have been understood. In both group and individual SCT, the crisis of hatred, which is expressed in a role-lock with the therapist, is an experience of paranoid rage fueled by sadism. Psychoanalytically oriented therapists refer to it as the negative transference; in group dynamics it is also known as "the authority issue." Bennis and Shepard (1956) called it a "barometric event."

The dynamics of the authority issue are the fulcrum dynamics of the process of change in all human systems, from simple to complex. Taking issue with authority occurs within the self, in dyads, in subgroups, in small groups, in large groups, and in the group-as-a-whole. It is common to individuals, families, social and business organizations, communities, and nations. It is as old as the human race and it fuels revolutions and wars. It never sleeps; a leviathan, it stirs restlessly in the depth of human experience and is easily aroused.

In group and individual therapy, the authority issue is the crucible in which the major defense of externalization is permanently altered. The defense of externalization projects onto others or the outside world the forces that restrain personal development, instead of confronting the difficulties of the change process in themselves. Externalization defenses put the locus of change energy outside the self and thus attribute the source of both good and bad to others. The result is a particularly intractable barrier experience. In SCT groups, the preparatory work of modifying resistance to change is done before the crisis of hatred by exploring the roles that members play out in the group, including the reciprocal role-locks of the defiant and compliant subgroups. Modifying resistance to change requires modifying the tendency to take things personally in a self-centered world and thus potentiates the ability to take responsibility for the self in a systems-centered world.

There are two major relationships to authority: positive and negative. The positive relationship is the half of the authority issue that can be contained and explored in subgroups with relative ease. This is not true of the negative relationship to authority, which fuels the crisis of hatred. The primal impulses underlying the negative relationship with authority are experienced as violent and murderous rage by patients who feel locked in a life-and-death struggle with the therapist. What is remarkable is that it is through accessing this primal rage that the transition is made from adversarial preoccupations to friendship, from hatred to love.

MANAGEMENT OF THE AUTHORITY ISSUE IN SCT

In SCT groups much of the preliminary work for moving through the transition from Phase One, the phase of authority, to Phase Two, the phase of intimacy, has already been done in that group members recognize how the retaliatory impulse is played out in one-up-one-down role-locks. The underlying dynamics explored in the authority issue are no different from those that were explored in these earlier experiences. What is different in the transitional phase is the depth of the exploration and the intensity of the experience. This depth and intensity leads group members to face the cost involved in externalizing conflicts with the self onto outside authorities: The cost is the disowning of one's personal authority.

There are four significant steps in the process of managing the authority issue: (1) understanding how the dynamics of sadomasochism relate to conflicts with authority, (2) exploring the paranoia and hatred involved in the impulses to scapegoat the therapist, (3) confronting the barrier experience of stubbornness, and (4) recognizing resistance to change.

Sadomasochism

The work of sadomasochism that was done in exploring the retaliatory impulse is revisited in the authority issue in ways that introduce a new dimension to subgroup work. It is at this stage that group members are encouraged to change subgroups so that they can explore first one and then the other side of the split. Members thus alternate between their feelings of power and control and their fears of being punished, revisit their guilt, and observe their guilty thoughts about their guilt-free feelings. As subgroup work deepens their experience, members join one subgroup to explore the pleasure in sadism, which relates to the feeling of power, control, and safety from the feelings of helplessness, and then "subgroup hop" to the other subgroup to explore compassion, toward those in whom they have caused pain as well as toward themselves for the pain that others have caused them. There is also a revisiting of the following double message, which comes from a condensed experience of love and hate and which is strangely unconflicted when it is understood: "I hate you for what you did to me and will get even by doing it to you; I love you as I do this to you because by experiencing what I experienced you will understand how you hurt me and will return the love so that you will love me as I love you."

Increased understanding of the projective identifications that underlie the acting out of sadomasochistic relationships develops the therapeutic potential to contain rather than respond and is therefore preparation for the powerful role suction of the authority issue. The hatred toward authority experienced during this phase springs not only from the object-related defiant and compliant transferences of Phase One of group development but also from the objectless transferences of primary experience. The defiant and compliant transferences are first explored as defensive role-locks. The objectless transference of primary experience (arising from the early atmosphere between the child and the mother that is unconsciously reproduced in relationship to the world and hence to the group-as-a-whole) is unlikely to surface until well into Phase Three, the phase of interdependent work. Both levels of transference, however, are mobilized in the crisis of hatred. Thus, the therapist's own countertransference responses (inevitably aroused in the role suction of the authority issue) will be to both the role transferences and the pervasive transference of primary experience.

In their own training experiences, therapists are likely to have familiarized themselves with the painful vulnerability to reciprocal role transferences. And, in fact, they will already have been challenged not to act out role-locks in the earlier phases of group development. The source of pervasive transference, however, is always unconscious, and the work of making the unconscious conscious never ends. Thus, the therapist will always be most vulnerable to the virulence of the negative transference whenever it manifests itself—and never more so than in the crucible of the authority issue.

One of the more difficult role-locks to recognize is when a dyad looks like a subgroup but is actually serving as a split-off container for a group projective identification. When the therapist is a member of the dyad, it is not only more difficult to maintain objectivity but sometimes impossible to even recognize that he or she is caught up in such a pairing. The clue for therapists is an increasing pressure in themselves to convert the member they are paired with, and the growing conviction that to impose their interpretation on the member is for the person's own good. At worst, the therapist can become convinced that the only thing wrong with the group is this particular patient, thus mirroring the patient's conviction that the only thing wrong with the group is the therapist. The phenomenon of being paired with a group member to contain the authority issue for the group happens to every therapist sooner or later—and more frequently for some than for others. The underlying dynamics include the projection from the group into the containing dyad and a negative transference and countertransference between the paired therapist and patient. Recognizing their experience as countertransference, with an underlying projective identification, is a difficult self-confrontation for therapists, who are usually under the impression that they are working with a patient's resistance when in reality they are scapegoating the patient.

This therapist–patient role-lock, endemic in the authority issue in groups, is best managed at the beginning, before the group has had the opportunity to consolidate the role-lock. This is relatively easy when the therapist has not taken the role-lock personally but difficult when he or she has and is in a barrier experience. The easiest way to avoid the role-lock is to rely on the group-level process of subgrouping. With subgroups working around similarities and identifying differences, there is an ongoing opportunity for the group to reabsorb the split-off pair and restore a working environment. Managing the impulses to pair and be paired, and maintaining individual member experience at a level that is no deeper than each subgroup can contain makes it less likely that the therapist will get caught in a role-lock with a member or with the group. Working through the authority issue is dependent on the therapist's being able to maintain the role boundaries in the group and to maintain subgroups as containers for the work.

If it should happen that the therapist is caught in a role-lock dyad and the group has projected into the role-lock and isolated the patient and therapist from the group, the therapist has few alternatives but to struggle as best they can, to contain the pressure to act out sometimes for weeks or even months until the transferences and countertransferences have been metabolized. An SCT alternative is for therapists to disclose to the patient their personal experience. In doing so, they are relying on the fact that their experiences, since they are in the same subgroup, will be more alike than different. In this case, the barrier that must be converted into a permeable boundary is between the patient and the therapist. Since it is unlikely that the patient will be able to initiate the rapprochement—and since the group cannot—it is the therapist who must find a way to change the communication pattern. Thus, in spite of the rule of thumb that therapist disclosure is likely to be used as ammunition rather than as information in the phase of authority, disclosure is worth a try. The therapist might say something like this:

> "I have a sense that you and I are having the same kind of experience. I am feeling that if you would only understand what I am saying to you, everything would be all right. I feel frustrated and angry—and frightened that we are never going to work this out. Do you resonate with any of what I have said? Do you feel that about me, too?"

Scapegoating the Therapist

Typically, in the crisis of hatred it is the group that actively scapegoats the therapist as the paranoid object, as opposed to the therapist's crisis of hatred, in which the therapist, caught in a role-lock, scapegoats a patient. The act of scapegoating the therapist expresses the sum of hatred and grief that was aroused in group members by early failures in mirroring, attunement, and empathy. It is the process of moving into and through the here-and-now group experience of scapegoating the therapist that modification is made to this early hatred and paranoia in group members. When members experience in the containment of the group the unconscious fantasies they had feared, something is permanently changed. An "awe-ful" unconscious has been made conscious, and the work of integration can begin.

This crisis of paranoid hatred that arises from the group and coalesces in the negative transference is familiar to most group leaders. Not only is it common in therapy groups; but also in training groups, as described by Bennis and Shepard (1956) and in today's Tavistock, A. K. Rice, and group-as-a-whole groups. Freud (1922) framed this crisis in terms of a primitive ritual murder of the leader: "These many individuals eventually banded themselves together, killed (the father) and cut him in pieces. . . . They then formed the totemistic community of brothers, all with equal rights and united by the totem prohibitions which were to preserve and to expiate the memory of the murder."

Many group therapists understand "prohibitions" to mean a solution to the problem of competition for power among the members of the community (or group), who would murder each other, as well as the father (leader), if their rivalry were not contained. Others interpret the term to mean a symbolic communion that takes the power of the leader—that is, the power that was projected onto the leader (a nascent democracy!)— into each member and also takes it back into the group-as-a-whole.

The dilemma for all group therapists, whatever their style, is how to contain the regressive, primitive, and often bloody and violent fantasies of destruction that emerge spontaneously. Sometimes the therapist is seen as some animal that is savaged, murdered, thrown into the middle of the group. Sometimes group members experience themselves as violent and bloody animals feeding on the carcass, with blood dripping from their faces. Other times the fantasy is that the therapist is thrown onto a pyre, danced around, roasted, and eaten. Sometimes a duality of impulse is experienced: a desire to rend and tear at flesh in savage hunger and, at the same time, to swallow and digest and grow satisfied and full inside. Often, the work is followed by a rush of gratitude and love that the therapist can contain so much hate; afterward, in the relief, there can be a profound feeling of group communion (Agazarian, 1994).

In my more chaotic moments in leading Tavistock small groups and in my earlier days of working with large groups, I experienced, as have many other leaders, moments when I was convinced that I would be killed (and maybe eaten!) by the group (Agazarian & Carter, 1993). The change in the depth of this experience came gradually for me as I developed the SCT methods of boundarying and accompanied many SCT groups into the experiences that lie underneath the destructive impulses, which I believed, up until recently, were the nexus of the authority issue. I am now convinced that how the underlying dynamics of the authority issue are manifested has less to do with the inherent destructiveness of the human race and more to do with how the hatred and paranoia in the group are boundaried. That is, it is not the virulence of the dynamics but the way the dynamics are contained that determines the resolution of issues with authority both in groups and individual therapy.

It is for this reason that it is particularly important in structuring the group through this phase that the therapist determine what regressions are useful and how they are to be contained. This is relevant not only to individual and group psychotherapy but also to training models. If ever there was a case for tempering the wind to the shorn lamb, the management of the authority issue is it. When setting up the structure for the management of the negative transference that is expressed in the authority issue, it is important for the therapist to remember that the greater the ambiguity and the greater the deprivation of feedback, the stronger the experience will be. The responsibility of SCT will be to research the methodology that establishes the boundaries of each phase of the developing systems in therapy and to continue to identify the driving and restraining forces for containing the impulse to act out. Much of the anguish in therapy and training arises from the therapist's failure to establish appropriate boundaries so that the negative transferences can be sufficiently contained to allow their components to be recognized and integrated.

Originally, a goal in SCT groups was simply to contain the full experience of hatred. More recently, the goal has been to have hatred transformed. In Pat de Mare's words, "hate . . . which in Greek also means grief . . . constitutes the basis for psychic energy . . . distinct from an instinctual process," and the "structuring of hate through dialogue constitutes transformation" (de Mare, Piper, & Thompson, 1991, p. 141).

Stubbornness

Stubbornness as a defense develops early and is therefore relatively primitive. In fact, stubbornness would be better named survival stubbornness, as it is the mechanism by which the remaining core of the original, spontaneous, primal self survives the socialization process. Stubbornness is a driving force in relationship to autonomy; it is essential to the individuation of each human being—and inconvenient to those in the role of socializer, as every parent of a 2-year-old knows. Stubbornness preserves the self-centered self and keeps a tenacious grip on life; we humans do not give up easily. It is a barrier experience when it is used to resist transformation, but it is a driving force toward development and transformation when it is in the service of the therapeutic task. Stubbornness involves endurance, tenacity, strength, courage, and will. It is stubbornness that fuels the grim, despairing determination to go on with life—or the decision to end it. Stubbornness is *the* driving force when survival is at stake. It is the survival mechanism that enables the system to continue when its natural energy is exhausted and it is not in a situation where it can regenerate itself, when its survival depends merely on continuing to work (a dynamic highly relevant to the workaholism of today's work world). Stubbornness enables human beings to stand up to pressure, to refuse to be bullied, to fight back against all odds, to endure the unendurable, to find their way out of jungles and deserts, to conquer the wilderness, and to survive concentration camps. Stubbornness is not something that a human being wills to switch on or off but a mechanism that switches on automatically. Indeed, it is very difficult to switch off, which is what makes it such a tragedy when the automatic pilot of stubbornness switches on as a restraining force governing the human system away from its natural drive.

Stubbornness is another one of the many human experiences that have such a bad name that people are typically reluctant to acknowledge them. Initial work in a therapy group in identifying stubbornness typically has a serious and heavy tone, with members tending to accuse themselves

or others of having this characteristic. The first step in the group, therefore, is to focus on legitimizing the reality of the experience of stubbornness. Exploring the stubbornness experience from the safety of subgroups
significantly reduces the criticality with which stubbornness is viewed.

The physical posture that telegraphs stubbornness is often obvious:
People fold their arms, cross their legs, and pull back their head; sometimes they glower, and often their whole body looks resistant. In spite of
the fact that this posture is so obvious to onlookers, people in this posture are often unaware that they are communicating stubbornness. The
next step after legitimizing the experience of stubbornness is to arouse
people's curiosity and ask them to experience the difference between sitting centered and "sitting stubborn." As soon as people are willing to
experiment with their posture, they are out of the barrier experience.

As probably every therapist knows, there is a great temptation to enter
into a deadlock with the patient or group that has retreated into
stubbornness. For this reason, it is extremely important for therapists to
understand the full dimensions of the issues around resistance to change.
When the strength and primitive nature of the impulses underlying the
resistance are better understood, it is easier for therapists to avoid reacting
to their own frustrations and entering into a stubborn, uphill power struggle with a patient or therapy group.

As in most defense modification, the criterion that signals the shift
from an ego-syntonic to an ego-dystonic relationship with stubbornness is a
change of attitude toward the defense. When sense of humor and common
sense are restored, the power of all restraining forces is reduced. What is
more, both sources of knowledge—the imagination of comprehension and
the intuition of apprehension—are again available. Table 11.1 depicts the
force field of major driving and restraining forces in stubbornness.

Stubbornness as a Barrier to Shame

Undoing stubbornness requires both intrapersonal (intrasystem) and
interpersonal (intersystem) work. The intrasystem work requires finding
a way to make the boundary permeable while the person is in the barrier

TABLE 11.1. The Force Field of Stubbornness

Driving forces—>	<—Restraining forces
Fortitude and tenacity—>	<—Stubbornness
Common sense—>	<—Closed mind
Sense of humor—>	<—Concrete thinking
Taking things in context—>	<—Taking things "just personally"

experience of stubbornness. Success or failure in this task rests heavily on how successfully the patient has learned about shame. It is important that feelings of embarrassment, humiliation, shame, or shyness are recognized as barrier feelings that protect a boundary and that they are not made into problems.

In the experience of stubbornness, the sense of shame is absent. In fact, stubbornness is often a defense against shame, and the process of coming out of stubbornness can easily reactivate the shame that has been avoided. Crossing through the turbulence at the boundary (going in and coming out over the thresholds of shame) is much easier in a subgroup, where the different kinds of mortification that are aroused in members can be shared and contained.

It is stubbornness that fuels the role-lock with authority. There is much at stake here. What the subgroups are at the edge of discovering is that the stubborn role-lock with authority masks the yearning to be able to depend on an authority to "fix" reality, as well as the bitter disappointment that results when life does not improve. Understanding how inherently frustrating and disappointing the world and life can be is a difficult boundary to cross. Even more difficult for members to discover is that the power struggle with outside authority is no different from the power struggle with their own inner authority. Indeed, the intractable stubborn role-lock with themselves mirrors the role-lock with authority that they have just resolved.

Once in stubbornness, it is almost impossible to change one's role, however strong the wish. For example, a therapy group member cried out, with some wry humor, to the leader, "You are telling me how to do exactly what I have always wanted to do, and I can see when others do it your way, they get exactly what they want—but however much I want to, I'll be damned if I am going to give in." This is a good illustration of how the struggle against one's own authority engages the same active defiance (or passive compliance) that characterizes one's struggle against others' authority. The stubborn defense against change is much easier done than undone. It is a poignant experience to recognize the dilemma and confront the costs of acting out. At the very instant that we become aware of how many of the problems in our work life and our love life we have created for ourselves, we experience great grief for the life we have not lived.

It is not until the stubborn struggle is detached from the relationship with outside authority and owned as a struggle against taking personal authority over one's own life that the true work of therapy begins. The conflict between the stubborn insistence that the forces inhibiting personal change are in the hands of outside authority and the powerful impulse to own one's own authority is experienced as a life-or-death struggle—and is a major resistance to change.

Resistance to Change

Resistance to change is always an attempt to maintain the system as it is. Whether it is useful or not depends on the goal. It is important to be able to resist change whenever the system is going through a period of integration and consolidation. It is important *not* to resist change when the system is at the edge of a transformation. Resistance to change is called stubbornness or obstinacy when it stands in the way of a socially approved goal; it is called tenacity or fortitude or determination when it is harnessed to achieving that goal.

Resistance has long been accepted as inherent to the process of therapy. From an SCT perspective, resistance is understood as inherent to the process of *change* in the context of therapy, not to the process of therapy itself. This is an important point in that it seems obvious that every form of therapy arouses some form of resistance. There are both driving and restraining forces inherent to the developmental process of every system. Defense modification systematically weakens the specific restraining forces that pace the development of the phases and subphases of the SCT group. SCT techniques for defense modification tend to pace both the phases of development of the group and the unfolding of the underlying dynamics. Because of SCT's use of the method of subgrouping, many of the resistances that are expected do not surface in a familiar form. This does not mean that SCT evokes less resistance. The same kinds of resistances are evoked, but these are managed differently. Where SCT differs from those therapies that "respect" resistance is in the methods it uses for modifying resistance.

The major resistance to change in all phases of SCT group development is the resistance to moving from certainty to uncertainty, from the known to the unknown. SCT addresses this from the beginning of therapy by encouraging members to "sit at the edge of the unknown" while they compare their experience of their defensive self (which they know well) with their experience of their undefended self (which they are in the process of discovering). Moreover, since patients are encouraged to work only when they experience resonance for work, resistance is not so readily mobilized.

In the authority phase of group development, the full strength of resistance to change is recognized. Members face both the fear of change and the fear of not changing. All the imprisoning rules and regulations a patient is rebelling against are also the only guidelines to living that he or she knows. This crisis within the self is essentially a solo journey, whether it is contained by the subgroup or by the individual therapist.

SAMPLE CASE

The following paragraphs describe one person's journey in individual therapy from imprisoning rules to freedom. The confrontation with resistance to change came at a point when the patient was almost ready to complete her therapy. First, there was a return of the authority issue. The patient resented any influence from me, and every question of mine was experienced as a command. An old role-lock returned in which the patient's impulse to set up a compliant role relationship set off deep resentment in her. In one session the resistance was deeper and more impassioned than usual. The patient was convinced that I was trying to govern how she thought, and she was ready to kill for her freedom— either herself or me. I responded by saying that many people throughout the ages had in fact died for intellectual freedom, that she was in their subgroup, and that I, apparently, was in a subgroup with the Grand Inquisition and McCarthy. The patient was not reassured. However, she did regain sufficient containment to be able to look at her conflict instead of remaining locked in stubborn defiance; her observing self-system was reestablished. Nevertheless, she was white with terror and could hardly bear her experience. Nor was she able to accept support from me.

Confronting her choices, the patient insisted that she was in an impossible position: On one side was the world of rules and regulations she could no longer bear to live in; on the other was the absolute unknown. Even the fleeting thought of letting go of the rules and regulations was, to her, like falling into an abyss. It was too terrifying, too "awe-ful," too much. She told me that it had been a mistake for her to come to therapy at all; that she should have remained in ignorance, that anything was better than seeing a choice she could not make. She asked me how I could have brought her to this point. When I told her it was because I was her therapist, she seemed to derive some small comfort from my response.

And so the patient sat, in conflict between having a choice and being too afraid to make it. She comprehended her dilemma but was too terrified to apprehend it. This was the moment of annihilation anxiety— what many people know as the terror of falling apart. All too often this is interpreted in therapy without giving patients the understanding that what is falling apart is not the self but their relationship to their adapted self, that what is happening is like the splitting of a chrysalis that allows a new being to emerge, one that can only be known after the transition has been made. This is the crux of the resistance to change. What fuels the resistance is a terror of the unknown that is so great that it is experienced as a threatened annihilation of everything. As we sat together in her terror, the patient gradually regained some color. She rediscovered her curiosity. A second or two later—an interval we experienced as an eternity—she apprehended what it meant to be herself.

I have used this experience from individual therapy to illustrate the seriousness of the work for people when they confront their resistance to change. Confronting resistance means giving up attributing the source of one's personal restrictions to the rules and regulations of external and inconsistent authority and facing instead the task of developing and accepting one's own authority. As my patient said, "There is an awesome responsibility to being yourself."

This same journey is easier for patients in subgroups. With subgroups to contain both sides of the experience, individual members can do the work that is appropriate to where they are in relation to becoming themselves; at the same time, they can see for themselves that those who have gone further have come to no harm. As in all other work in SCT, it is not that this work is any easier than the work performed by patients in other therapies but that it is done with less terror.

The consequences of working with the core of the resistance to change are permanent. When this patient returned for her next therapy session, she looked different. Her face was relaxed, it looked wider, somehow, and softer. I understood what people mean when they say someone looks radiant. I remarked to the patient that she looked different; I told her how pretty she looked. She, who seldom appreciated her looks, smiled and said, "I was just feeling pretty." She told me that she had enjoyed the weekend and had not wanted it to end, even though she had been alone, and that she had so much she wanted to do. She told me that her period had come and gone and that she did not have the migraine that inevitably accompanied it. She told me that her familiar moment of despair had occurred at the boundary between the end of her workweek and the beginning of the weekend but that she had said to herself, "This is just turbulence at the boundary," and had gone home smiling. She talked of a difficult meeting at work in which the atmosphere had been tense; of how curious she had been about what was causing the tension; and of how she had suddenly recognized the difference between just "being there and wondering" (containing her emotion and maintaining her curiosity) and taking things personally.

EVERYDAY RESISTANCE TO CHANGE

The full drama of the life-and-death experience of the human struggle is contained in the clinical vignette presented above. It is just such a peak moment in therapy that makes all the moments of frustration and despair, all the retrenching and starting again, worthwhile for both therapists and patients. This chapter ends, however, with the ongoing management of the resistance to change that must be addressed over and over again, every day. The dialogue below is probably all too familiar to every therapist, every group member, every patient, everyone. It seems to be a good way to end a chapter on resistance.

MEMBER 1: This work is too hard.

MEMBER 2: It's simply too hard.

MEMBER 3: I know what you mean. It never stops.

M1: You no sooner manage one thing and you're face-to-face with another.

MEMBER 4: I'm tired.

M2: Me, too.

M3: And fed up!

M1: There's got to be another way.

M4: Something easier.

M2: It should be easier.

M1: Why can't it be easier?

M4: I'm sure there's something wrong. Change shouldn't be this hard.

M2: You ought to be able to learn something and put it behind you.

T: Like the three questions for anxiety!

M1: Right on! You should be able to learn them and that's it.

M3: Learn them once and never have to use them.

M2: Well, at least not have to keep using them, over and over—

M4: Every time you get anxious—

M1: Ask those three stupid questions.

M3: Every time you make a negative prediction, make yourself believe your common sense.

M4: Every time you get preoccupied, vector your energy.

M2: Sit at the edge of the unknown, forever waiting.

M1: Get curious! Hah!

M3: Don't explain, explore! Hah!

M3: Can't even have a good depression anymore.

M2: Or enjoy a good outrage.

M1: It's not fair.

M4: Life's not fair.

M2: It's not my fault.

M3: It's somebody's fault.

M1: Somebody ought to be to blame.

M2: Somebody ought to make it easier.

M3: Somebody ought to do it for us.

M1: It shouldn't be all up to me.

M4: It shouldn't be all up to us!

Phase Two:
The Intimacy Issue

Chapter 12

Defenses against Separation and Individuation

ennis and Shepard (1956) compared the dynamics of the first and second phases of group development. They noted a parallel between the dependency conflicts in the first phase and the intimacy conflicts in the second. The conflict in the first phase splits between overdependent conformist and counterdependent rebel and is acted out in compliance and defiance. The conflict in the second phase splits between counterpersonal and overpersonal forces, which are acted out in blind mistrust and blind trust. These concepts were congruent with my own experiences while I was using a psychodynamic group-as-a-whole method and were a challenging reality when I began the transition into SCT (Agazarian & Peters, 1981; Agazarian, 1994).

Before I introduced the SCT method of complementary subgrouping, both my therapy and my training groups worked the two sides of each split separately and sequentially. Groups tended to spontaneously follow the Bennis and Shepard model: They entered the phase of intimacy in euphoric enchantment, passed through disappointment and suspicion, and ended in disenchantment. When I introduced SCT subgrouping and thus encouraged the group to explore both sides of the split together, the way the intimacy dynamics were manifested in the group changed. In the beginning it was very difficult indeed to have the group contain these powerful impulses without repressing one side while acting out the other. As groups became more familiar with subgroup work and members were discouraged from taking deep-sea dives into one side or the other, I learned how to keep both sides of the split conscious in the group-as-a-whole. Subgrouping made it easier to manage and monitor the depth and rate of the regressive forces.

The predisposition to manage the enchantment/disenchantment split sequentially still influences the group, but using the SCT methods to manage the two sides of a split together significantly influences how these two subphases play out. The group makes the transition into intimacy with great cohesion, with members bonding with each other's similarities. Similarities reinforce closeness. Differences introduce distance. Individual differences appear in members' preference for closeness or distance in relationships: "Not quite close enough" is already too close for some members, whose "keeping comfortably distant" may already be too far for others. Differences in preference for closeness and distance sooner or later introduce disappointment, and with disappointment, disenchantment and suspicion enter the group. The group loses its cohesion.

In my experience of working as a leader and supervisor of group-as-a-whole groups before I made the transition into SCT, I learned that the group that is basically cohesive can survive a phase that is characterized by noncohesiveness. Even after I learned this, it was important to remind myself (and others) to assess group cohesion to help manage my own (and the group's) response to the phase of disenchantment—when attendance may very well be sporadic and members apathetic. Groups with a background of strong cohesion are unlikely to lose members at this period; groups with a noncohesive background not only tend to lose members but sometimes even disintegrate under the stress.

Even though the behavior in the phase of disenchantment may look the same for both cohesive and noncohesive groups, their prognoses are different. As long as group leaders do not know the difference, the loss of their own internal cohesiveness may tempt them to act out their own disenchantment on the group. My supervisees and I came to understand that our own needs for control, affection, and inclusion were threatened. When we acted out our disenchantment, we found ourselves running after absentee group members with phone calls or letters. In more extreme manifestations, we would punish late or absent members when they came back to the group. Our most painful experiences occurred when we joined the underlying pessimism of the group members' prognosis for the survival of the group. Remembering that disenchantment is the other half of enchantment is helpful for both groups and therapists. Working the two together with subgrouping brings great relief for both the therapist and the group.

SCT therapists emphasize that one cannot have the relationships one wants but only the relationships one can make. Making a relationship requires being separate enough to experience both the similarities and the differences between the self and the other and being sufficiently individuated to integrate the differences into the system of each relationship. The challenge is to remain in valid communication in spite of the underlying fears of engulfment (in closeness) and of isolation (in distance).[1] The basic work to be done by members in Phase Two, the phase of intimacy, is the work of separation and individuation, namely, acquiring the ability to tolerate the similarities in closeness and the differences in distance.

SCT TECHNIQUES IN THE PHASE OF INTIMACY

As the group develops, the basic SCT techniques of defense modification remain the same. However, the complexity of the dynamics they address increases, and so does the depth of the defense modification (which in this phase is known as Module 4). In the first phase of group development, the goal of defense modification is to help people learn how to undo their own defenses and test their own reality as a step toward discovering themselves instead of explaining themselves. Defense modification involves methods for revising old maps[2] through testing reality. The fork-in-the-road technique discourages people from making new maps until after they have entered the unknown and explored it. In this sense, SCT patients are in training to learn how to make, and how to revise, their own maps.

There are always two kinds of unknown: the unknown destination and the unknown path. Apprehension relates to the unknown destination (self-knowledge), whereas anxiety relates to the path: that it cannot be found, that it is too difficult or dangerous to follow, or that it will take more courage, will, and stamina than is available. The SCT fork-in-the-road provides a method for finding the path; defense modification reduces the restraining forces to taking it. Throughout the early stages of therapy, exploring led to discovering what was already half known (preconscious rather than unconscious). In the phase of intimacy, however, the unknown is truly unknown; it is impossible to know before it is discovered. What is unknown is the transformational self, which will not be known until after it has transformed. Transformation is being through becoming. Many people have taken this journey and found their way. Some talk about what they have found; others also describe the road to finding it. In Phase Two of group development, which is different from the Phase One, SCT gives the group both a map of the path and a guide.

---

[1]Earle Hopper (1991) has posited another basic assumption—massification and aggregation—an approach–avoidance dynamic that underlies the closeness–distance conflict in systems.

[2]Korzybski (1948) first developed the idea of man the mapmaker and time-binder. He also recognized that "whatever one says a thing is, it is not"—a basis for his non-Aristotelian general Semantics and a reinforcement for the complementarity between driving and restraining forces and context.

The Distraction Exercise

The form of the distraction exercise (see Chapter 3) remains the same and is used at the beginning of every group session, no matter what phase the group is in. The communications that are filtered across the boundaries by the distraction exercise differ according to the context. Each time the group meets, it begins by crossing the boundary, discriminating between facts, opinions, and feelings; vectoring energy from outside to inside; and by reducing defensive responses that would otherwise obscure resonance with the work of that particular session. Initial defense modifications are centered around common experiences like performance anxiety and fear of acceptance. As intrapersonal defensiveness diminishes in the group, interpersonal defensiveness comes into focus. In the phase of intimacy, work at the boundaries begins to involve annihilation and separation anxiety. The dynamics of the anxiety-provoking thoughts increase in complexity. The simple techniques for undoing them, however, remain the same.

Subgrouping

In the earlier phases of group development, the management of defensive splitting was done either by subgrouping or through moderating the simpler of the projective defenses. The defenses were relatively easy to identify, and the management techniques were relatively simple to apply. The defensive splitting that occurs around separation and individuation in the later phases of group development is not so simple. Separation and individuation require working with the primary split, which is predefensive. Subgrouping as a method of containing a split manages conflict by increasing the discriminations and increasing the complexity in discrimination. Predefensive splitting, however, arises from a phase of individual development in which it was not possible for the organism to either make or integrate disparate discriminations. When infant experience is good, it is all good and there is no awareness of bad. This side of the split is the source of optimism, enchantment, and blind trust. If these are not tempered in reality, they are the source of addictive positive transferences that interfere with, and sometimes preclude, the work of separation in therapy.[3] Conversely, when the infant experience is bad, it is all bad and there is no awareness of good. This is

---

[3]Endorphins are stimulated both in addiction and during breast-feeding. This may be the source of the isomorphy between chemical addictions and emotional dependencies. This would explain why addicts are not able to use the information that they have about the bad effects of the "good" drug.

an experience of alienation, isolation, and grim, joyless survival. It is the other side of the split and the source of pessimism, disenchantment, and blind mistrust. Regression to the negative side of the preintegrative split fuels the intractable negative transference. Only a barrier experience is available to the person in the depths of either side of the split.[4] In the phase of intimacy, regression must be managed so that it does not slide past the anchoring relationship to the group-as-a-whole and descend into the grim, joyless, paranoid/schizoid world described so well by Melanie Klein (Hinshelwood, 1989).

Subgrouping continues to be the major method of conflict resolution. In the phase of intimacy, enchantment and disenchantment are split between two subgroups and are contained in the group-as-a-whole. A further development in subgrouping emerges in this phase: After the apparently different subgroups have worked through to recognizing the similarities between them, integration takes place as usual in the group-as-a-whole. The group-as-a-whole then continues the work of discrimination and integration, without splitting into subgroups. Thus, work in the phase of intimacy alternates between subgroup and group-as-a-whole work. This trend also appeared in the later stages of Phase One, when group members, acting as a group-as-a-whole, scapegoated the therapist. Now in Phase Two, the group takes the next step—working as a group-as-a-whole without the necessity of having an external enemy to enhance the cohesion.

Subgrouping is particularly useful in the earlier stages of the work on intimacy. By subgrouping, the group-as-a-whole retains knowledge that there are always two sides to good and evil, even when members in one or the other subgroup do not. In individual therapy, it is the therapist who reminds the patient that there are two sides to everything. The blind trust of enchantment derives from an overemphasis of similarities and a denial of differences. The blind mistrust of disenchantment is the opposite: It derives from an overemphasis on differences and a denial or denigration of similarities. In an SCT group, blind trust and mistrust are modified by testing members' expectations, that is, by testing the reality of their predictions about what will happen and what will not. It is through this process that members come to trust that the group-as-a-whole will maintain resonance with each subgroup, even when members

---

[4]Failure to recognize when the source of a negative or positive transference is the preintegrational split, and therefore exists as two separate, barrier experiences, can have tragic consequences in therapy. I am thinking particularly of a much-loved Brazilian therapist whose patient, in the process of terminating therapy in a positive transference, called on him at home and put a bullet into his heart. As we grieve, it is also important to understand and learn, so that the therapist will not have died in vain.

of a subgroup can no longer resonate with each other. It is at this point that there is enough basic trust for a working regression to take place in the group-as-a-whole itself as well as in its subgroups.

Regression

SCT conceptualizes the management of primary splitting as a regression under the aegis of each person's self-observing system. This conceptualization is based on the understanding that the roots of the split are not defensive but preintegrative. From this perspective, it is a mistake to encourage patients to explore their pessimism or optimism in detail— either as a defense or as a symptom. Rather, SCT works to manage the regression so that the experience is framed as a repetition of what all human infants experience before they have developed the capacity to recognize differences. In all SCT work, regression is seen as a dedifferentiating process that requires new discriminations and integrations each step of the way. Thus, the observing self system serves as an anchor as the regressive process accesses earlier and earlier experiences. The work in the group is to increase the capacity of individual members to maintain recognition of the fact that there *is* a split as they learn to access and integrate deeper and deeper regressive levels on first one and then the other side of trust and mistrust. This is the journey that requires members to acquire information through the emotional understanding of the apprehensive unconscious, where time and contradictions do not exist.

Eye Contact

In all groups, the signal that indicates that the group has made the transition into the phase of intimacy is a change in the way members make eye contact. In the phase of authority, eye contact is nearly always triangular: Members talk to each other and at the same time keep an eye on the therapist. As soon as the group enters into the phase of intimacy, these sidelong glances all but disappear, and group members' focus is on the relationships between themselves. Watching eye movements in the group is a useful guide to when intimacy in the group is predominantly a defensive maneuver in relation to issues around the leader and when it is, in fact, a new stage in members' ability to relate in the group. It is helpful for therapists to understand this difference as a shift in dependency relationships, from the therapist to the group-as-a-whole, and thus avoid taking personally the fact that in this phase the therapist is dropped. When intimacy in the group is mainly defensive, compliant and defiant role-locks, not intimacy itself, are the issues. When the group is actually in the phase of intimacy, the issues are interpersonal closeness and distance.

In making the transition from authority to intimacy, that is, from Phase One to Phase Two of group development, members come to the hard-won recognition that the frustrating struggle they have with outside authorities mirrors the struggle they have with their stubborn selves and that much of their own pain, as well as the pain they cause others, comes from acting out their defensive selves. They enter the phase of intimacy determined to turn from their defenses toward their true selves. There is an initial illusion that, with the new relationship to the self, relating to others will be easier and that the work of change is behind them, a feature of the first phase of development. One of the realities of change is that it is difficult to change at any phase. Although the course of defense modification in the phase of intimacy is simpler than before, it is not any easier.

The members' major motivation in the phase of authority is to avoid pain; in the phase of intimacy, the major motivation is the search for the transforming self. In the phase of authority, the goal of therapy is to moderate defenses and symptoms; in the phase of intimacy, the goal is to separate and to individuate. In both phases, the goal of SCT is to reduce the restraining forces to survival and development and to liberate the drive toward transformation.

Eye contact is particularly important to both the enchantment and disenchantment subphases of the phase of intimacy. The deeper the group explores enchantment, the greater the variation in eye contact. As the group explores enchantment, members experiment with looking and looking away. As they learn more about their own conflicts around "dropping" (abandoning) each other when they look away, they become less sensitive to being dropped. The group-as-a-whole becomes more proactive and less reactive as members become free to call for connection if people are not "behind their eyes," if they are not fully present for eye contact in the distraction exercise, or if they have drifted out of visual contact with their subgroup. The other aspect of increased proactivity in the group-as-a-whole is an increase in members' awareness of their experience of seeing. It introduces an added dimension to the group-as-a-whole when members are free to let their eyes wander, to allow themselves to look and gaze, and to take in through their eyes. At this level of experience, the group-as-a-whole contains the regression without the need for subgroups. There is a profound wonder at this level of regression, an apprehensive experience of contented pleasure and of knowledge without words. Later, when the group comes to comprehend what it has apprehended, there is a recognition of multiple levels of discrimination. Members report understanding the difference between the comprehensive experience in eye contact and the apprehensive experience in gazing and between meeting another's eyes, being behind one's own eyes, and seeing others behind their eyes. They are able to maintain an ever-deepening relationship with the self while relating deeply to others. Members can check out with each other with extraordinary accuracy their impressions of how close or how distant contacts between them are. Making and integrating these discriminations increases the threshold of identity at the boundary between isolation and fusion. This in turn increases the potential for a deep, contained regression in the subphase of disenchantment.

In the disillusionment of disenchantment, members react to the pain of separation with isolation instead of individuation. Members look down, look away, and withdraw into themselves in hopelessness and despair. Members who have experienced separation and individuation through gazing have an increased potential for maintaining eye contact and for following their subgroup into the experience in the group-as-a-whole. These group members let their eyes wander instead of withdrawing; by letting themselves look, they are able to see others mirroring the isolation in themselves. They allow themselves to gaze and to take in through their eyes the depth of human pain—their own, others', everyone's.

With intimacy, as with all other dimensions of SCT work, the subgroups increase the capacity for the group-as-a-whole to contain both sides of the split. Containing both enchantment and disenchantment, as they are explored separately in subgroups, increases the capacity for the group-as-a-whole to integrate layer after layer of regressive experience. As the group-as-a-whole integrates deeper levels of experience that were previously split, individual members are able to make discriminations at levels of experience that were not available to them before.

"Surprises and Learnings"

The SCT method of "surprises and learnings" (the review period before the end of a therapy session, when the session is reviewed for surprises, satisfactions, dissatisfactions, and discoveries) is particularly useful in the phase of intimacy in helping maintain integrational integrity, in spite of the isolating character of the primary split in this phase.

UNDERSTANDING DYNAMICS IN PHASE TWO

Work in the subgroups in exploring defensive enchantment and disenchantment leads to understanding some of the adaptations members made in the process of separation and individuation in their own development, adaptations that now prevent them from bringing their full selves into their present relationships, either with themselves or with others. The nucleus of the phase of intimacy is the search for the self. It is in this sense that all the work before Phase Two is a preparation for the true work in therapy, namely, separation from the false self and a reindividuation around discovered aspects of the spontaneous self.

Fears of being swallowed up, managed in passing in Phase One, are salient in Phase Two and escalate into fear that the price of group membership is the loss of the self. The underlying dynamics are the fears of both fusion and de-fusion, that is, fears of losing identity on the one hand and all meaning on the other. In Phase Two, when the common sense mechanisms are used to undo anxiety, the anxiety does not go away; neither does stress and hostility. Defenses are no longer characterological but transferential. Up until this phase, transference responses were sufficiently comprehensible to the observing self to free enough energy for group members to continue to work; fully addressing them had to wait until the basics of defense modification were acquired. In Phase Two the first steps are taken in surfacing the pervasive transference (see the Glossary).

WORK IN THE ENCHANTED SUBGROUP

The enchanted subgroup organizes around a sense of mastery and independence. Most members of the group-as-a-whole feel potent, resourceful, accomplished, and triumphant. It is during this period that new kinds of alliances are made between members and that individual members receive positive feedback from the group on how they are regarded as a particular resource to the group in furthering its growth and maintaining its ability to function. It is a time of cohesive good fellowship in group development. Characteristically, the group will work independently of the therapist; whereas the therapist was under attack for withholding help and resources during the authority conflicts, his or her help is now not only not sought but apparently not needed.

As the enchanted subgroup works, it discovers that it overemphasizes similarities at the expense of recognizing differences. Individual members gain insight into the phenomenon of being in love. They recognize that as long as the partners are each able to bask in each others' similarities, all is right with the world. When, however, ambiguities or contradictions are introduced into the relationship, fears of one's own negative reactions to differences are aroused. Anxiety at separation then floods the system. Unless the mirroring climate is restored, love is experienced as anguish, with an underlying terror of annihilation. Working in the subgroup, enchanted members learn to tolerate differences in each other and thus make the developmental shift from mirroring to attunement, resonating with each other in the same rhythm but with different shades and colors and tones (Stern, 1985). This ability to widen the range of resonance to differences is important to the group-as-a-whole, since it lays a foundation for resonance, which will be essential to the disenchanted members when their turn comes to explore their reluctance to subgroup around any similarities.

For those individuals whose formation of object relations was a delayed experience, the phase of enchantment provides a repetition of early symbiotic gratification. Their striving to become fused with the group and to merge their identity into the group identity intensifies the forces of group cohesion. In contrast, for those individuals whose early object relations were formed in disappointment and deprivation, or for those for whom too-early splitting of the object precipitated premature independence, the intense group cohesiveness precipitates fears for their own identity, fears that lead to alienation. It is then that members become aware of the defensive aspect of their enchantment, even those members who have centered more closely around maintaining the euphoria rather than expressing it. The enchanted group-as-a-whole is alerted to its denial—denial of guilt, denial of anxiety, denial of mistrust. The defensive aspects of the euphoric omnipotence, grandiosity, overestimation, and blissful symbiosis are recognized. Closeness becomes too close. At this point the balance in the group tips, and the disenchanted subgroup becomes activated and dominant. Conflict returns to the group. Group cohesion is disrupted, and the group enters the subphase of disenchantment.

WORK IN THE DISENCHANTED SUBGROUP

Disenchanted subgroups organize around a sense of disappointment and failure. The group-as-a-whole, but especially the members of the disenchanted subgroup, feel let down, anxious, distrustful, and isolated. For the optimists the disappointment is acute and is experienced as a tendency toward depression or as an impulse to externalize against the group, the therapist, or other members. For those who are more comfortable in pessimism, however, there is almost a relief that the world has returned to being as untrustworthy and disappointing as they had always believed it to be. Members report depression and disillusionment, loneliness, alienation, futility, hopelessness, and despair. If there is any acting out in this phase, it will be "in the form of tardiness and missed sessions.

Depression and Despair

The SCT approach makes an important distinction between depression as a defense, which is modified in the first phase of group development, and despair, which is addressed in the second. Depression is defined as a defense against hostility that turns the retaliatory impulse back on the self. Despair is defined as a defense against hope and an experience of profound disappointment, an endless mourning for the loss of the separate other and the split-off self. The distinction between depression and despair is relatively new to the literature (and is one of the SCT discriminations made in the process of operationalizing the theory). It is an important one. For example, the researchers of a recent study were astonished to find that hopelessness (despair) is not an extreme form of depression, as they had believed, but an independent variable which incurred different or more serious types of a variety of health problems than did depression (Everson, Goldberg, & Kaplan, 1996; Jenkins, 1996).[5]

MANAGING THE PHASE OF INTIMACY: CLINICAL EXAMPLES

In the phase of intimacy, as in all phases of group development, it is the SCT therapist's responsibility to identify the fork-in-the-road between the driving and restraining forces associated with the goals of the phase. Similarly, in this as in all other phases, which path of the fork-in-the-road to explore first is an informed choice that the member, the subgroup, or the group-as-a-whole has the responsibility to make. What makes the therapist's work easier is the SCT map that serves as a blueprint for practice. What makes the patients work easier is their now thorough familiarity with the SCT techniques and methods to use on the way.

In the phase of intimacy, the path to the split-off self is the feeling of dread, which is an emotion that is used as a guide that leads directly to what is dreaded. In the earlier stages of group development, dreadlike feelings are more likely to be generated by "dreadful thoughts" and are therefore modifiable by the three questions for anxiety (see Chapter 6). True dread is more likely to be related to fear, a compound experience of negative predictions and terror of the experiences to come. SCT predicts that following the course of dread will lead through emptiness to

---

[5]Hopelessness can be identified by a subject's response to two statements: "It is impossible to reach the goals I would like to strive for" and "The future seems to me to be hopeless, and I can't believe that things are changing for the better." This measure of hopelessness (on a 5-point Likert scale) is distinct from measures of depression (in the MMPI) and has shown a strong statistical link to an increased risk of incurring a variety of health problems (*Science News*, 1996)

the threat of falling apart. SCT understands this emptiness as the "absence feeling," the symptom of a disconnect that prevents access to the inner experience of emotion, to the sense of self. In the absence of a sense of self, there is despair. In despair, there is no hope, there is no dread, there is no shame. Shame serves as a barrier between the available self and the self that was split off in the original shaming. The experience of shame is terrible for everyone. SCT group members must become able to bear it if they are to discover that they themselves are generating the shame by continuing to shame themselves as they were once shamed. SCT frames shame as turbulence at the boundary between the available self and the split-off and encapsulated self. By going through the shame barrier, members break through to the spontaneous experience that was split off in the original shaming.

This work, of course, is greatly facilitated by the resonance between the members of a subgroup: One member's work takes the subgroup forward, and when that individual member can go no further, another member picks up and carries on. When one or two members have survived the fear of disintegration and of loss of the self and have crossed the boundary to discover the spontaneous experience behind the original shaming, the map is made for the group and other members can follow.

Given the road, its course is inevitably both painful and frightening—and remarkable in the way it elicits human courage and tenacity. The clinical example chosen to illustrate this journey can be understood in terms of both individual and group therapy. Much of the course of the journey is presented as it occurs in individual therapy. At those moments when subgrouping would make the journey easier, the comments of the "therapist-as-a-subgroup" in individual therapy as well as the communications from a subgroup in group therapy are given. The illustrations begin with a patient experiencing dread. The course is traced from the first moment of dread through to the discovery of the true self.

Dread

PATIENT IN INDIVIDUAL THERAPY: I'm feeling dread.

T: Dread is a useful feeling to follow. Which way is it going?

P: I feel dread in the pit of my stomach, and I'm afraid. I'm afraid I'm going to discover something awful.

T: Do you remember what you call that kind of thought?

P: Yes, a negative prediction. But I don't think that it's generating the feeling of dread. [The patient has internalized his experience of the three questions for anxiety (see Chapter 6) and is spontaneously vectoring his energy away from the anxiety-provoking thought.]

T: Is it making it harder for you to follow the feeling of dread?

P: Yes, it is doing that. If I don't pay attention to the thought and pay attention to the dread itself, I feel myself sinking. I'm apprehensive. No, I'm more than apprehensive, I'm thoroughly scared.

T: If you follow that sinking feeling, you will find out what you are dreading. Are you curious?

P: Not very!

Following dread calls for defense modification—but with a difference. Typically, patients are encouraged to modify defenses so that they can sit at the edge of the unknown with curiosity about the alternative. However, dread is not treated as a defense. When following dread, the path for the fork-in-the-road *toward* exploration and discovery is toward dread, not away from it. If the patient presented above were in group therapy, the therapist would at this point in the therapeutic process ask if other group members had feelings of dread. After receiving affirmative replies from other members, the therapist would identify for the group the object of the dread, namely, the unknown.

In individual therapy, the therapist joins the subgroup! For example:

T: You are experiencing the dread of the unknown. I understand. When I am at the edge of the unknown, trying to get my courage up to move toward what I am dreading, I fill up with dread and don't want to go on anymore. In a sense, I'm with you at the edge now. I'm reminding myself that what I'm experiencing is "only" turbulence at the boundary and that once I have made up my mind to cross, I'll be able to follow. I'll keep pace with you and will stay alert for my own sinking sensations to see where they lead.

P: You're saying you are experiencing this, too?

T: Yes, my own version. Remember, we do this work together. You don't go down alone. When we work at this level, I also experience my versions of dread of the unknown. That's when I try to remember to be curious.

P: It sounds good, but I'm not curious.

T: Curiosity is the signal that lets you know you're ready. It's a mistake to go before you're ready. Do you have a sense of what is in your way?

P: Yes, it's the sinking feeling in my stomach. It's making me queasy.

T: Are you at a fork-in-the-road?

P: Maybe. All I know is, I'm afraid I'm going to get still more queasy—well, that does sound as if I'm preparing to get a symptom.

T: Do you want to make plenty of space for your queasiness?

P: (*Centers and makes room for himself and begins to report his experience.*) I'm not so queasy now . . . and I am getting curious. I feel hollow . . . it's almost funny . . . I feel like a hollow tree.

T: Often, feeling hollow or empty is an absence of something. Is there also a feeling that something is missing?

P: Yes. It's not *me* exactly that's missing. It's more *what* I'm missing—I know! I'm missing my feelings! I feel hollowed out without them. I feel terribly sad, as if I am yearning for something I've lost.

T: Are you at a fork-in-the-road between yearning and a feeling of loss?

P: It's hard to separate the two.

T: Do you think this is similar to the work you did separating out your experience of wanting from your experiences of disappointment when you don't get what you want? The disappointment at not getting?

[This is an example of exploring yearning when it is not strongly defended against. Work with yearning follows the same form as work with wanting. Being encouraged to have the full experience of yearning, regardless of whether or not it will be gratified, will bring a strong, good feeling of life and identity. This patient is already on the way to exploring the positive side of the split—a life full of hope and positive predictions, where the glass is always at least half full. This will be explored next. Enchantment first, disenchantment second. Hope before despair.]

P: It might be! If I make space for the feeling of yearning, I can feel a spreading warmth inside. It suffuses the whole of me. I can feel a smile coming. I look at you, and you seem loving and kind.

T: If you keep following your feelings, what happens next?

Blind Trust

For people for whom blind trust is easier than blind mistrust, there is always hope and optimism. This part of the journey is then not so difficult. The first step with such patients is to access the experience of bliss that underlies the fundamental optimism. The second step is to recognize and modify the blind trust that makes them vulnerable to exploitation.

P: It's bliss! You and I seem as one . . . we're melting together . . . I have such a feeling of well-being and completion . . . I'm part of the universe . . . I'm the sun . . . you're the sun . . . we're full of the sun . . . I am dissolving.

The experience of bliss, reflecting one side of the split, comes with many sensations—of sunlight and warmth, of sucking, of warm milk in the mouth, of warm softness against the cheek, of being a small child in an adult's arms or of being a young animal at play with its litter mates or snuggled up against its mother. These experiences are not defensive but primary. They are the source of optimism, of confidence that the world is fundamentally good. However, this is only one side of the split. The therapeutic work for enchanted patients is to recognize their defenses. In blind trust, disappointing experience is denied or reversed into its opposite. This leads to a defense of merging, of susceptibility to symbiotic relationships in which there is a danger of exploitation or serious abuse, which will be endured under the name of love.

T: You look blissful. Keep making room for your experience . . . and when you are ready, ask yourself what you know.

P: I know that I am a loving, trusting person who is able to love with my whole heart. I give my whole heart. I've given my whole heart to you. I'm so glad you have my heart. I trust you with it completely.

T: Stay open to yourself, and see what you discover next.

P: I'm basking at the edge of the unknown.

T: Wait and see which way you take yourself.

P: I'm going deeper and deeper into trusting you.

T: What do you know about trusting me?

P: (*Hurriedly*) You'd never hurt me.

T: Did you notice, you answered that very fast? Keep a sense for the rhythm in yourself, and see what else you know about that.

[The therapist is relying on the patient's access to his apprehensive experience and is cuing him to be open to what he knows. If the patient is ready, he will know both the moments when he can trust the therapist and the moments when he is not so sure he can.]

P: Well, I know that you are constant and there for me and that you'll be there as I work . . . but . . . I know that sometimes you are a little bit off . . . and I know that when that happens, I don't want to know. I look the other way. I follow a direction that isn't really mine. I don't want you to be different from me, so I try not to be different from you. [The therapist remains silent so as not to distract the patient in any way as he begins to explore the other side of his split.] I'm getting a huge experience. It's hard to find words. All those times . . . all those people . . . it's happy but not happy. I'm seeing the difference. I can feel myself different. I'm different from you. It's very, very sad. It hurts. It's a good pain but it hurts. I feel guilty, like I'm betraying you. How will you be without me? I'll be all right without you. I'm going to be, even if I lose you. It hurts. It's a good hurt. I feel so strange. I feel like myself.

The patient is now ready to understand the different compromises he has made in himself to keep his relationships conflict free. He has begun the important task of a new level of separation and individuation. He is experiencing both pain and grief as he separates from others by recognizing how he differs from them. At the same time, he experiences the satisfaction of experiencing his true self.

From this point onward in both individual and group therapy, the leading edge of work is to continue both to increase individuation and to confront the different versions of how blind trust has been maintained. Undoing denial and recognizing the compromises in relationships that have been built on blind trust is painfully embarrassing and humiliating, and it arouses deep shame.

Blind Mistrust

The stronger the early disappointments a person has sustained, the stronger the rooting in basic mistrust. When dread is followed out of the hollow feeling, it leads to a void and a sense of great uneasiness and suspicion. Suspicion defends, by the projection of blind mistrust, against the bitter feeling of having been betrayed. It is only at the end of the journey that members discover that what has been betrayed is the part of the self that is split off and kept encapsulated within a barrier of shame. The steps in this experience need careful monitoring so that regression does not take the subgroup, or the individual patient, into a barrier experience. This is avoided in group therapy when the therapist consolidates the group's ability to observe the journey every step of the way. This is illustrated in the following dialogue:

MEMBER 1: I'm not so queasy now . . . and I am getting curious. I feel hollow . . . empty. I'm afraid. It's cold and dark and there's nothing there.

T: Often, feeling hollow or empty is an absence of something. Is there also a feeling that something is missing?

M1: No. It's just the empty place inside me. I know it all too well. It's somehow the core of my experience.

T: Anyone else resonating?

M2: Yes, I know what you mean. There's a huge emptiness which fills me up.

M1: I know that everything is futile, so I've come to terms with it.

M2: There's no point in having expectations. I know I'll be disappointed, but I'm not disappointed anymore because I don't expect anything anymore.

M1: There's nothing to look forward to.

M3: And you can't count on anybody.

M2: If you want something done, you have to do it yourself.

M3: I feel sorry for the suckers who think life is full of promise.

T: Is the subgroup exploring pessimism?

M3: I wouldn't call it pessimism.

T: Are you angry?

M3: No, fed up.

M2: Resigned.

M1: Right, pessimism isn't the right word.

M2: Resigned that life is just like that—getting through one day after another, nothing to look forward to except more work, more responsibility.

T: Would you call it despair?

M2: Despair is better.

M1: Like Sartre.

M2: Or Schopenhauer . . . or Nietzsche.

M3: It's not despair, it's reality.

T: Nothing will ever change for the better? Everything is hopeless? (*The subgroup agrees.*) You know, in SCT we think about despair as a defense against hope. Do you notice that you don't feel dread anymore? Would you be willing to explore the fork between despair, which you seem to know very well, and what happens if you try to find the other road?

M1: You're saying to follow the dread?

T: See if it leads somewhere.

The Shame Barrier

For the disenchanted, following dread into and out of the hollow feeling begins a cold and lonely journey. There will be vivid impressions of falling endlessly into a black hole; of being lost in outer space, tenuously tethered by a lifeline; of being cold in an ice age of empty, boundless, frozen wasteland. And always there is the experience of being alienated, isolated, hopeless, in despair. When defensive despair is addressed, there is a desperate holding on so that one does not "disintegrate" or "fall apart." When the group-as-a-whole is encouraged to regress into and through the feared disintegration, it reaches an experience of shared alienation, an existential common experience.

It is no coincidence that annihilation anxiety is aroused when these defenses are threatened. The group is in conflict between the courage to explore and the terror of exploring inner experience, which requires facing the fear of personal disintegration. There is typically a last-ditch defensive stand, a schizoid withdrawal, an implosion into the black hole, a turning away from any reexperiencing of the original annihilating shame. Hiding out in alternate realities or avoiding crossing through the barrier of shame constitutes the true loss of the self and the experience of despair. It is the loss of the self that creates the emptiness of alienation; it is the loss of the self that is grieved, not the world of disappointments in which the disenchanted fear to live.

The aspects of the self that were originally shamed are maintained by a barrier of shame. Shame functions as a barrier experience that not only creates an impermeable boundary between the self-centered system and its systems-centered context, but also splits off and encapsulates a part of the spontaneous self, a part to which the self-system no longer has access. Shame is not the only affect that reduces the permeability of intrapersonal and interpersonal boundaries. Barrier affects create management problems of their own. Guilt, embarrassment, humiliation, and shame are feelings that reduce the potential for knowing the self; shyness reduces the potential of being known by others. Barrier affects generate impulses to retreat from reality unless they are addressed for what they are—barriers that are potentially permeable, rather than problems in and of themselves. Accepting barrier affects as turbulence at the boundary, rather than as barriers, makes the difference between being imprisoned in the compromises of the adapted self and regaining the freedom of the spontaneous self that is hiding out. Consider the following dialogue:

P: I can feel myself withdrawing. I'm just too ashamed.

T: Shame is like a turbulence at the boundary. If you make it into a problem, it will be difficult to find out what part of you is hiding out
behind the shame.

P: That's all very well. You say, "Don't get stopped by shame or embarrassment or shyness." But going anywhere near those feelings is just
too hard.

T: I know it's hard. Shame is one of the worst feelings I know. The work
is very hard. But I do think its even harder never to find out about the
part of yourself that you became ashamed of.

P: I'd rather die than look. Anyway, I wouldn't even know where to look!

T: You could start by asking yourself what part of yourself you are afraid
to show!

What must be discovered by patients like this is that by avoiding
shame and humiliation, they are continuing to shame and humiliate
those originally shamed or humiliated aspects of themselves that thus
remain alien to their present experience. Through this process of discovery, they learn that guilt belongs to the irreality world of "shoulds"
and prevents them from facing, owning, and accepting responsibility for
their actions in the here-and-now and that shyness is the final barrier
behind which the secret self hides and is the no-man's-land between the
self and the other. One SCT group member, in the process of regaining
his full potential for sexual experience, became embarrassed that if he
opened up to this potential, he would not be able to contain it and would
have an orgasm in front of everyone. Being reminded that how and
where to discharge his sexual energy were his choices to make, freed him
to have his experience, contain it, and to share his triumph and joy with
the group.

The worst consequence of shame is the permanent absence of that
part of the self that is needed for intimate relationships, either with the
true self or with any significant other, an absence that results in schizoid
feelings of emptiness In truth, the self *has* been emptied out, and there
is inconsolable grief at its absence. It is the work in the phase of intimacy
that teaches people how to move through the barrier of shame and free
their original spontaneity.

That the defense of the shame barrier is upheld by denial rather
than depression is evidenced by the fact that when people access the
split-off part of the self that was shamed, they recognize it immediately as
if they have always known it was there but avoided being in touch with it
because of the pain.

Each defense is, of course, perfectly correlated with the experience against which it is defending. In a real sense that part of the self that was shamed was annihilated; for all intents and purposes, it died and was mourned. The group truth, of course, is that there are many other selves alive and well but in hiding. Group development calls on many different aspects of the self to reemerge and take part in the developing group.

Phase Three: Life and Interdependency

Chapter 13

Defenses and the Experienced SCT Group

*T*he advantage of an experienced SCT group is that all the SCT methods, techniques, and skills acquired in the different phases and subphases of group development are available to members for their work. This is true, not only for the experienced group members who built the SCT group, but also for the new members who enter an already established SCT therapeutic environment.

The challenges of everyday life mirror the challenges in the life of every group. The work of the group in its third and final phase will require further mastery of one or another of the challenges to human survival, development, and transformation. Group members will continue to discriminate and integrate the splits that occur naturally when people attempt to manage frustration and solve the problems of everyday life. Although the experienced group has already passed through the first two phases of development, different aspects of each phase will cycle and recycle throughout the life of the group. Within each phase, many different levels of defense occur. The defenses addressed, however, always follow the defense hierarchy, that is, defense modification progresses from the simpler to the more complex. Anxiety is always addressed before any other defensive response, no matter what phase of development the anxiety reaction occurs in, and its source is always pinpointed before undoing the next defense. Similarly, negative predictions are always modified before tension is addressed, and cognitive distortions and somatic symptoms are always modified before work is done with depression, hostility, and role-locks.

Learning how to modify defenses by addressing the simpler before tackling the more complex equips members to continue to do the work on their own. Furthermore, in rising to the ongoing challenge to not take things "just personally" members spend less time inside their barrier experiences and more time orienting themselves to the ever-challenging systems-centered context. SCT members have also learned, from the fork-in-the-road technique, that there are two sides to every problem. It is not sufficient, however, for members to learn specific defense modification techniques. It is also necessary for them to use the methods that increase their capacity to contain frustration at the edge of the unknown and to redirect their energy toward their inner experience, to learn to contain both sides of their conflicts and the full force of their impulses, and to continually rediscover authentic relationships with themselves and others.

The major challenge to the leader of the experienced group is to keep it working! Learning the methods and techniques that create an SCT group are hard won and the satisfaction of using them is a strong reinforcer for maintaining the norms of the group. Satisfaction, however, is not always enough. Maintaining the SCT methods as a driving force is a demanding discipline, and, like all complex disciplines, must be consistently reinforced. It requires a constant vectoring of energy to maintain the system in a state of change. As soon as the therapist recognizes the work that a member (or the group) is doing and experiences it as having the same flavor as previous work, it is likely to be redundant. Work that is redundant for one member may be a driving force for another or for the subgroup or group-as-a-whole. This is where knowing how to match the goals of a particular member to the phase of group development is an important skill for the SCT therapist. Throughout the course of group development, SCT therapists work with one part of their attention on the systems-centered group-as-a-whole and another part of their attention on each individual member of the group. Just as the SCT group has a leading edge of work so does each group session and so does each individual member. Maintaining the leading edge for both the group and its members is a boundarying responsibility for the therapist. The differentiating criterion is the amount and quality of repetition.

It is the ongoing work of crossing the boundaries from the past and the future into present reality that occupies the experienced group. Not only are group members' constructed realities of the future modified, but their attitude to the past and the constructed realities that serve as their "memories" of the past are subjected to scrutiny and changed. Rather than view the past as a source of emotional pain, rage, conflict, yearning, bitterness, and loss, members now spontaneously regard their past as a long period of training that has made it possible for them to be what they are. The mixed feelings that once were associated with past events change into an acceptance of the past. Gone also is the magnetism of old roles and defenses. Rather, at their most centered, members tend to calmly watch their impulses to defend come and go, their temptations are reported like any other piece of information that is brought across the boundaries into the here-and-now, and their full energy remains connected with the group.

Another major source of therapeutic benefit is the work performed by group members in accessing their inner resources and bringing them into the group. This work requires members to show themselves, to go through the self-consciousness that often accompanies owning and demonstrating one's competence, and to manage the shyness that often goes with showing pleasure in one's own competence.

In spite of the therapeutic progress so clearly shown by the experienced SCT group, there are nevertheless obstacles still to be overcome. There is never a time in an SCT group when the work of boundarying comes to an end. In moments of stress or fatigue, or simply when motivation is low, the defensive self takes over, and regression occurs. The danger of a slide into a barrier experience is omnipresent. Not using the SCT skills that have been learned is like stopping regular physical exercise: All the old stiffness, fatigue, and feelings of ill-being return. That is the bad news. The good news is that it is easy to regain a centered equilibrium. New skills, once learned, do not go away. Just as returning to physical exercise restores the feeling of well-being in relatively little time (compared to the amount of work it took to get fit the first time), so too is it easier to reacquire the skill of boundarying than to learn it as a beginner.

In all the developmental phases, groups have characteristic ways of sabotaging the therapeutic process, and Phase Three is no exception. One subtle way the experienced group can act out resistance is by a rigid adherence to rules and regulations. SCT methods and techniques can be followed slavishly instead of used as flexible guidelines that relate to the goals of the context. SCT techniques and methods can be misused by applying them in the right way for the wrong purpose. SCT is particularly vulnerable to these tendencies since, as its methods simultaneously reduce the restraining forces and increase the driving forces, the methods are equally powerful whether they are directed toward the goals of change or the goals of resistance to change.

MODULE 5: MODIFICATION OF DEFENSES AGAINST KNOWLEDGE AND COMMON SENSE

In SCT, common sense is closely related to emotional intelligence. Common sense combines the intuition of apprehension and the rationality of comprehension. Apprehensive knowledge is not verbal, comprehensive knowledge is. Apprehensive knowledge signals through symbols and intuition which can translate instantly into insight or can emerge so fragmented that, like Mendelbrott's squiggle, it can take years or a lifetime to understand. Comprehensive knowledge develops through the process of collecting information, forming and testing hypotheses, and making and revising cognitive maps. The work of the experienced SCT group is focused on reducing the restraining forces to communication between these two kinds of knowledge.

Emotional intelligence (Goleman, 1995) is the bridge between apprehensive and comprehensive knowledge; that is, it is the link between the apprehensive experience of our phylogenetic inheritance and our ability to put our experience into words. Access to emotional intelligence is essential if we are not, like Phineas Gage, to lose all access to our common sense and our ability to make decisions and implement them (Damasio, 1995). Emotional intelligence is the insight, the hunch, or the feeling of certainty that directs our choice of what to do and when, where, and how to do it. It is the vector that determines which branch of the fork-in-the-road to take first. Emotion connects man to his goals, and common sense enables him to choose his path.

In the experienced group, curiosity is the major driving force that fuels the process of modifying the major defenses against comprehension, apprehension, and emotion. Fear of the physical experience of emotion is one of the major restraining forces against accessing the apprehensive knowledge it contains. Early in the first phase of development, tension is recognized as the defense that constricts the physical sensations that signal emotion. Later in the first phase, SCT group members discover that subliminal intention movements signal the physical experience of emotion. As members become aware of their intention movements they gain access to the full potency of their emotional experience. Accessing emotional experience does more than lead members to the experience of being full of their own potency. It also develops the path for accessing apprehensive knowledge of the self.

Defenses against connection with the self maintain the split between comprehensive and apprehensive knowledge. Making the boundary appropriately permeable between comprehension and apprehension requires an increase in the ability to tolerate the turbulence of a transition that can be experienced as a falling apart. The major defenses against connection with the self are addressed in the phase of intimacy. In the work of exploring experience without externalizing it, group members encounter the affective experiences of dread, emptiness, and falling apart. As members become increasingly familiar with these experiences *as defenses* that can be expected to occur each time the chaos of the unknown is entered, they find it easier to mobilize the energy of curiosity and to regard their defensive experiences simply as turbulence at the boundary. As one member put it: "In order for me to become me, I have to let go!"

Group members who have worked their way through the first four defense modification modules are well equipped to address the challenges in the fifth. They have learned to contain their potential energy without discharging or constricting it, to temper their apprehension with curiosity, and to vector their energy across the boundaries between apprehension and comprehension. It is through a nondefensive communication between apprehension and comprehension that the final work of therapy is done. An ongoing nondefensive relationship is established between primary and secondary experience (secondary experience arises from imagination and comprehension, primary experience from apprehension, or intuition). This is achieved by group members who are able to develop a greater and greater capacity to tolerate the chaos of primary experience, organize it, and communicate it comprehensively.

Access to Comprehension

Defenses against comprehension are failures in reality testing. Such failures were addressed from the very beginning of the phase of flight in the development of the SCT group. The common sense methods of undoing negative predictions and mind reading introduced norms of reality testing to the group. Group members learned methods for testing their expectations instead of trusting their wishes and fears. It is the experienced group's ability to test reality that enables it to contain group and individual regressions within the group structure, no matter the depth to which the group gains access.

Access to Apprehension

Defenses against apprehension are failures in containing. The work of containing was begun at the boundaries of the first meeting of the SCT group, when members were asked to discriminate between explaining and exploring. Discrimination requires self-observation, the prerequisite for the development of the self-observing system. Self-observation requires containment of the self while it is being observed. Recognizing the thinking self as different from the feeling self requires the ability to contain each as simultaneously separate and integrated. Recognizing the difference between the self and its context requires the ability to contain the self-centered system in the systems-centered context. Recognizing the difference between the self, the observing self, and the self that takes on membership in a subgroup and in the group-as-a-whole involves containing the experience of a hierarchy of systems, each of which has a different goal and requires a different role. Group members must contain the apprehensive chaos while what is known goes through the unknown into what will be known next. Undoing the defenses against this process began at the beginning of the group as members learned to separate out facts from feelings, and continued in the second phase of group development, when members learned the pain of separation that comes from overdetermining differences and the terror of the loss of identity that comes from overdetermining similarities. The major difference between the third phase and the preceding two is that the third phase provides the context in which the primary transferences as well as the secondary transferences can be recognized and modified.

TRANSFERENCE MODIFICATION
IN THE EXPERIENCED GROUP

Like psychodynamic groups, SCT groups take the phenomenon of transference very seriously. Unlike psychodynamic groups, SCT methods for using transference therapeutically are significantly different. From the beginning of group development, secondary transference is differentiated from primary transference. Unlike primary transference, secondary transferences are accessible to conscious and preconscious experience. In SCT the ability to access and work with primary transference is dependent upon the quality of the preliminary work with the secondary transference. SCT groups are rarely ready to address primary transference manifestations before the third phase of development.

Primary and Secondary Transference

SCT identifies three kinds of secondary transference: stereotype social role relationship transference; authority role relationship transference; and intimacy role relationship transference. *Stereotype role relationship transferences* replicate early family norms, govern the way that the impulses to scapegoat differences are expressed, and serve to establish and maintain the social status quo. *Authority role relationship transferences* repeat the pattern developed in managing *one-up–one-down* relationships between the self and the other. These manifest in compliance or defiance and defend against disappointments in functional dependency. *Intimacy role relationship transferences* replicate the vicissitudes of attachment and loss in the relationship between the infant self and the other. They manifest as attachments characterized by blind trust, merging love, and fusion or as blind suspicion, alienation, hate, and despair.

Whereas the source of secondary transferences are early role relationships, primary transferences are not role boundaried. The source of primary transference arises before human infants have developed the capacity to differentiate themselves from their mother and before they develop the ability to contain and integrate differences. SCT differentiates between two primary transference phenomena: *pervasive transference* that arises from partially differentiated states and *pretransference* that arises from predifferentiated and undifferentiated states.

The pervasive transference is understood, in both SCT and psychodynamic literature, to have its source in infant experience before the development of the ability to experience a universe that contains differences. Infants experience either satisfaction and bliss or dissatisfaction and chaos. Because this is a primal split, there can be no transaction across the boundary. When bad exists there is no good, and when good exists there is no bad. This is reexperienced later as an all pervasive mood in which the person feels that a half-full glass will never be full enough or a half-empty glass will always be more than enough. The pervasive transference is the precursor to the secondary intimacy role relationship transferences. As the twig was bent, so will the branch grow. Each of us has a predisposition toward optimism or pessimism, toward blind trust or blind mistrust. Bringing to consciousness the pervasive transferences that permeate experience increases the range within which differences are discriminated and integrated and increases the ability to contain opposites together in one experience instead of splitting them apart, projecting out, or denying one of them.

Predifferentiated experience is different from the pervasive transference in that it has no boundaries and is experienced as oceanic apprehension, a feeling of being one with the universe. Without boundaries there are no contradictions, and one can be simultaneously omnipotent and impotent, grandiose and insignificant. This level of experience can be accessed through regressions caused by drug use, trauma, and mental illness. It can also be accessed through expanded consciousness that accompanies meditation, mystical or peak experiences, and such pathways as SCT.

Like the primal ooze from which life emerged, *undifferentiated experience* is the raw material for apprehensive understanding (and all transferences). In this experience there are no boundaries around consciousness. Knowledge of the undifferentiated experience is our leading edge in phylogenetic inheritance. It is also the source of the chaos of the unknown. We have no words to contain or explain this experience.

The ongoing work of developing the self-centered system in a systems-centered context uses the energy of this level of experience, and the SCT discipline of containing is one of the methods by which that energy is accessed.

Management of Transference

One of the major differences between systems-centered and psychodynamic groups is the management of transference. Projections increase in complexity from phase to phase and every projection has a transferential component. In the SCT approach to the phases of group development, transference manifestations are immediately made conscious by modifying those defensive projections that are appropriate to each phase and subphase. Social transferences, for example, are explicitly addressed at the beginning of Phase One whereas intimacy transferences are not explicitly addressed until Phase Two.

SCT methods and techniques systematically bring transferential responses into awareness rather than allowing them to fuel the transference neurosis, either in the group-as-a-whole or in its members. For example, functional subgrouping discourages the development of transference manifestations in the group by requiring members to resonate with the subgroup experience rather than withdraw into their own experience and act out their unconscious transference in role pairs. Boundarying also reduces the potential for developing the transference neurosis. Requiring the "facts" of distractions to be stated and separated from the feelings brings the observing self-system into the associative process. The SCT methods for undoing defenses and testing the reality of inner and outer experience make the preconscious conscious, reducing secondary transference phenomena and containing the primary transference.

In the early stages of group development, unconscious transferential role signals are immediately made conscious by drawing the members' attention to them. This is the first step towards enabling members to connect the signals to the impulses that lie behind them, and ultimately to identify what past role is being imported as a defense against the present. SCT techniques discourage rather than encourage transferential experience. For example, SCT therapists address members' associations to their past by drawing their attention to how their present experience is different from the past. Thus, rather than encouraging associations that direct members away from their present into their past, the process of discriminating the differences encourages members to integrate past experience in the present. Thus, in SCT, the group's ability to maintain regression within the boundaries of the observing self-system is developed (regression in the service of the ego).

Although SCT recognizes that secondary transference manifestations have deeper sources, access to these sources of transference requires regressions that the SCT group entering the third phase of group development has not yet developed structures to contain. The

SCT approach is to develop the structure first, so that the work of discrimination and integration can be continued at every level of regression. There are failures in containing, of course, in all phases of group development. These failures occur when members take things "just personally" and precipitate a barrier experience in themselves. Barrier experiences involve an encapsulated subsystem contained within the self-centered system. There is a transfer into the present of earlier role-locks in relationship to authority and intimacy. While members are in a barrier experience, that experience *is* their reality, and they have no choice but to act out in their behavior the cognitive misconstructions that fuel that experience. Members of groups in the third phase of group development are more accustomed than members of groups in earlier phases to recognizing the barrier experience and therefore have a better chance of helping each other out of it. Barrier experiences are essentially transference experiences in that they precipitate regressions to earlier and more primitive modes of consciousness. Containing and self-centering makes it possible for members to observe how they act out secondary transferences when they are in a barrier experience. Exploring the deeper levels of the barrier experience, in subgroups or through self-centering and containing, develops capacities in the members of experienced group and is also the route that leads members to discovering their primary transferences.

SELF-CENTERING AND CONTAINING

Self-centering is in itself a healing process. It is the process of "containing" the self at the edge of the unknown. Containing is the experience of knowing the self in the here-and-now and beyond: knowing the self as self-centered in a systems-centered context with the capacity to see the many contexts in the systems-centered hierarchy. Centering in the SCT group first takes place when members learn how to sit centered. This is followed by learning how to stay centered and contain, how to be "ready" to discover what in the self is being defended against. This is the aim of self-centering containment. Remaining centered requires vectoring energy away from the defenses and back into the self-centering state. In the experienced SCT group, most members can contain for a considerable length of time, continually recentering and waiting to resonate with themselves and others.

The ease with which experienced SCT group members can solve their own problems is illustrated by a clinical vignette: A member of an experienced group came to a group therapy session saying that she could hardly wait to "get centered" so that she could sort out her feelings and understand her problem. She was sure she had to break up with her boyfriend. "He's swallowing me up," she told the group. As she centered she began to understand that she had been spending too much time in his house and not enough time in her own. She knew without any doubt that she was losing herself—not because of her boyfriend but because she was not taking enough time for herself. She realized that what was best for her was to invite her boyfriend to her house more often and to stay at his house less. With this insight and resolution, she was no longer in a barrier experience and had regained her common sense (and her relationship!). What members know when they are centered is often dramatically different from what they know when they are not.

The ability to apprehend as well as comprehend is acquired as the ability to contain and center develops. SCT containing and centering are both similar to and different from the discipline of meditation. In both the SCT and the meditation experience the boundaries of space and time are transcended. However, the SCT centering experience both transcends the boundaries of space and time and locates experience in the context of here-and-now by bringing awareness of the self-centered system into the systems-centered context. Centering accesses both the apprehensive and comprehensive levels of knowing. The hierarchy of living human systems is apprehended; the implications of context are comprehended.

Centering is reached through consistently reducing the defenses and opening up to authentic experience. Learning to "fill up with oneself" without defending against the experience begins early in the work of the developing SCT group and involves paying attention to the sensations of emotion. These experiences are often new, unusual, and very satisfying for both patients and SCT trainees. As tensions melt, sensations increase, and new sensations enter awareness. It is through discovering sensation that members discover their physical body. Subgrouping around sensation is an important transition between experiencing oneself in one's full sense of being and following oneself into the experience of the unknown.

Through centering, SCT members also discover how to access and increase their experience of pleasure. Discovering pleasure is a therapeutic goal that can easily be overlooked if the therapeutic focus is on pain, a pitfall that the fork-in-the-road technique helps SCT patients avoid. However, centering may open the way to a different pitfall. Focusing on the pleasure of centering can preempt its purpose. What is a driving force in meditation is sometimes a restraining force in SCT: When apprehensive experience becomes a goal in itself, the work of continuing to comprehend and test the realities of apprehensive experience stops.

Subgrouping around pleasure can be either a restraining force or a driving force in the experienced SCT group: It is a driving force when the goal of the work is to discover how to experience pleasure. It becomes a restraining force when pleasure becomes an end in itself. Consider this exchange:

P: I've been sitting centered here all during the group session feeling so full of pleasure that I didn't even have to join a subgroup.

T: Do you know whether you have been working to have pleasure for the sake of pleasure or whether you have been working to have pleasure for the sake of learning how to experience deeper and more meaningful pleasure and satisfaction?

Making this discrimination is important in all SCT self-discovery work. It is a judgment call for the therapist to decide when work on self-centering is at the leading edge of change, at the transition into deeper levels of experience and knowing, and when it has been done enough and has become redundant. When a patient seems to have succumbed to focusing on the pleasure of self-centering at the expense of its purpose, the therapist may say something like the following:

"I am not sure that describing the physical experience of your pleasure is still your leading edge. It seems to me that making space for pleasure and allowing yourself to fill up with it fully is something that you now do quite easily. Your leading edge may be the next step, which is to center yourself in the pleasure, sit at the edge, and wait to see what else you discover about yourself in this state?"

Although an individual member's work may be breaking new ground for the subgroup, the therapist must watch for when it is in fact going over old ground for the member. In boundarying, part of the SCT therapist's job is to identify the next step in defense modification for each individual member as well as for the group. For experienced group members in the interdependent working group, learning how to make these discriminations for themselves is also part of their leading edge.

THE DISTRACTION EXERCISE IN THE EXPERIENCED GROUP

Every session of an SCT group is expected to start with the distraction exercise (see Chapter 3). This exercise is nearly always the best indicator of the state of the group as issues in the distraction exercise reliably parallel the developmental issues and defenses that are relevant to the present of the group.

There are more mixed feelings about the distraction exercise than about any other SCT technique. On the one hand, it takes time away from the interactive part of group work and is a challenge to individual members to stay focused and connected to the person who is working on his or her distraction. On the other hand, it is the most effective way to bring working energy across the boundaries for both individual members and the group-as-a-whole. The distraction exercise makes space for individuals to describe outside issues and, at the same time, to bring their emotional involvement into the group. (One therapy group modified the distraction exercise to contain both distractions and "news." Factually reporting news brings into the group information that is important to individual members, and to the group, without the risk of filling up the group work time with "storytelling.")

In therapy groups, both novice and experienced, it is in the distraction exercise that the major work is done in moderating anxiety. Fundamental to the method is the discrimination between facts and opinions, which significantly reduces ambiguity, which is itself a major source of anxiety. The distraction exercise also teaches the elementary rules of problem solving. Separating out facts from feelings orients facts to reality, and modifying cognitive distortions introduces reality testing. Relating feelings to facts rather than to distortions makes the information in feelings available. In the experienced SCT group, the distraction exercise also functions as interpersonal feedback. Members have the opportunity not only to check out their impressions as they make eye contact but also to identify interpersonal comforts or discomforts that they can use later as data in separating out their projections from reality.

Monitoring Fitness for Work

Another important piece of work that occurs in the distraction exercise at the boundary involves members' well-being and physical health. Issues about physical well-being and the person's fundamental relationship to these issues are explored at different levels throughout the different phases of development of the SCT group, and are an ongoing focus in the interdependent work phase of the group.

Somatic symptoms are the second defense in the triad of symptomatic defenses. Modifying tension symptoms is always an important transition between modifying cognitive distortions and managing the retaliatory impulse. Members working in the experienced group have learned to take responsibility for reporting tension-generated symptoms whenever they occur so that they can be immediately modified before they become a restraining force to work.

Throughout the course of group development, the methods of the distraction exercise lend themselves to helping patients discriminate between tension symptoms that can be immediately modified, somatic symptoms that will require a plan for deconditioning, and physical symptoms that are related to medical problems. Patients often do not discriminate between psychological and physiological discomfort. Many all too easily attribute medical problems to psychological causes and then neglect them.

The impulse to interpret symptoms is rerouted by requiring facts, not thoughts. Sometimes, members' distractions involve a physical predisposition to certain kinds of tension, or even a chronic condition. Then they are encouraged to bring their common sense to bear upon the problem. Members with bad backs, for example, are encouraged to review ways to ameliorate the difficulty of sitting for an extended period of time during a group session and to follow treatment strategies recommended by their physician. Some members bring pillows, some bring footstools, some stand up for a while, and many recognize that the posture that their physician has recommended for their back is the same as sitting centered! (One member in her 7th month of pregnancy reported that she had predicted that sitting centered would make her back ache, but that when she tried it she discovered she could work the whole session without discomfort.) When a member must stand up intermittently to relieve pressure, there is negotiation with the group as to which position makes it easier to maintain eye contact. (This same negotiation took place when one member's arthritis was severe enough to require him to lie down during group meetings.)

Throughout all phases of group development members learn to take their self-centered system seriously as the primary source of energy for systems-centered work. SCT members know that their responsibility is not to work in unnecessary discomfort but to report it when it becomes a distraction (suffering in silence and "being brave" is as much a restraining force as complaining). Unnecessary discomfort then becomes a reality which can be addressed with common sense (e.g., members know that it is important to go to the bathroom when necessary rather than to try to vector their energy on group work when the bladder or bowel is full). This goal-oriented approach to discomfort has had a significant impact upon members' attitude toward their physical health and emphasizes how seriously SCT requires members to vector their energy into their work and not into their symptoms.

Although somatic issues may surface during the distraction exercise in the earlier phases of group development, work on the more serious relationship of the self to the symptoms is undertaken later. As the group matures, members tend to make significant changes in the way they take responsibility for their physical well-being. This is particularly important in groups where patients tend to substitute psychological interpretations (and the hope of a magical cure) for common sense. For example, sometimes it is reassuring, sometimes annoying, but always important to connect fatigue with too little sleep, or hunger to having skipped a meal.

The advantage for patients working in an experienced group is that the focus is less on defense and symptom modification and more on character modification. When there are medical problems, detailed reality testing is initiated not only as a method of making a diagnosis but also as a means of teaching patients how to interact responsibly with themselves and their physician. The following dialogue is from a mature SCT group:

P: I've given up going to see my doctor because nothing he does is any good. I'm at a fork-in-the-road. I can give up basketball and be pain free, or I can play and suffer.

T: Do you have a diagnosis?

P: It's getting worse, and I'm afraid I will have to stop playing basketball.

T: Is that your physician's recommendation? [Notice that when a negative prediction is not directly related to the goal of work, it is bypassed. The goal here is to check medical reality.]

P: He doesn't know.

T: Then is that a self-diagnosis?

P: Well, in a way.

T: Is it or isn't it?

P: It's a self-diagnosis.

T: Do you believe you are qualified to make a medical diagnosis about your knee?

P: No.

T: The fact is that there are specialists in knee problems and several different approaches to treatment. What other avenues have you tried?

The happy ending is that the patient went to a knee clinic, was given exercises, and has been playing basketball without pain and without danger to himself ever since. The bonus is that the group became more alert to exploring options before accepting limitations.

Another member of this group coughed persistently for a month while insisting that she was under a physician's care. During the distraction exercise, it was established that her physician had diagnosed walking pneumonia, had given her medication, and had told her to return in 6 weeks. At the end of the fact-finding questioning, she recognized that there might be other causes for her persistent coughing besides pneumonia (like allergies or asthma). The patient called her physician the next day and was referred to a specialist who diagnosed reflux. After proper treatment, her cough disappeared. This patient was then motivated to explore her attitude toward doctors and her health in general. She recognized that she had a tendency to ignore her physical symptoms or to defer to her doctor's judgment even when she failed to give her doctor the information that her symptoms were not responding to treatment! This patient's explanatory work turned into important subgroup work for the group.

Dream Work

In experienced groups, the distraction exercise is a useful tool for dream work. In SCT, dreams are not used as a major therapeutic tool until after the defenses in the triad of symptomatic defenses (see Table 4.4) have been modified. It is at this point that dream work may well be useful to help members understand their relationship not only to therapy and themselves but also to the group.

The following format for dream work also works well in individual therapy: The patient first reports the whole dream. The dream is then worked in the same way that the distraction exercise is worked, with an emphasis on "microreporting" each feature of the dream together with the feeling that is generated by that feature. In the following dialogue, a member of an advanced SCT group is reporting a dream:

P: I entered the room.

T: You entered the room. Your feeling?

P: I felt excited. And then I started talking—

T: Excuse me. You entered the room, feeling excited. Before you started talking, did you notice anything about the room in your dream?

P: Well, yes. It had brown walls, a red carpet, and a man that I didn't know standing by a window.

T: Brown walls. Did you have a feeling about the walls?

P: Yes, I thought they were too dark.

T: Was there a feeling that went with that impression?

P: A small amount of displeasure.

T: And the red carpet?

P: Pleasure! It felt springy under my feet as I crossed the room toward the man at the window.

By the time a group member finishes reporting a dream, the group usually understands it. Although they sometimes comprehend the dream's meaning, more often their understanding is apprehensive, with the multidimensional implications at different levels of knowing that is characteristic of apprehensive understanding. Members who are familiar with the method of free association and interpretation in dream analysis have reported that the SCT method controls tendencies to speculate, interpret, or explain and that there seems to be a significant increase in the frequency of intuitive flashes of apprehensive and comprehensive understanding.

SUBGROUPING IN THE EXPERIENCED GROUP

Subgrouping is a powerful technique that does more than manage conflict; it also promotes the work of separation and individuation. In the early stages of subgrouping, members take two important steps in the process of separating and individuating. The first is the work of staying separate from the group and connected with themselves so that they can deepen their own experience. The second step involves staying loyal to the subgroup, which provides a supportive environment for them while they learn how to maintain their individual experience in the face of new developments in the group. This lays the foundation for staying separate enough to maintain individuated feeling states while at the same time remaining connected to others with resonance and empathy. Thus, patients (and trainees) learn how to stay in relationship with both the self and the other without losing either.

In the experienced group, the work of separation–individuation is more complex and requires more complex subgrouping techniques. For the experienced group, it is not sufficient to increase individuation simply by maintaining resonance with the part of themselves that is resonating with their subgroup. Rather, they are required to be aware when they experience an integration of their own work even though the subgroup is still working. Their next step requires changing subgroups or starting a new one. This aspect of the separation process not only involves individuation of the self as related to others, but also individuation of the self in the different contexts of time, space, and role. Experienced members increase their awareness of their experience in the present, by discovering that when experience is freed from associations to the past and predictions about the future, there is an increased consciousness of the rhythm of feeling in the present, in their subgroup, in the group-as-a-whole, and in themselves. Once acquired, following the internal rhythm of resonance with the present becomes a natural process.

Gaining experience in judging when to change subgroups is also the context in which experienced members learn, not only to individuate themselves from their subgroup, but also individuation of role through an increased awareness of how their group role changes as their perception of the context changes. Members come to recognize that when their role in subgroup work becomes personally redundant, the challenge is to start a new subgroup that is relevant to both their member role and also to their role in the group-as-a-whole. As members individuate they become the pathfinders of the work that the group can do next.

SUMMING UP: SCT INNOVATIONS FOR GROUP THERAPY

Systems-centered therapy was developed from a theory of living human systems and tests the hypothesis that systematic modification of defenses in the context of the phases of group development will reduce the forces in patients that inhibit change and will release the inherent driving force so that it can be directed toward the goals of change. Clear outcome criteria for each step in the sequence of defense modification locates the patient in the SCT treatment plan. Because each defense modification addresses a specific symptom, therapy can be delivered either continuously or separated into modules. SCT can therefore be applied to the goals of both short-term and long-term therapy.

The formal practice of SCT is still relatively new. Therapists in SCT groups have noticed that expected dynamics are often manifested in unexpected ways. The relative absence in the SCT group of acting out by creating identified patients or by scapegoating has already been mentioned. SCT groups also differ from the expected in their responses to new members. The discipline of functional subgrouping appears to reduce the turbulence of introducing a new member for both the group and the member. When a new member joins a subgroup he or she has the immediate support of the subgroup (for a new member who is already acquainted with SCT therapy, there is a feeling of coming home). New members of SCT groups, as compared to other therapy groups, have less difficulty recognizing the norms as the group structure (boundarying and subgrouping) is the same in all SCT groups. When a group is begun with a population of members who are already experienced in SCT therapy, the group tends to bypass the expected phases of group-as-a-whole development. That is, new groups that are formed from members who are experienced in the methods of SCT tend to function like a mature, experienced group. (The SCT methods of boundarying and functional subgrouping can also be applied successfully to other kinds of groups, like training groups, special interest groups, and work groups in organizations.)

The innovation of functional subgrouping has had a significant and immediate impact on the therapeutic process. By subgrouping functionally, therapy groups do not develop a status hierarchy based on stereotypes, authentic communication is potentiated between the members, the capacity of the group-as-a-whole to contain regression is increased, and the probability that individual members will become victims to regressive role suction is reduced.

Another major innovation introduced into group therapy by SCT is the five modules of defense modification and the manner in which each modification is coordinated to a specific phase of group development. Modifying defenses sequentially from simple to complex increases the potential for exploring rather than acting out the different defensive impulses that are triggered in the different phases and subphases of group development.

Systems-centered therapy assumes that self-centeredness is the major source of all personal and interpersonal pain. SCT enables a shift from self-centeredness to an increased awareness of the self in a systems-centered context. In the process of becoming systems-centered, members learn that every context has its own goals and that every change in goal requires a corresponding change in role if they are to live in a goal-oriented way. SCT members learn to orient themselves inside the different roles as they shift awareness from being a separate individual to being a member of a subgroup to being a member of the group-as-a-whole. They learn that when they take things "just personally" they lose sight of all other contexts and are imprisoned in a barrier experience inside their self-centered system. By discriminating between self-centeredness and the systems-centered context, members increase their ability to make the transitions in relationships that are required in the multiple contexts of everyday life.

The major driving force in the systems-centered orientation to therapy is its emphasis on the discrimination and integration of differences. This process alone consistently reduces both the severity and frequency of the pain that is generated by defenses. SCT techniques of splitting conflicts and deliberately choosing to explore one side at a time definitely increases a group member's potential for regaining access to the undefended self. The fork-in-the-road technique enables people to direct their energy away from their defenses. In SCT work, members constantly practice containing their potential energy without discharging or constricting it; they increase their capacity to recognize their internal experiences; and they explore the frustrations, conflicts, and impulses they are defending themselves from. When the restraining forces to internal knowledge are reduced, people regain their common sense, their sense of proportion and their cosmic sense of humor, as well as their ability to access the joy (and the pain) of living in the here-and-now.

Glossary of SCT Terms

Acting Out: Acting on a conflict, a defense, or an impulse without taking into account the different system contexts and thus precipitating behavior without understanding the implications it has for the individual person, the member, the subgroup, or the group-as-a-whole systems.

Anxiety: A psychophysiological response to system disruption (a restraining force) characterized by some or all of the following symptoms: dry mouth, cold hands, rapid heart beat. In SCT, the source of anxiety is attributed to one of three causes: (1) anxiety-provoking thoughts, (2) physiological experience of emotion, (3) normal excitation at the edge of the unknown. Psychosomatic symptoms (cognitive disruptions, fainting, etc.) are deconditioned before defense modification.

Ambiguity: See Information Theory (Shannon & Weaver, 1964).

Apprehension: Intuitive understanding: nonverbal, noncognitive, it has to be translated into words before it can be integrated into comprehension. The anxiety-like experience that accompanies the process of discrimination and integration of chaotic information into meaning. The anxiety-like experience that accompanies the chaotic transition from one integration to another.

Attunement: Psychophysiological resonance. Synchronized and in tune with another's internal rhythm and experience.

Authority: Throughout this book the word "authority" has the meaning of "the right to work." This then ties in with the SCT definition of the word "energy" as "the ability to do work."

Barrier Alert: A signal that the observing self-system is losing the ability to perceive the self in either a self-centered or a systems-centered context. A cognitive disruption; the boomerang defense or taking something personally are examples of barrier alerts.

Barrier Experience: The experience generated by a defensive, encapsulated, subsystem, formed within the self-centered system. The self-system loses the facility to observe the self in either its self-centered or systems-centered contexts. All differences are experienced by the person as cognitive dissonance. Perception is selective and self-reinforcing. The sense of space and time is impaired, as is the ability to take on the different roles and goals relevant to the systems of member, subgroup, and group-as-a-whole systems.

Boomerang Defense: The fleetingly experienced or denied retaliatory impulse toward some frustrating person, thing, or event that is turned back as an attack on the self in the form of mind reading, negative predictions, tension, psychosomatic symptoms (including psychomotor retardation), and depression.

Boundaries: The system structure within which information is located in space, time, reality, and role.

Boundaries, Reality: Discriminate between reality that is consensually validated through reliable reality testing methods and hypothetical reality (irreality).

Boundaries, Role: Define the different system roles that shift as the context and goals of systems shift (e.g., the different roles and goals of the systems of member, subgroup, and group-as-a-whole in the system hierarchy).

Boundaries, Space: Determine the subsystem parameters within, between, and among systems in the hierarchy.

Boundaries, Time: Determine the system parameters of past, present, and future.

Boundarying: The application of the systems-centered methods and techniques that reduce the restraining forces to communication at the boundaries within, between, and among systems in the hierarchy and increase the probability that information (energy) will be transferred.

Boundarying and Vectoring: Boundarying makes boundaries permeable to information, and vectoring directs the information toward the primary and secondary system goals.

Centering: Vectoring energy toward the psychophysiological "center" (physiologically, the diaphragm and lower abdomen), with the intention of accessing spontaneous, apprehensive understanding of the relationship of the self to the context and goals of the present. Centering increases boundary permeability between apprehension and comprehension.

Cognitive Dissonance Theory: Festinger's theory of cognitive dissonance postulates that cognitive dissonance occurs when the mental map does not fit the realities of the territory. Cognitive dissonance is reduced either by redrawing the map or by maladaptively changing the perception of reality to fit the map.

Cognitive Distortions: Misconstructed mental maps of the world that are organized around unchecked assumptions, like negative or positive predictions; mind reading; and other judgments based on wishes and fears rather than on reality testing.

Common Sense: Intuitively logical or "instinctive" responses to reality that increase as the permeability of boundaries is appropriately increased or decreased between comprehensive and apprehensive knowledge.

Comprehension: Knowledge arrived at through cognitive processes of thinking and imagination.

Communication: Transfers of matter/energy across system boundaries.

Constructed Reality: The cognitive maps of reality that result from the person's organization of their information about reality and whose reliability influence the appropriateness of a person's role behaviors in relationship to their system goals.

Containing: Potential energy maintained within a relaxed state of focused alertness and readiness.

Context: The environment of the system in space and time. The phase of development in which the work of an SCT group takes place.

Contextualizing: Capacity to see more than one context at a time. In SCT, individuals experience themselves in the context of the member, subgroup, and group-as-a-whole systems. Contextualizing requires the vectoring of energy into the roles and goals that are appropriate to the different systems of the hierarchy.

Deconditioning: Routing energy away from defensive cognitive or somatic responses to stimuli and rerouting energy into authentic, emotional experience of conflicts or primary impulses.

Defenses: Restraining forces that inhibit the inherent system drive toward the goals of survival, development, and transformation of living human systems. Defensive experience generates a secondary "as if" reality and diverts energy away from the authentic experience of conflicts, impulses, and emotions generated by the challenges of primary reality.

Defense Modification: A predetermined sequence of SCT methods and techniques which systematically undo defenses against intrapersonal and interpersonal experience in the context of the phases of group development.

Depression: A masochistic defense that constricts and revectors the retaliatory impulse away from an outside target (e.g., a person, object, or thing) toward the self. The self becomes the target, not only of the retaliatory, aggressive, or sadistic thoughts or actions, but also of disapproval of the impulse itself.

Despair: A regressive experience of the unpleasurable side of the preintegrated split in which pleasure has no reality, and in which survival is experienced as a hopeless, grim, and meaningless life sentence.

Discovering Reality: Differentiating the reality of the experience from the defenses against it. The defenses against reality are, in fact, often the source of the pain about reality.

Distraction Exercise: An SCT boundarying technique used when a distraction is vectoring members' energy out of the group, requiring discriminations between thoughts and feelings so that emotional energy can be revectored into the here-and-now reality of the group.

Dread: A sinking feeling, which, when followed rather than avoided, leads to the apprehensive experience of what is dreaded and typically there is a reintegration of a split-off part of the shamed or emotional self.

Driving Forces: Vectors in the force field that direct the life force toward the primary goals of survival, development, and transformation and the secondary goals of environmental mastery.

Edge of the Unknown: The apprehensive experience of being in uncertainty, often mixed with dread and anxiety about not knowing what is going to happen next. When curiosity about the unknown is aroused, energy is revectored and the experience transformed from dread and/or anxiety into excitement, anticipation and wonder, which is labelled as apprehension at the "edge" of the unknown.

Emotion: In SCT, the words "emotion" and "feeling" have different meanings. Emotion is a physiological response and understood as a combination of affect, sensation, and motion that is always accompanied by an intention movement (often subliminal) that signals an impulse to action. Emotion is a primary, apprehensive process; feelings are a secondary, comprehensive process by which emotions are described and labelled cognitively.

Emotional Intelligence: Common sense.

Emptiness: The experience of the loss of the split-off parts of the self.

Energy: The ability to work, which in SCT is defined in terms of the transfer of information in communication transactions (matter/energy) across the boundaries within, between, and among the hierarchy of systems.

Energy, Actualized: Information that is vectored in relationship toward implicit and explicit goals in a reality context in space and time.

Energy, Potential: Information that is available but not actively vectored toward implicit and explicit goals in a reality context of space and time.

Feeling: A secondary, comprehensive process which enables emotion to be verbalized. Feelings have two sources: emotions and thoughts. Primary emotional experience translates into feeling words ("grief," "rage," "joy," etc.). Secondary emotional experience generated by thoughts also translates into feeling words (as "grief" generated by sad thoughts; "rage" generated by moral outrage; "joy" generated by positive predictions). Interpretations of experience (like "abandoned," "betrayed," etc.) also generate feelings. Feelings generated by thoughts "feel" the same as feelings generated by emotions but have different psychophysiological sources.

Field Theory: Lewin's (1951) field theory postulates that all behavior is a function of the perceptual map (the life space) of the path to the goal, and that knowing the map makes it possible to predict behavior.

Force Field: A field of equal and opposite driving and restraining forces which define the system's structure at a moment in time. Driving forces are vectored toward the system goals of survival, development, and transformation. Restraining forces reduce the permeability of the boundaries to the energy (information) in the driving forces.

Fork-in-the-Road: A metaphor for the forced choices presented to SCT members, first between explaining and exploring (i.e., elaborating on the known vs. discovering the unknown) and then between exploring the defenses against reality versus discovering the reality of experience, conflicts, or impulses that are defended against.

Function: The defined purpose of the system, which is to survive, develop, and transform. A theory of living human systems postulates a single dynamic: the process of recognizing and integrating differences, explaining the process by which living systems travel along the path to the goal, solving the problems that lie in the way. By recognizing differences in the apparently similar and similarities in the apparently different, all living systems survive, develop, and transform from simple to complex. In SCT, this function is operationalized by functional subgrouping.

General Systems Theory: Von Bertalanffy (1968) postulates that all living systems in the same hierarchy can be defined isomorphically.

Goals: Heuristically, living human systems are defined as goal-directed and self-correcting in relationship to primary and secondary goals. The quasistationary equilibrium (the place of rest) of the system in relationship to its goals in a moment in time can be diagnosed through the use of the force field model.

Goals, Primary: Primary goals of living human systems are survival, development, and transformation. The primary goal of SCT groups is to develop the system structure of member, subgroup and group-as-a-whole systems and to transform through discriminating and integrating information (energy) within, between, and among the system hierarchy.

Goals, Secondary: Secondary goals of living human systems are environmental mastery: the explicit goals that are stated for a particular system. In an SCT group the secondary goals are to develop into a problem-solving group-as-a-whole system by modifying the hierarchy of defenses in the context of the phases of group development.

Group-as-a-Whole System: Contains the subgroup systems and vectors energy toward primary and secondary goals.

Grief: The emotion aroused in the process of crossing the boundary between irreality and reality and adjusting to a sad fact of life, such as grief at the loss of a loved one; at an impairment or loss of function or capacity; at the loss of a fantasy or an illusion; or from the recognition of what one's defenses have cost in terms of missed and sabotaged opportunities, relationships, and self-development.

Guilt: The signal of a conflict between a judgment about what one ought to or should be, do, think, or feel and a contradictory impulse, emotion, feeling, or wish. In SCT guilt is addressed by making the conflict between irreality and reality explicit, and directing attention to containing and centering the reality experience rather than acting upon it or criticizing it.

Hostile Discharge Defense : Avoidance of the retaliatory impulse by discharging into hostile and/or sadistic acting out of the retaliatory impulse with targeted or random discharges of irritability, frustration, and arousal. Symptoms generated: depression and hostile actions.

Hierarchy: The structure in which each system exists in the environment of the system above it and is the environment for the system below it.

Individuation: See Separation and Individuation.

Individuation Defenses: Defenses against recognizing and integrating similarities in the apparently different. Disenchantment; contempt; alienation; suspicion; disassociation; despair; mistrust of self, others, and groups are the major defenses against individuation. Symptoms generated: paranoia, isolation, despair.

Information Theory: Postulates that there is an inverse relationship between noise (ambiguities, contradictions, and redundancy) that introduces entropic forces into the communication process and the probability that the information in the communication will be transferred across system boundaries.

Insight: Comprehensive and/or apprehensive integration of information that changes understanding through cognitive processing (intellectual insight) or through instant knowledge.

Intention Movements: The nonverbal cues that people send that signal their emotional responses in relationship to themselves and others: from Tinbergen's (1951) observation that birds and animals signal their intention to act before they act. These intention movements can be interactive. For example, when a chick observes an "attack intention" in an adult bird, it inhibits the attack by assuming a submissive posture.

Intimacy: Discriminating between self-centered relationships and systems-centered relationships: transforming the relationship that one "wants" into the relationship that one can "make" in reality through the process of separation, individuation, and integration.

Interpersonal: The relationship between the self and others.

Intersystem: Relationships across the boundaries between systems in the hierarchy of systems.

Intrasystem: The system-as-a-whole in relationship to its subsystems.

Intrapersonal: The relationship between the self and the different parts of the self (internal subgroups).

Isomorphy: Similarities in structure and function of systems in the same hierarchy.

Knowledge and Common Sense Defenses: (1) Defenses against comprehensive and apprehensive knowledge generating symptoms like impairment of decision making and implementation abilities; loss of common sense and humor. (2) Defenses against reality testing generating symptoms like self-centeredness at the expense of the environment.

Life Space: A cognitive map, defined by Lewin (1951) as a function of the person's perception of the environment.

Masochism: Making oneself the victim of the retaliatory impulse. Turning the retaliatory impulse back on oneself and taking on the role of victim, victim's victim, or scapegoat.

Member System: An SCT concept that is actualized when an individual contains self-centered system energy and vectors it into a subgroup.

Methods of SCT: Boundarying, subgrouping, vectoring and the hierarchy of defense modification which bring into being the systems-centered group.

Mirroring: Reflecting (as in a mirror) another's facial expressions, posture, and mood.

Modules of Defense Modification: Five modules that define the series of defenses which are modified sequentially in the contexts of phases of group development.

Module 1. The social defenses and the triad of symptomatic defenses modified in the flight subphase, in the transition between the flight and fight subphases, and in the fight subphase of SCT group development. See Acting Out, Cognitive Distortions, Depression, Tension.

Module 2. Role-lock defenses modified in the fight subphase of group development. See Role-Lock Defenses.

Module 3. Resistance to change defenses: modified in the transition between Phase One (authority) and Phase Two (intimacy) of group development. See Resistance-to-Change Defenses.

Module 4. Defenses against separation and individuation in intimacy: modified in Phase Two of group development. See Separation Defenses and Individuation Defenses.

Module 5. Defenses against knowledge and common sense modified in everyday life. See Knowledge and Common Sense Defenses.

Noise: Ambiguities, redundancies, and contradictions that serve as restraining forces to the transfer of information across system boundaries; also known as entropy or dissonance.

Pervasive Transference: The objectless transference of primary experience arising from the early atmosphere between the child and the mother that generates a pervasive orientation to experience.

Reality, Constructed: Comprehensive mental schema that represent organizations of sensory data, like mental maps, which serve as the basis for interpreting inner and outer reality and which guide responses and actions and predictions. See Field Theory.

Reality, Misconstructed: Comprehensive mental maps that are generated by wishes and fears about reality and are relatively impervious to, or in contradiction with, sensory data. Misconstructed maps serve to guide maladaptive responses, actions, and predictions in relationship to reality.

Reality, Primary: Direct, sensory, and apprehensive experience of inner and outer reality; the raw data for comprehension.

Reality, Secondary: Discriminations and integrations of primary data through the data organizing processes that result in comprehension.

Reframing: In SCT, rewording the meaning of events in the group so that they are related to general human dynamics and not to specific individual psychodynamics. Reframing is used to depathologize, normalize, legitimize, and humanize, and to discourage members from taking their experiences "just" personally.

Regression as a Driving Force: Reexperiencing the past in the context of the present, so that information is available from *both* the past and the present for the work of discrimination and integration and is related to the present context.

Regression as a Restraining Force: Reexperiencing the past "as if" it were the present. Resources for discrimination and integration are governed by the level of development of the regression.

Remorse: The experience of regret at the consequences of an action, often coupled with compassion for the people involved in the consequences.

Resistance to Change: Closing boundaries to differences within, between, or among systems in a defined hierarchy. Resistance effectively disrupts the process of discriminating and integrating differences — the transformational dynamic in system survival and development.

Resistance-to-Change Defenses: Module 3 defenses modified in the transition stage between Phase One and Phase Two of group development. These defenses include (1) externalizing conflicts with authority—defensive stubbornness and suspicion that splits good and bad and blames the bad on authorities or society from the righteous and complaining position—(which results in sabotage of social and personal goals; (2) Disowning authority—defensive stubbornness and suspicion of self that splits good and bad and blames personal incompetence—which results in sabotage of personal goals.

Resonating: Experiencing emotionally the core synchronicity between oneself and a part of oneself; between a part of oneself and another; and sometimes, when resonating with the system hierarchy, centering oneself in the system-as-a-whole. Resonating is an affective experience and is the criteria for joining a subgroup.

Responsibility: Behaving appropriately to the role one is in, to the context that one is in while performing the role, and to the goals of both the context and the role.

Restraining forces: Vectors in a force field that oppose the driving forces and reduce the permeability of the boundaries to the driving life force.

Role: An identifiable collection of behaviors that serve as driving forces toward the goal, appropriate to the context. It is a construct that is independent of the people who take on the role. One person changes their role many times a day: parent, spouse, employee, driver, guest, and so on.

Role-lock Defenses: Module 2 defenses modified in the fight subphase of group development. Defensive projections and projective identifications into one-up–one-down role relationships(e.g., identified patient and helper; scapegoat and scapegoater, victim and bully, and other defiant/compliant splits that repeat old roles). Symptoms generated: repetitive stereotypical interpersonal relationships at work and at home.

Sadism: Thoughts, words, and deeds that target others with the retaliatory impulse without compassion for them as victims.

SCT: See Systems-Centered Therapy.

Self-Centered System: SCT definition for intrapersonal personality and character; the source of potential energy for developing the systems-centered hierarchy. The self-centered system and the systems-centered system are isomorphic.

Self-Observing System: The "eye" of the systems-centered self. The discriminatory and integrational function of the system hierarchy. Surveys the subsystems in the self-centered system and the self-centered system in systems-centered contexts. Discriminates between thinking (comprehensive knowledge) and emotion (apprehensive knowledge) in the self-centered system. The source of common sense.

Separation Defenses: Defenses against recognizing and integrating differences in the apparently similar. Enchantment; idealization; merging; love addiction; blind faith; hope; and trust in others, self, and groups are the major defenses against separation. Symptoms generated include exploitability and dependency at the expense of interdependence and independence.

Separation and Individuation: The process of discriminating and integrating differences in the apparently similar and similarities in the apparently different.

Social Defenses: Avoidance of unpredictable interpersonal reality by defensive, stereotypical, social communications. Symptoms generated: inauthenticity.

STDP: Habib Davanloo's formulation and methods of Short-Term Dynamic Psychotherapy.

Structure: The boundaries of a system in space and time. System boundaries discriminate between its inside and its outside, place it in its hierarchy of systems, and differentiate it from the subsystem components inside its boundaries and from the larger system of which it is a component.

Subgrouping, Functional: A conflict resolution technique in which members are deliberately encouraged to form subgroups around two (or more) sides of a conflict. Conflict is thus split and contained in the group-as-a-whole rather than within its members. Subgroup members work together within their own subgroup to explore their similarities (rather than to scapegoat differences). As each subgroup works, members discover differences in the apparent similarities within their own subgroups and then recognize similarities between the different subgroups. As similarities in the apparently different are recognized, integration takes place in the group-as-a-whole.

Subgrouping, Stereotype: A natural phenomenon in which people in groups tend to come together around similarities and to split away from differences.

Subgroups, Explicit: Members who are formally working toward a clear goal in the group.

Subgroups, Implicit: Members who, through an observer's eyes, appear to be working together, though members themselves may not be conscious of it. For example, all of the members who are using fighting behaviors make up an implicit subgroup, even if they do not recognize that fighting each other meets the criteria for a "fighting" subgroup.

Subgroup System: Boundaried within the group-as-a-whole and boundarying the member systems. Contains splitting in the group-as-a-whole and uses the functional conflict resolution method of splitting, discriminating, and integrating differences at all levels of the system hierarchy.

Suspicion: The experience generated from an expectation that the environment is potentially exploitive, harmful, or dangerous. Perceptions are selective and are organized into cognitive misconstructions that reinforce mistrust. Suspicion is transformed into a paranoid barrier experience when information is organized into a comprehensive map that reflects the primary split of basic mistrust.

Systems-Centered Therapy: The process of subgrouping, boundarying, vectoring, and defense modification carried out in a systematized sequence in the context of phases of system development.

Tension: Second defense in the triad of symptomatic defenses: avoidance of arousal and emotional experience through constriction of the striated muscles (central nervous system). Benign symptoms generated: stiffness in neck, back pain, and a tight abdomen or chest, as well as muscle pain, tics, twitches, and so on. When tension is discharged into the autonomic nervous system secondary, non-benign, psychosomatic symptoms are generated (e.g., irritable bowel syndrome).

Theory of Living Human System: Defines a hierarchy of isomorphic systems that are energy-organizing, self-correcting, and goal-directed. Structurally, each system in the hierarchy is defined by its boundaries; functionally, systems survive, develop, and transform through splitting, containing, and integrating differences.

Theory of Stress: Howard and Scott (1965) postulate that all human behavior is goal-directed behavior that either approaches or avoids the problems that lie on the path to goal.

Transference: The transfer of a past system function into the context of the present in a closed feedback loop. Transference is defined as having two components: (1) unconscious memories of past emotional reality and (2) unconscious, preconscious, and conscious interpretation of the present context to replicate the criteria of past irreality.

Transference, Primary: Transference related to past system function in relation to the primary goals of survival and development and reflecting the transformation from living systems into the living human system: (1) pervasive transference is experienced as a pervasive atmosphere (e.g., an orientation toward optimism or pessimism); (2) preintegrative transference which dichotomizes good and bad/hope and despair/blind trust and blind mistrust into discrete experiences—each of which precludes awareness of its opposite; (3) predifferentiated transference—a transcendental experience of primary consciousness, in which there are no boundaries between self and other, animal or human, space and time, energy, or matter; (4) undifferentiated transference—undifferentiated information (matter-energy) experienced as chaos.

Transference, Secondary: Transference is related to past system function in relation to the social and environmental contexts, including (1) stereotype social role relationship transferences, (2) defensive role postures (defiant, compliant, scapegoat, etc.) and (3) interdependent role-locks in authority and intimacy.

Transformation: A function of discrimination and integration. ($T = f\{d,i\}$). This hypothesis is common to many theorists. For example, as early as 1862, Herbert Spencer stated that evolution is a change from an indefinite, incoherent homogeneity, to a definite, coherent heterogeneity, through continuous differentiation and integration.

Triad of Symptomatic Defenses: Defenses against anxiety, tension, irritability, and frustration that generate most of the symptoms that initially bring people into therapy and include (1) the cognitive defenses against anxiety that generate more anxiety; (2) the somatic defenses of tension that create psychosomatic and somatic symptoms which increase stress which increases tension(both cognitive and somatic defenses increase frustration and irritability); (3) the defenses against irritability and frustration, which arouse the retaliatory impulse which is defended against by depression or hostile acting out.

Trust: Defined in SCT as a function of tested expectations.

Turbulence at the Boundary: An SCT descriptor for the normal dissonance that occurs at the threshold of a boundary between the known and the unknown. Turbulence is experienced as apprehension; as inhibiting feelings, like shyness or embarrassment (intersystem boundaries); or as shame or dread (intrasystem boundaries) which, when reframed as turbulence, depathologizes and normalizes the process.

Vectoring: Directing working energy across the boundaries toward the goal.

Vectors: Arrows in flight have a direction, a force, and a target or goal (point of application). Driving and restraining forces are vectors with opposing goals. When behavior is framed in terms of vectors, then all behavior is interpreted as a vectorial output of the system. Thus, diagnosis reveals the direction in which the system is travelling, the amount of energy (motivation) for the journey, and the goal that the system is traveling toward.

Wariness: Potential energy, alertness and acuity accompanied by a scanning of environment for information and readiness to respond appropriately to environmental conditions.

Work: Transfer of matter/energy, which is the same as Miller's (1978) definition for communication.

References

Agazarian, Y. M. (1969a). A Theory of Verbal Behavior and Information Transfer. *Classroom Interaction Newsletter, 4*(2), 22–33.

Agazarian, Y. M. (1969b). The Agency as a Change Agent. In A. H. Goldberg (Ed.), *Blindness Research: The Expanding Frontiers.* University Park, PA: Penn State Press.

Agazarian, Y. M. (1972a). A System for Analyzing Verbal Behavior (SAVI) Applied to Staff Training in Milieu Treatment. *Devereux Schools Forum, 7*(1), 5–18.

Agazarian, Y. M. (1972b). Communication through the Group Process: An Approach to Humanization. *The Devereux Papers, 1*(1).

Agazarian, Y. M. (1982). Role as a Bridge Construct in Understanding the Relationship Between the Individual and the Group. In M. Pines & L. Rafaelson (Eds.), *The Individual and the Group: Boundaries and Interrelations: Vol. I. Theory.* New York: Plenum Press.

Agazarian, Y. M. (1983a). Theory of Invisible Group Applied to Individual and Group-as-a-Whole Interpretations. *Group: The Journal of the Eastern Group Psychotherapy Society, 7*(2).

Agazarian, Y. M. (1983b). Some Advantages of Applying Multi-Dimensional Thinking to the Teaching, Practice and Outcomes of Group Psychotherapy. *International Journal of Group Psychotherapy, 33*(2).

Agazarian, Y. M. (1986). Application of Lewin's Life Space Concept to the Individual and Group-as-a-Whole Systems in Psychotherapy. In E. Stivers & S. Wheelan (Eds.), *The Lewin Legacy: Field Theory in Current Practice.* New York: Springer-Verlag.

Agazarian, Y. M. (1987a). The Difficult Patient, the Difficult Group. Symposium: A Discussion of the Videotapes of a Difficult Group. *Group: The Journal of the Eastern Group Psychotherapy Society, 2*(4).

Agazarian, Y. M. (1987b). *Bion, the Tavistock Method and the Group-as-a-Whole.* Guest Lecture, Department of Continuing Education, sponsored by Massachusetts General Hospital.

Agazarian, Y. M. (1988a, Spring). Analysis of a Script of a Demonstration Group from the Perspective of the Group-as-a-Whole. *Friends Hospital Group Psychotherapy Training Monograph.*

Agazarian, Y. M. (1988b). *Application of a Modified Force Field Analysis to the Diagnosis of Implicit Group Goals.* Unpublished paper presented at the Third International Kurt Lewin Conference of the Society for the Advancement of Field Theory.

Agazarian, Y. M. (1989a, February). *Pathogenic Beliefs and Implicit Goals: Discussion of "The Mount Zion Group: The Therapeutic Process and Applicability of the Group's Work to Psychotherapy"* (Paper presented by Harold Sampson and Joseph Weiss, Slavson Memorial Lecture). Paper presented at the meeting of the American Group Psychotherapy Association, San Francisco.

Agazarian, Y. M. (1989b). Group-as-a-Whole Systems Theory and Practice. *Group: The Journal of the Eastern Group Psychotherapy Society, 13*(3–4), 131–155.

Agazarian, Y. M. (1989c). The Invisible Group: An Integrational Theory of Group-as-a-Whole. *Group Analysis: The Journal of Group Analytic Psychotherapy, 22*(4), 355–369.

Agazarian, Y. M. (Ed.). (1989d). The Group-as-a-Whole [Special Issue]. *Group: The Journal of the Eastern Group Psychotherapy Society, 13*(3–4).

Agazarian, Y. M. (1991). Systems Theory and Group Psychotherapy: From There-and-Then to Here-and-Now. *International Forum of Group Psychotherapy, 1*(3), 2–3.

Agazarian, Y. M. (1992a). Contemporary Theories of Group Psychotherapy: A Systems Approach to the Group-as-a-Whole. *International Journal of Group Psychotherapy, 42*(2), 177–204.

Agazarian, Y. M. (1992b). Book Review of *Koinonia: From Hate, through Dialogue, to Culture in the Large Group*, by Patrick de Mare, Robin Piper, and Sheila Thompson. *International Journal of Group Psychotherapy, 42*(3).

Agazarian, Y. M. (1993a). Reframing the Group-as-a-Whole Group. In T. Hugg, N. Carson, & T. Lipgar (Eds.), *Changing Group Relations: The Next Twenty-Five Years in America.* Jupiter, FL: A. K. Rice Institute.

Agazarian, Y. M. (1993b). Discussions on the Large Group. *Group: The Journal of the Eastern Group Psychotherapy Society, 17*(3), 210–234.

Agazarian, Y. M. (1994). The Phases of Development and the Systems-Centered Group. In M. Pines & V. Schermer (Eds.), *Ring of Fire: Primitive Object Relations and Affect in Group Psychotherapy.* London: Routledge, Chapman & Hall.

Agazarian, Y. M., Boyer, G. F., Simon, A., & White, P. F. (1973). *Documenting Development* (3 vols.). Philadelphia: Research for Better Schools.

Agazarian, Y. M., & Carter, F. (1993). The Large Group and Systems-Centered Theory. *Group: The Journal of the Eastern Group Psychotherapy Society, 17*(4), 210–234.

Agazarian, Y. M., & Janoff, S. (1993). Systems Theory and Small Groups. In I. Kaplan & B. Sadock (Eds.), *Comprehensive Textbook of Group Psychotherapy* (3rd ed.). Baltimore: Williams & Wilkins.

Agazarian, Y. M., & Peters, R. (1981). *The Visible and Invisible Group: Two Perspectives on Group Psychotherapy and Group Process.* London: Routlege & Kegan Paul.

Agazarian, Y. M., & Simon, A. (1989, February). *An Analysis of Excerpts from the Chicago Group Script of a Psychotherapy Group by SAVI, a Behavioral Observation System.* Unpublished paper presented at the meeting of the American Group Psychotherapy Association, San Francisco.

Asch, S. (1960). Effects of Group Pressure upon the Modification and Distortion of Judgments. In D. Cartwright & A. Zander (Eds.), *Group Dynamics Research and Theory* (2nd ed.). Elmsford, NY: Row, Peterson.

Bales, R., Borgatta, E., & Hare, A. (Eds.). (1955). *Small Groups: Studies in Social Interaction.* New York: Knopf.

Bandler R., & Grindler, J., (1975). *Patterns of the Hypnotic Techniques of Milton H. Erickson, M.D.* (Vols. 1 & 2). Cupertino, CA: META.

Bandler R., & Grindler, J., (1979). *Frogs into Princes: Neurolinguistic Programming.* Moab, UT: Real People Press.

Bateson, G. (1972). *Steps to an Ecology of Mind.* New York: Ballantine.

Bavelas, A. (1960). Communication Patterns in Task Oriented Groups. In D. Cartwright & A. Zander (Eds.), *Group Dynamics Research and Theory* (2nd ed.). Elmsford, NY: Row, Peterson.

Beck, A. (1976). *Cognitive Therapy and the Emotional Disorders.* New York: International Universities Press.

Beck, A. P. (1981). A Study of Group Phase Development and Emergent Leadership. *Group: The Journal of the Eastern Group Psychotherapy Society,* 5(4).

Benedict, R. (1934). *Patterns of Culture.* New York: Houghton Mifflin.

Bennis, W. G., & Shepard, H. A. (1957). A Theory of Group Development. *Human Relations,* 9(4), 415–437.

Berne, E. (1964). *Games People Play.* New York: Grove Press.

Bion, W. R. (1959). *Experiences in Groups,* London: Tavistock.

Bion, W. (1985). Container and Contained. In R. Colman & M. Geller (Eds.), *The Group Relations Reader,* 2. Washington, DC: A. K. Rice Institute.

Birdwhistle, R. (1960). Kinesics in Communication. In E. Carpernter & M. McLuhan (Eds.), *Explorations in Communication.* Boston: Beacon Press.

Bowlby, J. (1969). Instinctive Behavior: An Alternative Model. In *Attachment and Loss: Vol. 1. Attachment.* New York: Basic Books.

Burns, D. (1981). *Feeling Good: The New Mood Therapy.* New York: Signet.

Cartwright, D., & Zander, A. (Eds.). (1960). *Group Dynamics Research and Theory* (2nd ed.). Elmsford, NY: Row, Peterson.

Coch, L., & French, J. (1960). Overcoming Resistance to Change. In D. Cartwright & A. Zander (Eds.), *Group Dynamics Research and Theory* (2nd ed.). Elmsford NY: Row, Peterson.

Damasio, A. R. (1995). *Descartes' Error: Emotion, Reason and the Human Brain.* New York: Putnam.

Davanloo, H. (1987). Clinical Manifestations of Superego Pathology. *International Journal of Short-Term Psychotherapy,* 2, 225–254.

de Mare, P. B. (1989). The History of Large Group Phenomena in Relation to Group Analytic Psychotherapy: The Story of the Median Group. *Group: The Journal of the Eastern Group Psychotherapy Society,* 13(3,4), 131–155.

de Mare, P., Piper, R., & Thompson, S. (1991). *Koinonia: From Hate, through Dialogue, to Culture in the Large Group.* London: Karnac Books.

Durkin, H. (1964). *The Group in Depth.* New York: International Universities Press.

Durkin, H. E. (1972). Group Therapy and General Systems Theory. In C. J. Sager & H. S. Kaplan (Eds.), *Progress in Group and Family Therapy.* New York: Brunner/Mazel.

Durkin, J. E. (Ed.). (1981). *Living Groups: Group Psychotherapy and General System Theory.* New York: Brunner/Mazel.

Ekman, P. (1964). Body Position, Facial Expression, and Verbal Behavior during Interviews. *Journal of Abnormal and Social Psychology, 68*, 295.

Ekman, P. (1992). Facial Expressions of Emotion: New Findings, New Questions. *Psychological Science, 3*, 34–38.

Emery, F. (Ed.). (1969). *Systems Thinking.* Harmondsworth, England: Penguin.

Everson, S. A., Golderg, D. E., & Kaplan, G. A. (1996). Hopelessness and Risk of Mortality and Incidence of Myocardial Infarction and Cancer. *Psychosomatic Medicine, 58*, 113–121.

Festinger, L. (1957). *A Theory of Cognitive Dissonance.* Evanston, IL: Row, Peterson.

Festinger, L. (1960). Informal Social Communication. In D. Cartwright & A. Zander (Eds.), *Group Dynamics Research and Theory* (2nd ed.). Elmsford, NY: Row, Peterson.

Festinger, L., & Aronson, E. (1960). The Arousal and Reduction of Dissonance in Social Contexts. In D. Cartwright & A. Zander (Eds.), *Group Dynamics Research and Theory* (2nd ed.). Elmsford, NY: Row, Peterson.

Festinger, L., Riecken, H., & Schacter, S. (1956).*When Prophecy Fails.* Minneapolis: University of Minnesota Press.

Freud, A. (1936). *The Ego and the Mechanisms of Defense.* New York: International Universities Press.

Freud, S. (1921). *Group Psychology and the Analysis of the Ego.* In J. Strachey (Ed. & Trans.), *The Standard Edition of the Complete Psychological Works of Sigmund Freud* (Vol. 18). London: Hogarth Press, 1955.

Gibb, J. (1956, August). *Factors Producing Defensive Behavior within Groups.* Boulder: Group Process Laboratory, University of Colorado.

Goleman, D. (1995). *Emotional Intelligence.* New York: Bantam.

Hare, A. (1967). *Handbook of Small Group: Research.* New York: Free Press.

Hare, A., Borgatta, E., & Bales, R. (1955). *Small Groups; Studies in Social Interaction.* New York: Knopf.

Hinshelwood, R. D. (1989). *A Dictionary of Kleinian Thought.* London: Free Association Books.

Hopper, E. (1991). Encapsulation as a Defense against the Fear of Annihilation. *International Journal of Psycho-Analysis, 72*, 607–624.

Horwitz, L. (1977a). Group centered approach to group psychotherapy. *International Journal of Group Psychotherapy, 27*(2), 423–439.

Horwitz, L. (1977b). Projective identification in diads and groups. *International Journal of Group Psychotherapy, 33*(1), 259–279.

Howard, A., & Scott, R. A. (1965). A Proposed Framework for the Analysis of Stress in the Human Organism. *Journal of Applied Behavioral Science, 10*, 141–160.

Huang, C. A. (1988). *Embrace the Tiger, Return to Mountain: Essence of Tai Ji.* Berkeley, CA: Celestial Arts.

Jenkins, D. (1996). While There's Hope, There's Life [Editorial Comment]. *Psychosomatic Medicine, 58*, 122–124.

Kohler, W. (1947). *Gestalt Psychology.* New York: Liveright.

Korzybski, A. (1948). *Science and Sanity: An Introduction to Non-Aristotelian Systems and General Semantics* (3rd ed.). Lakeville. CT: International Non-Aristotelian Library, Institute of General Semantics.

Kreeger, L.C. (Ed.). (1975). *The Large Group: Dynamics and Therapy*. London: Constable & Co.

Levenson, R. W., Ekman, P., & Frieson, W. V. (1978). Voluntary Facial Action Generates Emotion-Specific Autonomous Nervous System Activity. *Psychophysiology, 27*.

Lewin, K. (1935). *A Dynamic Theory of Personality: Selected Papers*. New York: McGraw-Hill.

Lewin, K. (1936). *Principles of Topological Psychology*. New York: McGraw-Hill.

Lewin, K. (1951). *Field Theory in Social Science*. New York: Harper & Row.

Lewin, K., Lippit, R., & White, R. (1939). Patterns of Aggressive Behavior in Experimentally Created "Social Climate." *Journal of Psychology, 10*, 271–299.

Lewin, R. (1969). *Complexity. Life on the Edge of Chaos*. New York: Macmillan.

Lippit, R., & White, R. (1960). Leader Behavior and Member Reaction in Three Social Climates. In D. Cartwright & A. Zander (Eds.), *Group Dynamics Research and Theory* (2nd ed.). Elmsford NY: Row, Peterson.

McCullough, L. (1995). Short Term Dynamic Psychotherapy: A Cross Theoretical Analysis of Change Mechanisms. In R. Curtis & G. Striker (Eds.), *How People Change*. New York: Plenum Press.

Milgram, S. (1974). *Obedience to Authority: An Experimental View*. New York: Harper & Row.

Miller, J. (1961). *Information Input Overload: Self-Organizing Systems*. Washington, DC: Washington Press.

Miller, J. (1978). *Living Systems*. New York: McGraw-Hill.

Pennov, D. (1978). *Love and Limerance*. New York: Steine & Day.

Raven, B., & Rietsama, J. (1960). The Effects of Varied Clarity of Group Goal and Group Path upon the Individual and His Relation to His Group. In D. Cartwright & A. Zander (Eds.), *Group Dynamics Research and Theory* (2nd ed.). Elmsford NY: Row, Peterson.

Pines, M. (Ed.). (1985). *Bion and Group Psychotherapy*. London: Routledge & Kegan Paul.

Rothman, M. A. (1992). *The Science Gap, Dispelling the Myths and Understanding the Reality of Science*. Buffalo, NY: Prometheus.

Ruesch, J., & Bateson, G. (1951). *Communication: The Social Matrix of Society*. New York: Norton.

Scheff, T. (1963). The Role of the Mentally Ill and the Dynamics of Mental Disorder. *Sociometry, 26*, 426–435.

Scheflen, A. (1973). *Communicational Structure: Analysis of a Psychotherapy Transition*. Bloomington: Indiana University Press.

Sechehaye, M. A. (1951). *Symbolic Realization: A New Method of Psychotherapy Applied to a Case of Schizophrenia*. New York: International Universities Press.

Science News. (1996, April 13). *149*, p. 230.

Shannon, C. E., & Weaver, W. (1964). *The Mathematical Theory of Communication*. Urbana: University of Illinois Press.

Simon, A. (1993). Using SAVI (System for Analyzing Verbal Interaction) for Couples Therapy. *Journal of Family Psychotherapy, 4*(3), 39–62.

Simon, A., & Agazarian, Y. M. (1967). *SAVI: Sequential Analysis of Verbal Interaction*. Philadelphia: Research for Better Schools.

Skinner, B. (1957). *Verbal Behavior.* New York: Appleton Century Crofts.

Stern, D. (1985). *The Interpersonal World of the Infant.* New York: Basic Books.

Szasz, T. (1970). *The Manufacture of Madness.* New York: Harper & Row.

Tinbergen, N. (1951). *The Study of Instinct.* Oxford, UK: Clarendon Press.

von Bertalanffy, L. (1968). *General System Theory* (rev. ed.). New York: George Braziller.

Watzlawick, P. (1976). *How Real Is Real? Communication, Disinformation: A Study of Interactive Patterns, Pathologies, and Paradoxes.* New York: Norton.

Watzlawick, P. (1990). *Munchausen's Pigtail or Psychotherapy and Reality.* New York: Norton.

Watzlawick, P., Beavin, J., & Jackson, D. (1967). *Pragmatics of Human Communication.* New York: Norton.

Weiss, J., & Sampson, H. (1986). *The Psychoanalytic Process: Theory, Clinical Observation, and Empirical Research.* New York: Guilford Press.

Whitaker, D. S. (1985). *Using Groups to Help People.* London: Routledge & Kegan Paul.

Whitely, J. S., & Gordon, J. (1979). *Group Approaches in Psychiatry.* London: Routledge & Kegan Paul.

Wiener, N. (1961). *Cybernetics* (2nd ed.). New York: Wiley.

Winnicott, D. W. (1951). Transitional Objects and Transitional Phenomena. *In Playing and Reality.* London: Tavistock.

Wolpe, J. (1958). *Psychotherapy by Reciprocal Inhibition.* Stanford, CA: Stanford University Press.

Zuckerman, S. (1981). *The Social Life of Monkeys and Apes* (2nd ed.). London: Routledge & Kegan Paul.

Index

Depressive defenses (*continued*)
  despair distinction, 266, 267
  in flight to fight subphase
      transition, 102, 103
  fork-in-the-road approach, 200–202
  and masochism, 103, 105
  symptoms, 99
  triggers, 201
  undoing of, 103–105, 190, 199, 200,
      203
Description technique
  anxiety undoing, 150, 151, 153
  tension-related symptoms, 173
Desensitization
  definition, 182
  in sexual dysfunction, 182–186
Despair
  as defense against hope, 267
  depression distinction, 266, 267
  in disenchanted groups, 266, 267
  shame relationship, 268
Differences, in systems, 19, 20
Disclosure, 244, 245
"Discoveries" method, 72
"Discovering reality" technique, 136
Discrimination technique
  in flight to fight subphase
      transition, 101, 102
  flooding containment, 88, 89
  and frustration tolerance, 101, 102
  and separation–individuation
      process, 110, 111
Disenchantment subphase
  despair in, 266, 267
  dynamics, 257–259
  eye contact, 263, 264
  group prognosis factor, 258
  regression in, 263, 264
  subgrouping in, 261
Distancing, 56
Distraction exercise, 73–79
  and anxiety, 73, 74, 77, 78, 290
  defense modification, 73, 74
  dream work tool, 293
  in experienced groups, 289–295
  functional subgrouping
      relationship, 87

  in intimacy phase, 260
  in social communication
      modification, 97
  and somatic symptoms, 290–293
  steps in, 75–79
Distress signals, 130
Doctor–patient relationship
  initial interview status defense,
      131–133
  one-up–one-down role, 128, 129,
      131–133
Dread, 267–270, 272–274
Dream work, 293, 294
Driving forces
  and communicative behaviors, 129
  in defense modification, 37
  vectoring, 31

E

Educational methods
  anger management, 207
  anxiety management, 151
Egocentricity, 9
Emotional intelligence, 87, 143, 144,
      281, 282
Emotions
  components, 144, 145
  containment of, 76
  and defense modification, 87, 88
  and distraction exercise, 74–76
  feelings distinction, 87, 88
  and intention movements, 87, 88
Enchantment subphase
  dynamics, 257–259, 265, 266
  eye contact in, 263, 264
  and object relations, 266
  resonance in, 265, 266
  separation–individuation issues,
      110, 111, 257, 258
  subgrouping in, 261
Endogenous depression, 200
Energy
  and defense modification, 90
  experience of, 198, 199
  frustration link, 197–199